New Scots

Studies in Scottish and Irish Migration

Series Editors: T. M. Devine, University of Edinburgh, and
Angela McCarthy, University of Otago

From the 1600s to the current day, millions of Scottish and Irish
migrants have sought new lives around the world. Scotland and
Ireland have also received returning migrants and newcomers of
diverse ethnicities. This series will examine the causes, consequences,
representations and legacies of these movements on the homelands,
the migrants and the destinations in which they settled. The series
incorporates not just the inward and outward movement of people,
but of ideas, products and objects. It specifically encourages cross-
disciplinary, comparative and/or transnational approaches across
groups, space and time.

New Scots

Scotland's Immigrant Communities since 1945

Edited by T. M. Devine and Angela McCarthy

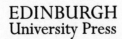

EDINBURGH
University Press

Edinburgh University Press is one of the leading university presses in the UK. We publish academic books and journals in our selected subject areas across the humanities and social sciences, combining cutting-edge scholarship with high editorial and production values to produce academic works of lasting importance. For more information visit our website: edinburghuniversitypress.com

Edinburgh University Press Ltd
The Tun – Holyrood Road
12 (2f) Jackson's Entry
Edinburgh EH8 8PJ

Typeset in 10.5/13pt Sabon by
Servis Filmsetting Ltd, Stockport, Cheshire
and printed and bound in Great Britain

A CIP record for this book is available from the British Library

ISBN 978 1 4744 3787 5 (hardback)
ISBN 978 1 4744 3788 2 (paperback)
ISBN 978 1 4744 3789 9 (webready PDF)
ISBN 978 1 4744 3790 5 (epub)

Contents

Figures

Tables

The Contributors

Eona Bell has a PhD in Social Anthropology from the London School of Economics and Political Science.

Stefano Bonino is the author of *Muslims in Scotland: The Making of Community in a Post 9/11 World*, published by Edinburgh University Press in 2016.

Chris Carman is the Stevenson Professor of Citizenship at the University of Glasgow.

Enda Delaney is Professor of Modern History at the University of Edinburgh.

T. M. Devine is Sir William Fraser Professor of Scottish History and Palaeography Emeritus at the University of Edinburgh.

Nicholas J. Evans is Lecturer in Diaspora History at the University of Hull.

Ailsa Henderson is Professor of Political Science at the University of Edinburgh.

Ima Jackson is Senior Lecturer in the School of Health and Life Sciences at Glasgow Caledonian University.

Rob Johns is Professor of Politics at the University of Essex.

Angela McCarthy is Professor of Scottish and Irish History and Director of the Centre for Global Migrations at the University of Otago, New Zealand.

James Mitchell is Professor of Public Policy and Director of the Academy of Government at the University of Edinburgh.

Ashli Mullen is a PhD researcher in Sociology at the University of Glasgow, studying the racialisation of Roma in Scotland.

Teresa Piacentini is Lecturer in Sociology at the University of Glasgow.

Emilia Piętka-Nykaza is Senior Lecturer in Sociology and Social Policy at the University of the West of Scotland.

Acknowledgements

We are grateful to the Economic and Social Research Council for three-year funding for our seminar series on 'Scotland's Diasporas in Comparative International Perspective' (a joint initiative of Angela McCarthy, Tom Devine and Nicholas J. Evans). This book is the outcome of one of those seminars, held in June 2016. We would like to thank the Mitchell Library in Glasgow for providing the stimulating environment within which the symposium took place and all those speakers and chairs who participated. In addition, we thank other partners of the event: the Coalition for Racial Equality and Rights and the Scottish Refugee Council.

We are deeply appreciative of Professor Enda Delaney who read all the chapters in this book and provided a comparative viewpoint in the final chapter. Angela would like to acknowledge her period as a Visiting Fellow at the Institute for Advanced Studies in the Humanities at the University of Edinburgh in 2017, during which time she completed her contributions in this volume and edited the collection.

T. M. Devine and Angela McCarthy

Series Editors' Introduction

Most studies of Scotland's migration history focus on the outward flow of people from late medieval times, or their inward movement during the nineteenth and early twentieth centuries. By contrast, the experience of newcomers from the 1940s has not attracted scholarly attention to anything like the same extent. This pioneering volume, *New Scots*, is a cross-disciplinary collection and the first to provide a wide-ranging overview of immigration to Scotland in recent history and its impact on both the newcomers and the host society. It examines key themes relating to post-war migration by considering the experiences of those who have come from England, Poland, India, Pakistan, China, the Caribbean and the African continent. *New Scots* also features analyses of asylum seekers and refugees, along with Jewish and Roma migrants, and includes a chapter on migrant voting patterns during the independence referendum of 2014.

The book makes a particular contribution in its multidisciplinary approach, ranging widely across history, sociology, social anthropology, criminology and politics. This is a salutary reminder that the study of migration and related fields crosses subject boundaries just as people, ideas and objects cross territorial ones. This will be a key feature of future volumes in *Studies in Scottish and Irish Migration*. Such a varied disciplinary approach, however, does not mean the loss of intellectual coherence. That is maintained by focused engagement with key themes such as community formation, family life, religion, labour, constitutional issues, cross-cultural encounters, identities and belonging. Contributors to *New Scots*, for example, examine issues of integration, prejudice, racism, the specifics of Scottish responses to inward movement from 'new' migrants, political preferences of immigrants and why the challenges of multi-ethnic immigration have been seemingly less acute than in much of England.

Its wide-ranging approach also enables the authors to showcase a wide array of sources such as government papers, the press, and social and political surveys. In addition, several chapters draw evocatively on the rich written and oral testimony of the migrants themselves. The different methodologies not only bring out similarities and differences between migrant groups, but importantly also of diversity within them in terms of religion, class, place of origin and language. That many of the authors situate their contributions within a longer timeframe enables critical continuity and change over time to be assessed. The ethnic and territorial origins of migrants to Scotland have altered considerably from the nineteenth century, but many aspects of their inward movement endure down to the present.

New Scots engages with aspects of mass international migration, one of the most important political, economic and social issues in the world today, by making a path-breaking contribution to modern Scottish history and society, migration studies and the experience of recent immigrants in the United Kingdom. It is to be hoped that the exploration of inward migration to Scotland continues to develop and facilitates a reconsideration of Scotland's past and present, in the same way as the recent 'diasporic turn' has done through key studies of outward migration.

T. M. Devine and Angela McCarthy

1

Introduction: The Historical and Contemporary Context of Immigration to Scotland since 1945

T. M. Devine and Angela McCarthy

In early medieval times, Scotland was one of several countries in Europe to experience the impact of immigration of foreign peoples, many of them coming from Scandinavia, Ireland and England. Eventually, from these early movements and subsequent intermingling with the indigenous population, the kingdom of Scotland came into being. In origin, therefore, as the author William McIlvanney once memorably remarked, the Scots were from the beginning truly a mongrel nation.[1] Immigration mainly tailed off for several centuries afterwards but the economic miracle enjoyed by Scotland between the middle decades of the eighteenth century and the Great War led once again to a significant increase in inward movement. These new migrants saw Scotland as a land of opportunity where the linked processes of massive industrialisation and urbanisation held out the promise of both more work and higher wages, especially for those from countries of deep poverty, persecution or ethnic harassment. The 1911 census recorded the presence of almost 400,000 people who had been born outside the country, a figure that approached one in ten of Scotland's total population at the time. The largest ethnic groups were Catholic and Protestant Irish, English, Lithuanians, Poles, Italians and Jews.[2]

The Great War inevitably constrained this influx, which also went into long-term decline during the 1920s and 1930s when economic crisis and rising unemployment made Scotland a much less appealing prospect for potential immigrants. Significantly, the numbers of Irish, who had been by far the country's biggest migrant group during Victorian times, fell away dramatically during 1914–18 and subsequently fell to a trickle after hostilities came to an end. Irish migrants now overwhelmingly looked elsewhere to the United States, Canada, England and Australasia and, by the 1920s and thereafter, the English-born had replaced them as the country's largest immigrant group. In a more general sense, the demographic history of Scotland after the First World War became one of dramatic growth in emigration rather than immigration. Indeed, during the 1920s the haemorrhage became so great that the recorded population of the nation fell in absolute terms for the first time since the eighteenth century. That exodus persisted after 1945, albeit on a somewhat reduced scale, and only started to ebb away to lower numbers in the early 1990s.[3]

From the 1950s, however, immigration to Scotland once again assumed numerical and social significance, though in large part the nature of the influx differed considerably from the earlier movements of the nineteenth century. The migrants now increasingly came from South Asia, central and eastern Europe, Africa and the Caribbean, as well as from some of the more familiar places of earlier times.[4] This Introduction seeks to explain the general dynamics of that process while also setting the scene for the more detailed studies that follow in the book by placing them within a global, European and Scottish context.

THE GLOBAL PICTURE

Some commentators interpret the global migrations of the last four decades of the twentieth century as unprecedented since the number of international migrants is estimated to have risen from c. 79 million in 1960 to almost 250 million by 2015. Yet, while current worldwide movement suggests transformation in origin, nature, direction and short-term increase, its scale, relative to total global numbers, is broadly similar to that of a century ago.[5] Today's international migrant flows are estimated at around 3 per cent of the world population, while the minimum of 60 million reckoned to have moved countries between 1820 and 1940 ranged between 5 per cent of global numbers in 1820 and 3 per cent in 1940.[6] Over that timeframe, as today, those earlier immigration streams often proved to be highly contentious and controversial, and were resisted by various action groups in host countries such as the USA and UK. Also nowadays, as then, immigration has moved to the top of the political agenda in the developed world. This is not simply a result of the perception of massive increase in volume, but also because the phenomenon is depicted as a movement in overwhelming numbers of the poor, displaced, dispossessed and ethnically different, who are fleeing from the southern hemisphere to the richer north and from very disadvantaged regions to more affluent countries within the Americas and Europe. The realities of that perception are questionable since international migration requires resources to move, and most migration is not from the poorest countries or poorest social classes. For those who do leave poorer countries, movement is often the result of inequality, violence and the lack of human rights. The role of the West in contributing to this situation through its record of colonialism is frequently elided.[7]

The dynamics of rapid globalisation have, however, been powerful factors in this process. Fundamental advances in all forms of communication and transportation meant distances between countries and continents became of rapidly declining significance. Of equal relevance has been further growth in material disparities between developed and developing nations across the world. In 1900 the estimated ratio of average income of the five richest economies to the five to ten poorest was reckoned to be around 9:1. By 2015 the gulf between richest and poorest states had widened dramatically according to some estimates to 100:1.[8] Not surprisingly, perhaps, a key result of this extraordinary maldistribution in the riches of the earth was that in the five years 2000 to 2005 alone, the more developed regions of the world gained an estimated 2.6 million migrants annually from poorer countries. Indeed, the figure approached 13.1 million immigrants in all over that period.[9]

Conflict within and between nation states also triggered global human movement. Between 1990 and 1995 it is reckoned over seventy countries were involved in ninety-three great or small wars. The vast surges in the numbers of refugees and asylum seekers, which have dominated the international media since that decade, can be largely attributed to this widespread incidence of global violence and the human misery and demographic displacement associated with it. By 2015 there were an estimated 21.3 million refugees globally, but in addition, cases were pending for a further 3.2 million asylum seekers across the world.[10] Again, however, historical perspective is useful. At least 9.5 million refugees were counted in Europe after the First World War, while the Second World War generated more than 60 million displaced persons. However, the refugee problem in both those conflicts primarily existed and was managed within the boundaries of the European continent. Nowadays the pattern is different, with untold numbers fleeing from multiple zones of conflict in Africa and the Middle East to several countries in Europe.[11]

Political decisions, which have allowed freer movement across national borders, have also facilitated migration. The most important development affecting the UK was the expansion in the membership of the European Union, culminating in the accession of a further eight states in 2004 and two more three years later. By 2017 the EU had grown to a total membership of twenty-eight nations, so allowing workers within the Common Travel Area to move more freely across much of the continent unimpeded by most controls. These migrant peoples not only include citizens of European states but also refugees and asylum seekers who had originally moved to Europe from further afield.

But recent economic difficulties within the Eurozone itself, exacerbated by the financial crisis of 2008 and its aftermath, also accelerated human mobility between low- and high-performing countries. Indeed, the problems affecting some European economies were so acute that long-term structural unemployment, especially among young adults, was an inevitable result. In November 2016, for instance, unemployment among all working-age groups throughout the Eurozone was 9.8 per cent, the lowest rate since July 2009. However, the jobless level for young people (under the age of twenty-five) stood at 21 per cent at the end of 2016, with the highest figures recorded in Spain (44.4 per cent), Greece (41.1 per cent) and Italy (39.4 per cent). At the other end of the spectrum, only 6.7 per cent of young people in Germany were jobless at that time.[12] The patterns in the UK, however, were somewhat better, with 4.8 per cent unemployment for all age groups at the end of 2016 and 11.5 per cent for young people not in full-time education.[13] These marked differentials between the labour markets in Britain and several European countries were likely to be an obvious incentive for the migration of working-age men and women to the UK.

A SCOTTISH FOCUS

The primary purpose of this book is to consider the nature and impact of these global trends and European developments on Scotland, with a particular focus on the 'new' post-1945 immigrant communities. Though Irish, Jews and Italians continued to come to Scotland, as they had done in large numbers in the past, they have been collectively outnumbered in recent decades by migrants from Poland, India, Germany and Pakistan, and other east European nationalities. The only significant continuity from the decades before the Second World War is the persistent numerical dominance of the English-born in Scotland. In fact, at the census of 2011, they accounted for more than all other migrant ethnicities to Scotland combined.

A brief outline of Scotland's immigrant history since the end of the Second World War suggests some salient trends. One of the most striking of these was that it took some time for the global migration

Table 1.1 Net migration from Scotland, 1951–89 (in thousands)

Decade	To the UK	Overseas
1951–61	210,000	10,000
1961–71	140,000	142,000
1971–81	52,000	99,000
1981–9	70,000	47,000

Source: Annual Reports of the Registrar General Scotland, 1951–89

revolution to have any significant impact on the country. The dominant Scottish demographic narrative between 1950 and the 1980s remained one of large-scale emigration rather than immigration. During those decades, England experienced particularly high levels of net inward movement, especially after the 1948 Nationality Act, which enabled the settlement of migrants from the British colonies and former colonies in the Commonwealth. North of the border the opposite was the case, with on average almost 6 per cent of the population leaving Scotland in each decade over that period, a level of haemorrhage unmatched in any other part of the mainland UK.

The fact that many of the nation's own younger and more active people were themselves leaving the country of their birth suggests that the employment opportunities in Scotland, at least compared to the rest of the UK, were not enough to attract immigrants in large numbers. Tellingly, that fact can be confirmed in relation to the history of New Commonwealth immigrants who had a deeply significant impact on several parts of England in those years. The demographic historian Michael Anderson noted that even by 1981, the percentage of the Scottish population in the census of that year who were born in Jamaica, Pakistan and India was a mere 0.01 per cent, 0.14 per cent and 0.18 per cent respectively. The simple truth was, of course, that a relatively stagnant Scottish economy with higher unemployment levels and fewer new economic prospects than most of England did not need additional supplies of migrant labour or proved capable of generating the opportunities to attract them. Migrants from different parts of the New Commonwealth showed a marked tendency to focus initially on different and highly specific UK labour markets to which they were often attracted by targeted recruitment campaigns in their country of origin or by high demand for low-paid semi-skilled labour in some areas of Britain. These were almost entirely located in a relatively small number of major urban areas in England and none were in Scotland. As Anderson summarised:

So, for example, in 1971, 55 per cent of all the West Indies-born migrants in Britain were living in Greater London, and another 33 per cent in Birmingham – but just 0.1 per cent in the Central Clydeside Conurbation (and 0.5 per cent in the whole of Scotland). Of migrants born in Pakistan living in Britain in the same year, 22 per cent were in London, 16 per cent in Birmingham, 16 per cent in the West Riding of Yorkshire, but less than 2 per cent in the Clydeside Conurbation (and less than 3 per cent in Scotland). A similar pattern continued into the 1970s with major flows of East Africans highly focused on Leicester and Peterborough in England, and south Asians into the Lancashire textile areas.[14]

The striking exception to this pattern of low levels of immigration was the continuous movement of English people of working age into Scotland. In fact, there had been significant net in-migration of the English-born in every decade since the Great War with the exception of the 1920s. The 1991 census recorded over 22,000 English-born 'corporate managers and administrators', around 9,800 science and engineering professionals, 11,780 teachers, over 14,000 clerical workers and 10,000 others employed in iron, steel and engineering. The reasons why they came north of the border in such numbers, despite very limited inward movement from elsewhere, are explored by T. M. Devine in Chapter 2.

Nonetheless, though much smaller in scale than their movement to England, Indians, Pakistanis, Chinese and others did move to Scotland from the 1950s, especially from their original settlement south of the border (though small numbers had been in Scotland before 1945). They soon began to make an economic, social and cultural mark on different parts of Scotland. The first South Asian immigrants after the Second World War were mainly engaged in the peddling trade and some became familiar figures in the Lowland countryside and the Highlands and Islands as they carried their bulging suitcases packed with small consumer items even into the most remote parts of Scotland. By the 1960s South Asian businesses specialising in catering, cash and carry and groceries were also opening in several Scottish cities and towns as the community started to disperse across the country in order to reduce ethnic over-competition in early places of settlement. By the early 1980s the different South Asian populations numbered around 25,000 in all, with 65 per cent of both Indians and Pakistanis already owning their own businesses by that time. Corner shops, restaurants, takeaways and the building of both Muslim mosques and Hindu temples became familiar parts of the Scottish town and cityscape, as described and analysed in Chapter 4 by Stefano Bonino. It remains an open question, however, whether the Asian focus on self-employment was caused, in whole or in part, by real or perceived discrimination in the labour market or by factors within the communities themselves which made for a more enterprising culture or, indeed, by a combination of both influences.

Also in the 1960s, Chinese restaurants and takeaways were set up in several Scottish towns, even though the roots of that ethnic migration lay as far back as the aftermath of the Communist Revolution of 1949. Several thousand Hakka and Cantonese refugees fled to Hong Kong and the New Territories from the regime, causing unemployment in these British colonies to soar and pressures on housing to intensify. In response, the colonial government adopted a strategy of encouraging emigration to the UK, firstly of young men from the poorest villages and then from more affluent areas. In the first instance, the migration trail led to London, where there was already an established Chinese community, which sometimes had kin connections with the new arrivals. That was then followed by a secondary movement in which some families began to fan out across the rest of the UK, including some coming to Scotland. Eona Bell charts their story in Chapter 7. By the census of 2011 there were 33,706 people of Chinese birth in Scotland. Significantly, however, around three-quarters of them had arrived in the four years before the census, which suggests a high level of student migration rather than of those who intended to settle permanently in the country. Indeed, one recent conclusion from the 2011 census data suggests that nearly half of all the Chinese in Scotland at that date were students in higher education.[15]

Only from the late 1990s, however, was migration to Scotland by non-UK ethnicities transformed both in scale and diversity of country of origin. The English movement was not only maintained but developed further, while Poland and other countries in eastern Europe began to contribute more migrants than ever before. Central to this development were political decisions made in 2004 by the European Union to extend membership to other nations on the continent. The accession of these so-called A8 countries to the European Union in that year had significant effects on migration to the UK as a whole. Movement from all of the eight – Poland, Lithuania, Estonia, Latvia, Czech Republic, Slovakia, Hungary and Slovenia – soon increased, though by different orders of magnitude from each country. The impact in Scotland was marked. Between 2001 and 2011, the non-UK element effectively doubled, from 191,571 to 369,997. This meant that the foreign-born component of the country's total population increased from 3.8 per cent in 2001 to 7 per cent in 2011.

A small but illuminating microcosm of changing times was the ethnic mix in 2017 of the congregation of the Catholic parish of St Mary's in the town of Hamilton, South Lanarkshire, and the background of pupils attending St Bride's Primary School in Govanhill, Glasgow, an area long an epicentre of immigration to the city reaching back to the days of the incoming Irish. On the school roll it is reckoned that in 2016 there were children from no fewer than thirty different nationalities. The Hamilton parish was created in the 1840s to serve the needs of the growing numbers of poor Irish who came to work in the many collieries and textile manufactures of the area during the Victorian era. For generations afterwards, their descendants continued to dominate the membership of the local church, and Scots from an Irish background still do so to this day. However, in recent years a minor cosmopolitanism has blossomed in the congregation with people attending from a range of countries including England, Poland, Lithuania, Italy, Spain, Germany, Latvia, the USA, Nigeria, South Africa, the Philippines, Australia and India.[16]

Indeed, in relation to the base populations of the two countries, increased immigration across Scotland was greater than that of England from 2001 to 2011: a 92.8 per cent rise in its foreign-born population compared to England's 61 per cent. The size of Scotland's Polish community expanded particularly dramatically with an increase of 2,105 per cent over the decade 2001 to 2011. After the English, Poles are now the country's biggest immigrant group, outnumbering the next largest non-British Isles group, the Indian-born, by more than two to one. They

Table 1.2 Scotland's top twelve migrant groups, 2001 and 2011

	2001	2011
England	408,948	459,486
Poland	2,505	55,231
Northern Ireland	33,528	36,655
Republic of Ireland	21,774	22,952
India	10,523	23,489
Germany	18,703	22,274
Pakistan	12,645	20,039
Wales	16,623	17,381
USA	11,149	15,919
China	3,329	15,338
South Africa	7,803	10,607
Nigeria		9,458

Source: UK censuses, 2001 and 2011.

also comprise a larger share of the foreign-born in Scotland than their numbers in Britain as a whole.[17] Emilia Piętka-Nykaza looks in detail at the settlement of Polish people and their experience in Scotland in Chapter 6.

Comparison with England's top foreign-born groups also illustrates some contrasts between the two countries. First, the absolute number of migrants in England easily surpassed that of Scotland. Second, apart from the top six groups, England attracted many more immigrants from Bangladesh, Nigeria and Jamaica than Scotland. Moreover, whereas the non-UK-born in Scotland increased by over 90 per cent between 2001 and 2011, England's increase, albeit, of course, within a much larger population, was 61 per cent, the lowest of the four UK constituent nations.[18] This meant that the overall percentage of the non-UK-born among England's total population rose from 9.26 per cent in 2001 to 13.9 per cent in 2011, whereas in Scotland that figure doubled in relative size from a much lower baseline.

Third, the relative numbers of foreign-born in both Scotland and England pale somewhat in comparison to immigrants in some other nations across the world. A notable example is New Zealand, a country with a slightly smaller population than Scotland. Immigrants in 2015 formed around one-quarter of New Zealand's total population, with

Table 1.3 England's top fifteen migrant groups, 2001 and 2011

	2001	2011
Scotland	794,577	708,872
India	450,493	682,274
Poland	56,679	561,098
Wales	609,711	506,619
Pakistan	304,706	476,684
Northern Ireland	215,124	206,735
Republic of Ireland	459,662	395,182
Germany	233,418	262,356
Bangladesh	150,057	206,331
Nigeria	86,370	188,690
South Africa	129,302	186,355
USA	141,198	173,470
Jamaica	145,234	158,630
China	47,201	146,202
Kenya	126,119	135,966

Source: 2001 and 2011 censuses, as calculated from Wikipedia and the Migration Observatory: http://www.migrationobservatory.ox.ac.uk/resources/briefings/england-census-profile/; https://en.wikipedia.org/wiki/Demography_of_England.

movement from England and Scotland traditionally a considerable part of that inflow. In recent years the policy of the country has been much more favourable to immigration from elsewhere. New Zealand is also unique among host nations in allowing foreign citizens the right to vote in general elections despite a legacy of hostility to immigration earlier in the twentieth century.[19] This more positive approach can partly be explained by a selection process which systematically targets economic migrants based on the skills and professional expertise which they can offer. Another factor is that, unlike more hostile reactions in the USA and Europe, neither the media nor mainstream political parties have sought to demonise immigrants. Instead, they are seen as critical to New Zealand's future economic prospects, a perspective which, as discussed below, is also shared by the current government of Scotland. One estimate has suggested that if New Zealand was to close its doors entirely to migrants, the national population would decline by almost 10 per cent, GDP would fall by 11.3 per cent and average per capita income would contract by $1,000.[20]

Place of birth, however, excludes the importance of ethnicity and religion, and the distinctions these reveal between Scotland and England. In the 2011 census, 85 per cent of England's population saw themselves as of white ethnicity compared with 96 per cent in Scotland. At a city level, London and Birmingham have 60 per cent white ethnicity compared with Glasgow's 88 per cent.[21] Ross Bond's work in this area reveals that most ethnic Irish and Pakistanis were born in the UK, while most Chinese and Indians were born abroad.[22] The Jewish community, a long-established migrant group in Scotland, was also dominated by the Scottish-born. Nicholas Evans and Angela McCarthy outline in Chapter 3 the changing dynamic of that community, including the influx of 'New' Jews from origins quite different from the earlier period, and their perceptions of anti-Semitism in Scottish society.

A8 IMMIGRANTS AND SCOTLAND

The recent influx of A8 migrants to the UK has undeniably stirred political controversy, and in the view of some analysts has been a prime factor causing the whole issue of immigration to rapidly move up the British political agenda. It is also apparent that fears over existing and future migration trends in some areas of the UK were key to the historic Brexit decision taken in the referendum of 2016.[23] Scotland, however, voted decisively by a margin of 62 per cent to 38 per cent to remain in the EU. An important question, therefore, is whether that different response was influenced in part by Scotland's distinctive history of immigration since 1945. Two authoritative investigations allow that hypothesis to be tested. The first was conducted by the reputable Migration Observatory at Oxford University and published in 2014.[24] The second was work carried out by the National Institute of Economic and Social Research on recent migration into Scotland. Its report appeared in 2009.[25]

After the completion of the research, the Director of the Migration Observatory noted that its enquiry was the first-ever major survey about attitudes to immigration in Scotland: 'Pretty much all the previous work has been based on small numbers of respondents and a small number of questions.'[26] The study was conducted by the polling organisation YouGov, which questioned a large sample of 2,000 respondents in Scotland. Its key finding was that Scottish attitudes to immigration did indeed differ from the rest of the UK but not to the extent that some had previously assumed. A majority (58 per cent) supported reduced movement into Scotland but more respondents thought immigration was good (41 per cent) than bad (31 per cent) for the country. By contrast, in England and Wales 75 per cent of respondents wished to see immigration fall and also saw the issue as the second most important political priority facing the UK. The subject did not, however, have the same salience north of the border where immigration was considered fourth in terms of relative political significance after the constitutional question, the economy and the health service.[27]

Other findings also suggested that the Scots had their own distinctive opinions. Support for a reduction in numbers was strongest in relation to low-skilled migrants, while only a minority wished to see stricter controls on higher-skilled workers and university students. Overall, then, the survey suggested that Scots did favour a fall in levels of immigration but attitudes in general were somewhat less hostile and negative than south of the border. In sum, of all regions in the UK, apart from London, Scotland was least opposed to immigration.[28] The Migration Observatory commented on its findings thus:

public opinion in Scotland is indeed less negative toward immigration that [sic] opinion [in] the rest of Britain. In Scotland compared with the rest of Britain, people are less likely to want immigration reduced, more likely to see it as good for their country, and less likely to see it as one of the most important issues facing the country. It is important, however, not to exaggerate these differences. A majority in Scotland still support reduced immigration, and the issue ranks high on the public agenda even if not as high as in Britain. And there is little support for a policy that is more open to immigration than the rest of the UK, at least when respondents are asked about immigration as a whole.[29]

There are a number of possible explanations for these Scottish responses but the two most favoured by commentators are demographic and political. Robert Wright, a Professor of Economics at Strathclyde University, argued that the historically low level of migration into Scotland in the twentieth century was a crucial factor. He suggested the country had not really been tested by the impact of mass immigration to anything like the same extent as parts of England:

> I think the difference between Scotland and the rest of the UK really boils down to the fact that there has been less immigration in Scotland than the UK for a significant period of time. So the fact there is more tolerance here is because there has been less of it. That does not mean there will be tolerance in the future when there is more immigration, so this will be a hurdle we have to jump later.[30]

As indicated earlier, New Commonwealth migration to the UK from the 1950s concentrated on London and the English Midlands and had only limited impact north of the border. The vast majority of Scotland's immigrants over that period were white, English-born and economically active, rather than families from the Caribbean, India, Pakistan or Africa.[31] At the 2011 census, one person in six living in Scotland had not been born in the country but most were the 459,486 people of English birth. Of the rest, about 37,000 were born in Northern Ireland and 23,000 in the Irish Republic, with a substantial number likely to have been students. The largest non-British Isles immigrant group were the Poles, 55,000 in number, followed by those who had come from India, Germany and Pakistan. Despite the publicity given to the A8 influx, therefore, Scotland still remained far down the league table of countries in the world according to total immigrant stock, although it was not at all near the bottom of that list. In terms of the share of international migrants in countries with at least 50,000 of them living within national borders, Scotland in 2014 ranked 68th out of 154 countries globally.[32]

The political context of migration also differs in Scotland from the rest of the UK. For some time since devolution in 1999, Scottish administrations of different political stripes have considered increased immigration a necessary corrective to the nation's problem of an ageing and, potentially in the long term, falling population. As already noted, until nearly the end of the twentieth century, emigration was significantly greater than immigration, although the differences started to converge from the late 1970s. Only in the first decade of the twenty-first century, however, did the balance finally become a positive one in favour of inward movement.[33] In 2007 the new SNP government set out its Economic Strategy, which was to match average European population growth over the ten-year period from then until 2017.[34] The SNP is therefore the only nationalist party in Europe that has a positive policy towards immigration, with an explicit commitment to encourage further movement into Scotland.

Indeed, some economists reckon that Scotland's population needs to grow by over 30,000 a year just to keep pace with the average for the rest of Europe.[35] Substantial migration from the A8 countries could therefore be seen as consistent with the long-term immigration strategy of the government.[36] Yet the Scotland Act of 1998, which set the ground rules for devolution, reserved control of immigration to Westminster, which has a rather different approach to the question from the Edinburgh administration. Scottish Government attempts after the Brexit vote in 2016 for some kind of bespoke devolution of powers over immigration north of the border have thus far been emphatically rebuffed by London ministers.

A detailed report on the short-term impact of the new influx from Europe came to mainly positive conclusions. It noted that 'employers value migrants for their positive traits of reliability, flexibility and productivity'. The A8 migrants were also seen to be meeting needs for low-skilled and semi-skilled labour, which had been difficult to recruit from the native-born population as a result of relatively low unemployment levels in Scotland. The migrants were not only willing to accept low pay but also poor conditions and broken working hours. They were also considered to possess a work ethic beyond that of local labour; several firms, especially in rural areas, admitted that they simply would not be able to function without them.[37]

On the other hand, migrant workers were said to have suffered from breaches of working hours regulations, social isolation when living in country areas, and were vulnerable to some hostility and criminal behaviour. For instance, 17 per cent of A8 migrants in a Glasgow-based study reported they had received verbal threats, while 7 per cent admitted they had experienced physical attack. In addition, one in four of more than 900 migrants interviewed in Fife said they had been verbally abused. Under-reporting of these offences by immigrants was very likely, in part because of traditional distrust of police in some of their home countries, where the forces of law and order had a less acceptable reputation than that of their UK counterparts. While many found Scotland 'a pleasant and friendly place to live in' and thought 'the Scottish public more welcoming to migrants than in other parts of the UK, excluding London',[38] this was not the experience of everyone:

Research on the experiences of young people and children from families seeking asylum in Glasgow discovered abuse and violence to be common, both in local communities and sometimes in schools. Research by Save the Children found that young people of secondary school age rated 'feeling safe' to be the hardest aspect of life in Glasgow. Parents expressed concern about their children's safely because of racism in the local community. Asylum seekers and refugee families were found to be anxious about the extent of drug and alcohol addiction in their local areas. Other issues related to the quality of housing and generally poor condition of the neighbourhoods in which asylum seekers and refugees have been housed. Later research confirmed these findings and noted that statutory agencies were not always aware of the extent and impact of racism experienced by refugees and asylum seekers.[39]

Teresa Piacentini's examination, in Chapter 8, of the recent history of asylum seekers from some African countries reaches similar conclusions to those cited above. Ima Jackson further shows in Chapter 5 that refugee and asylum-seeking nurses in Scotland confront discrimination and prejudice. A recent book on diverse Muslim experiences in Scotland also outlines various incidents of discrimination and Muslim acts of resistance.[40]

Roma, one of the most marginalised communities in Europe, have long endured deep prejudice in the lands of their birth. In recent years, some 1,800 Roma from Slovenia and elsewhere have settled in Govanhill in Glasgow. *The Herald* newspaper reported in November 2013 of the public reactions that they triggered in the city: 'They are society's bogeymen, women and children . . . the last community about which you may be racist and no one will blink. The Roma exist beside society, the perfect canvas onto which rumour and horror story may be painted.'[41] Ashli Mullen examines in Chapter 9 such media representations of the Roma community and their association with issues seen as symptomatic of the ills of Govanhill.

While some immigrant groups, such as the Poles, Indians and Pakistanis, have generally integrated into Scottish society, the experience of some more recent arrivals have not had the same positive experience to date. As Crown Office data on hate crimes confirm, racism remains a significant problem in Scotland, though perhaps less virulent than in some other parts the UK. The spike in hate crimes south of the border after the Brexit referendum was not replicated north of it. Nevertheless, in 2014–15 racial criminality remained the most commonly reported hate offence in Scotland, with 3,785 charges. This was more than four times the second most common type, sexual orientation aggravated crime, on which there were 841 charges.[42] Such statistics suggest that

Scotland should not be complacent in uncritically accepting a political rhetoric that portrays the country as always welcoming migrants.

Indeed, Scotland's history of inward migration before 1945 undermines cosy assumptions that Scotland's traditional culture is more welcoming to immigrants than in other societies. Irish Catholics, for instance, were targeted for their religion and seen as causing a range of social ills such as housing pressure and squalor, perceived outcomes of their associations with disease, poverty and criminality. Lithuanians were also subjected to hostile responses due to their perceived linkages to crime and drunkenness. Italians, meanwhile, were accused of being morally corrupt for opening their cafes on the Sabbath and were smeared as treacherous during wartime.[43]

IMMIGRATION, BREXIT AND THE RESPONSE OF THE SCOTTISH PARLIAMENT

In the wake of the Brexit referendum result and concerns about the future for Scottish citizens in Europe and EU citizens in Scotland, the all-party Culture, Tourism, Europe and External Relations Committee of the Scottish Parliament carried out a detailed review of the issues involved, drawing on the research of and evidence from a range of academic experts. Its report was published in early 2017.[44] The thorough consideration of the impact on Scotland of the 181,000 Europeans living in the country at the time was even more emphatic in stressing their value to Scottish society than the earlier investigations already cited. The effect, in the view of the MSPs of all parties on the Committee, had been positive at virtually all levels. Migrants had helped reverse the nation's decline in population, which had caused political anxieties in the past. Their role in several sectors of the economy from catering and agriculture to high tech companies and the health services was judged to be of crucial importance. It was argued that any contraction of migrant numbers in the labour force would have adverse economic consequences. The social impact of immigration was especially received in favourable terms: 'they have settled in our communities, enriched our lives and broadened our cultural horizons'.[45]

Since the majority of these migrants were of working age they had also to an extent offset the effects of an ageing population. Their higher levels of fertility than the Scots-born worked to the same positive end. Moreover, evidence provided by the University and College Union showed that 16 per cent of academic staff in higher education were EU citizens. In research-only posts, they filled almost a quarter of key positions. The relatively young average age of the migrants meant that their use of the health service was also low compared to the Scots-born. No clear link was established between immigrants from Europe and reported crime. In education, some schools had had to adapt to changing needs for language provision and especially for English as an additional language. But in the opinion of academic researchers who gave evidence to the Committee, migrants, despite such pressures, could also bring benefits into the classroom:

> there was a strong feeling among education authorities that having pupils from elsewhere around the world assisted with the aspirations of, and possibilities for, Scottish-born children, particularly in areas of multiple deprivation where Scottish-born children might have fairly limited experience of life beyond Glasgow, never mind of the wider world.[46]

Perhaps also the fact that these young Scots had experience over several years of children from other ethnic backgrounds in the classroom and playground might also in later life give them a more positive approach to people of other ethnicities.

Indeed, the emphatic consensus among the researchers who were interviewed was that immigrants from Europe paid much more into the system than they took out because the vast majority were young and in some kind of employment. There was a determination on the part of the experts to refute media misinformation about the impact of immigration. As one put it:

> there is no evidence that such immigrants are somehow stealing jobs from Scots or sponging on the welfare state. In fact, the position is the opposite by a significant margin, if we believe the research. At the end of the day, that is another reason why we can say that immigrants are very important economically. We get rhetoric from the anti-immigration lobby, but some very good research shows that the situation is the opposite of what that rhetoric claims.[47]

Yet there is a crucial caveat. In some parts of England a deep feeling has existed in some communities that their very sense of historic identity as well as the economic prospects for their young people has been threatened by the sheer scale of immigration in recent years. Thus far, in general terms, that reaction has not occurred to any significant extent north of the border. In part, as suggested earlier, the reason may be because the magnitude of influx has been considerably less than in England. However, that might not be the entire explanation. Some of the new immigrant communities in the early twentieth century were able to connect to the rise of Scottish nationalism, the most important political development in the country in the later twentieth century, as discussed by Ailsa Henderson and colleagues in Chapter 10. Rather than being passive spectators, sitting as it were on the proverbial fence, many Asians not only identified with the cause for independence, but also became actively involved in the debate before the 2014 referendum. Whatever the political views of the immigrants, their activism and interest were evidence of a degree of integration into Scottish society and concern for an issue in which native Scots had also become deeply involved. The SNP's jettisoning of ethnic nationalism of the exclusive 'blood and soil' type in favour of civic and inclusive nationalism where anyone who is a resident can join the nation likely also aids a sense of migrant integration. As summarised elsewhere, 'comparative academic research has shown that Scottish Muslims have stronger national sentiments towards Scotland than English Muslims have towards England'.[48]

This book, then, examines a number of key themes relating to migration to Scotland since 1945, including identities, discrimination and racism. We do not set out an overarching theory or typology of these concepts but rather allow our contributors to present their perspective, as every migrant group encounters and expresses them in different ways. Even so, the book reveals that most migrant groups experienced some form of racist reaction, be it through discrimination based on socially constructed markers of difference or through structural racism. However, the extent of overt hostility shown varied considerably among them. Neither does the book include every migrant group in Scotland. It does, however, include the main ethnicities and new areas of scholarship in the field.[49] With research on immigrants in post-1945 Scotland continuing to attract attention, the findings in the chapters that follow will further benefit from future comparative investigation across other migrant groups. The benefits of such an approach are outlined in Enda Delaney's final reflective chapter.

NOTES

1. 'Glorious diversity of our mongrel nation', *Scotsman*, 5 January 2008.
2. The most recent overview is Ben Braber, 'Immigrants', in T. M. Devine and Jenny Wormald (eds), *The Oxford Handbook of Modern Scottish History* (Oxford: Oxford University Press, 2012), pp. 491–509.
3. T. M. Devine, *To the Ends of the Earth: Scotland's Global Diaspora 1750–2010* (London: Allen Lane, 2011), pp. 270–88.
4. Regrettably, we have been unable to locate any scholar to contribute a chapter in this book on the contemporary Irish-born in Scotland.

5. Jan Lucassen, Leo Lucassen and Patrick Manning, 'Migration history: Multidisciplinary approaches', in Jan Lucassen, Leo Lucassen and Patrick Manning (eds), *Migration History in World History: Multidisciplinary Approaches* (Leiden: Brill, 2010), p. 3.

6. Donna R. Gabaccia, 'Migration history in the Americas', in Steven J. Gold and Stephanie J. Nawyn (eds), *Routledge International Handbook of Migration Studies* (London and New York: Routledge, 2013), p. 67.

7. Stephen Castles, Hein de Hass and Mark J. Miller, *The Age of Migration: International Population Movements in the Modern World* (Basingstoke: Palgrave, 2014, 5th edn), pp. 6, 7, 89, 199.

8. United Nations, *International Migration 2006*, Department of Economic and Social Affairs, Population Division, 2006.

9. Ibid.

10. UNHCR, *Global Trends: Forced Displacement in 2015* (2015), p. 2, online at http://www.unhcr.org/576408cd7.pdf

11. Michael R. Marrus, *The Unwanted: European Refugees in the Twentieth Century* (New York and Oxford: Oxford University Press, 1985), p. 4.

12. Euro area unemployment rate, 1995–2017, www.trading economics.com/euro-area/unemployment-rate (accessed 17 January 2017).

13. UK Labour Market-Office for National Statistics, 14 December 2016. www.ons.gov.uk/unemploymentandlabourmarket/December2016;   M. O'Neill and J. Mirza-Davies, 'Youth unemployment statistics' (House of Commons Library, Number 5871, 2016).

14. The analysis which follows primarily draws on Michael Anderson, 'Migrants in Scotland's population histories since 1850', in *Scotland's Population – The Registrar General's Annual Review of Demographic Trends* (2015), pp. 79–106; M. Watson, 'The English diaspora: Discovering Scotland's invisible migrants 1945 to 2000', *Scottish Economic and Social History*, 22 (2002), pp. 23–49; D. A. Coleman and J. Salt, *The British Population: Patterns, Trends and Processes* (Oxford: Oxford University Press, 1992).

15. Ross Bond, 'Minorities and diversity in Scotland: Evidence from the 2011 Census', *Scottish Affairs*, 26:1 (2017), p. 37. See also N. Bailey, A. Bows and D. Sim, 'The Chinese community in Scotland', *Scottish Geographical Magazine*, 110:2 (1994), pp. 66–75.

16. https://en.wikipedia.org/wiki/Demography_of_Scotland; information from Hugh MacDonald of *The Herald* newspaper, 27 February 2017, and Fr. Henry O'Brien, parish priest, St Mary's Hamilton, 25 February 2017.

17. 'Commentary: The relative and the real: A decade of migration in Scotland', *The Migration Observatory at the University of Oxford*, 3 December 2013.

18. http://www.migrationobservatory.ox.ac.uk/press/changes-to-the-migrant-population-of-scotland-2001-2011/

19. Paul Spoonley and Richard Bedford, *Welcome to Our World? Immigration and the Reshaping of New Zealand* (Auckland: Dunmore, 2012), p. 267.

20. Ibid., pp. 279, 207.

21. Bond, 'Minorities and diversity', p. 24.

22. Ibid., p. 31.

23. Kirby Swales, 'Understanding the Leave vote', NatCen, December 2016.

24. Report, 'Immigration and independence: Public opinion on immigration in Scotland in the context of the referendum debate', *The Migration Observatory*, 10 February 2014, online at http://www.migrationobservat ory.ox.ac.uk/wp-content/uploads/2016/04/Report-Immigration_Indepen dence.pdf

25. Heather Rolfe and Hilary Metcalf, 'Recent migration into Scotland: The evidence base', Scottish Government Social Research, Edinburgh, 2009.

26. 'Immigration: Is Scotland really different?', www.bbc.co.uk/news/uk-Scotland-25910947 (accessed 6 December 2016). See D. A. McCollum, D. A. Findlay, D. Bell and J. Bijak, 'Patterns and perceptions of migration: Is Scotland distinct from the rest of the UK?', CPC Briefing Paper 10, ESRC Centre for Population Change, Southampton, 2013.

27. Ibid.

28. C. Bromley, J. Curtice and L. Green, *Attitudes to Discrimination in Scotland: 2006 Scottish Social Attitudes Survey* (Edinburgh: Scottish Government Social Research, 2007).

29. 'Immigration and independence', p. 24.

30. Quoted in 'Immigration: Is Scotland really different?', p. 6.

31. Anderson, 'Migrants in Scotland's population histories', pp. 80–1.

32. Migration Observatory, 'Briefing: Global international migration stock: Scotland in international comparison', 4 March 2014, p. 5.

33. Anderson, 'Migrants in Scotland's population histories', p. 84.

34. Rolfe and Metcalf, 'Recent migration into Scotland', p. 1.

35. 'Immigration: Is Scotland really different', p. 5.

36. Rolfe and Metcalf, 'Recent migration into Scotland', p. 1.

37. P. de Lima, B. Jentsch and R. Whelton, *Migrant Workers in the Highlands and Islands* (Inverness, 2005); A. Metcalf, H. Rolfe and A. Dhudwar, *Employment of Migrant Workers* (Edinburgh, 2009).

38. Rolfe and Metcalf, 'Recent migration into Scotland', p. 1.

39. Ibid., para 4.60; Save the Children, *My Mum is Now My Best Friend: Asylum-Seeker and Refugee Families in Glasgow* (Glasgow, 2004), www. savethechildren.org.uk

40. Peter Hopkins (ed.), *Scotland's Muslims: Society, Politics and Identity* (Edinburgh: Edinburgh University Press, 2017).

41. *The Herald*, 22 November 2013.

42. Hate Crime in Scotland 2014–15, www.copfs.gov.uk/images/HateCrimein Scotland2014-15.pdf, downloaded 4 February 2017.

43. T. M. Devine, *The Scottish Nation, 1700–2000* (London: Penguin, 1999), ch. 21.

44. Culture, Tourism, Europe and External Relations Committee of the Scottish Parliament, EU Migration and EU Citizens' Rights, 3rd Report, 2017

(Session 5), http://www.parliament.scot/S5_European/Reports/CTEERCS 052017R03Rev.pdf

45. Ibid., Convener's Foreword, p. 2.

46. Ibid., Evidence of Professor Rebecca Kay of the Glasgow Asylum and Refugee Network, p. 27.

47. Ibid., Evidence of Professor Robert Wright, Strathclyde University, p. 27.

48. Cited in Omar Shaikh and Stefano Bonino, 'Heritage: Feeling Scottish and being Muslim: Findings from the Colourful Heritage Project', in Hopkins (ed.), *Scotland's Muslims*, p. 176.

49. An obvious gap in this book relates to the Irish-born. Yet, despite consulting Professor Enda Delaney of the University of Edinburgh, the leading historian of the post-1945 Irish migrant experience in Britain, we could not locate a scholar undertaking research on a new area of investigation relating to this migrant group.

2

Invisible Migrants? English People in Modern Scotland

T. M. Devine

English people in Scotland are now acknowledged to be by far the country's largest migrant group in modern times. Indeed, at the census of 2011, the 477,000 English- and Welsh-born who were enumerated outnumbered all other first-generation migrants to Scotland put together. Not all, of course, would necessarily be of white English ethnicity. Some were the children of Indians, Pakistanis, Chinese and West Indian parents who had moved to Scotland after first settling in London and the English Midlands. The marked increase in movement from across the border since the 1970s is an important reason why, after centuries of net population loss through emigration, Scotland in the last two decades or so has experienced net immigration.

This chapter begins by exploring the nature of English migration and the reasons for its sustained increase from the 1970s. The analysis then moves to a consideration of the areas of English settlement, class and occupational structure, and the response of Scots to the migrants in their midst, including two short case-studies of the English-born in two quite different Scottish settings.

I

The English in Scotland first started to attract serious scholarly attention in the 1990s. For a very long time they had fallen well below the research radar and their presence was hardly mentioned in studies of modern Scottish history.[1] Some writers had indeed acknowledged that, long before, skilled workers from England played a key role in the transfer of the new techniques of iron-making and textile manufacture during the early phases of the Industrial Revolution in Scotland between c. 1760 and c. 1830.[2] After that period, however, English migrants in general faded from scholarly attention. This oversight has given the erroneous impression that they can now be regarded as 'new' settlers to Scotland. However, if there is some novelty in their story it is rather to be found in the significant increase in their inward movement from the 1970s and the fact that, at long last, the English in Scotland are beginning to attract serious attention from researchers.

As Table 1 confirms, the English-born have been coming to Scotland for generations. Indeed, from the census of 1921 they occupied an even larger share of the non-Scots-born than the Irish who had tradition-ally dominated inward migration to Scotland from the late eighteenth century. For instance, the English presence in Edinburgh, often com-mented on nowadays, had very long antecedents. As early as 1881, the census of that year recorded that the number of English-born in the capital for the first time exceeded that of first-generation Irish.[3] Yet, so far as is known, that significant change elicited little reaction. At the time, the English remained 'invisible migrants'.

Table 2.1 Population of Scotland, 1861–2001, showing birthplaces

Year	Total Population	Born in (%)			
		Scotland	England	NI*	Irish Rep.**
2001	5,062,011	87.1	8.1	0.5	0.5
1991	4,998,567*	89.1	7.1	0.5	0.5
1981	5,035,315	90.3	5.9	0.5	0.7
1971	5,228,965	91.0	5.3	0.6	0.6
1961	5,179,344	91.8	4.6	0.8	0.7
1951	5,096,415	92.1	4.4	0.9	0.8
1931	4,842,980	92.8	3.4	1.2	1.4
1921	4,882,497	91.5	3.9		3.2
1911	4,760,904	91.7	3.4		3.7
1901	4,472,103	91.4	2.9		4.6
1891	4,025,647	91.6	2.7		4.8
1881	3,735,573	91.0	2.4		5.9
1871	3,360,018	91.1	2.1		6.2
1861	3,062,294	91.0	1.8		6.7

Source: McIntosh, Robertson and Sim, *English People in Scotland*, p. 2
Notes:
* This is the figure which is published in the various census volumes. Later recalculations were carried out to allow for undercounting but, in this table, the published figure is used.
** Persons enumerated from 1931 onwards, who gave their birthplace simply as 'Ireland', are included within the Republic total. Prior to 1931, figures are for Ireland as a whole.

From the 1950s, the numbers of English-born increased in each sub-sequent decade thereafter, rising from 222,161 in 1951 to 408,948 in 2001, an overall rate of growth of 84 per cent over the half century. During the shorter period 1971 to 2001, the increase was of the order of 48 per cent.[4] Further, although increased immigration to Scotland from India, Pakistan, Poland and elsewhere was a striking feature of the second half of the twentieth century, the English rate of growth remained exceptional. The English-born expanded from around equal numbers, in comparison with all other migrants combined, to nearly twice the size of other ethnicities by the end of the twentieth century.[5]

For some time, it was a popular belief that most of those who came to Scotland were well-heeled retirees from London and the South East or younger people in search of a higher quality of life who settled in scenic parts of the Highlands and Islands.[6] That such migrants did and do exist is undeniable and their significance, especially in rural Scotland, will be discussed later in the chapter. But the evidence suggests that neither in terms of place of residence nor occupational choices are these types representative of the majority of the English in Scotland in 2015. Instead, at the census of 2001, nearly one quarter of a million English-born lived in the urban central Lowlands, with another 92,000 or so in the North East region. In contrast, the Inner and Outer Hebrides overall attracted just over 7,000.[7] These settlement patterns, in rough proportionate terms, had changed little over the previous half century.[8] Moreover, the vast majority of English heads of households were economically active rather than living in leisured retirement. A range of interviews with this group conducted over recent years revealed that employment opportunities and career development were by far the key motivating factors in their decision to move to Scotland.[9] Nonetheless, all these studies also confirm that the reasons for living north of the border were complex and the hope of a better quality of life was also influential. Having said that, economic drivers remained of paramount significance for most people of working age who came from the south.

To understand why job opportunities in Scotland encouraged more English migration than ever before, a brief overview of Scottish economic change since the 1980s is helpful. It was the transforma-tions of that time, above all else, which generated new possibilities for working-age English people. Over that period the labour market in Scotland radically altered.[10] Until the 1970s, the traditional heavy industries of coal, shipbuilding, steel and heavy engineering, though in increasing difficulty, still remained dominant, as they had done since the middle decades of the nineteenth century. Then, with astonishing speed, they all virtually disappeared in a matter of years in the 1980s. Unemployment in some areas rocketed to levels not seen since the dark days of the 1930s, and manufacturing became less prominent in the Scottish economy by the 1990s than at any period since early Victorian times. In 1980 industry and mining together employed 800,000 Scots. A decade later that figure had fallen by more than a half. By the start of the new millennium, Scotland had a lower proportion of the labour force employed in manufacturing than the average for the UK as a whole. Deindustrialisation was a global process at the time but a small country like Scotland, which had disproportionate activity in the old economy, suffered especially badly.

But that process, though a traumatic and devastating experience for countless families in the old industrial heartlands of the country in the west-central Lowlands and the mining districts of Fife and West Lothian, did not result in permanent or absolute national economic decline. Instead, in these years the economy was transformed, which in the medium term led to a veritable revolution in employment patterns. The number of workers in manufacturing, agriculture and fisheries fell by almost 50 per cent between 1979 and 1994, while those with jobs in finance and in public services rose dramatically. The service sector now became by far the most dynamic in the economy. Demonstrably, a new economic system was rising out of the ashes of the old, though regrettably, not always in the same areas where traditional manufacturing and mining had once flourished. The modern drivers were a rapidly expanding public sector, with health, higher education and social services to the fore, along with finance, banking and insurance (by 1994 ten of the fifteen largest companies in Scotland were in financial services), tourism, light engineering, electronics and oil and gas.[11]

These transformative developments were likely to connect with increased English migration, and especially that of skilled, semi-skilled and professional people, at several levels. In parallel with the changes in Scotland, globalisation triggered an increased mobility among the service-class of managers and administrators, employed by multinational corporations and state institutions, from metropolitan headquarters to regional and local hubs across the UK.[12] Enhanced ownership of firms in the periphery by large companies in the metropolis also routinely led to expert management being seconded to local branches from head office. The expansion of this service-class, which overwhelmingly moved from place to place for reasons of employment or promotion, had several implications for the movement of economically active English people to Scotland.

First, the influence of English conglomerates in the Scottish economy had grown significantly throughout the last three decades of the twentieth century. Already in 1973 a research sample revealed that of 318 branch plants operating in Scotland, 184, or 58 per cent, were headquartered in England. Sixteen years later the Scottish Trades Union Congress reported that in manufacturing alone most control of Scottish firms in the sector rested in the City of London and English-based companies.[13]

Second, especially in the National Health Service, higher education and public administration, an internal UK labour market prevailed which helped to embed migration flows from south to north. In the universities, for instance, over the last forty years or so the old elite system has been replaced by mass higher education. As late as 1960, only the four ancient universities of Aberdeen, Edinburgh, Glasgow and St Andrews offered degrees, while the rate of participation of the relevant age cohort was little more than 5 per cent.[14] By 2015 the universities had expanded to fifteen in number, together with another three higher educational institutions which had the authority to award degrees. Student numbers soared to 281,285 by 2014–15, and the participation rate at that point hovered around 55.4 per cent of the age group.[15] Some institutions, such as Edinburgh, Glasgow, Strathclyde and Aberdeen, now employed many thousands of academic and administrative staff. Edinburgh, for instance, with 12,000 staff, became the third-biggest employer in the capital. This revolution in higher education provision was on such a scale that it could not have taken place without extensive recruitment of professors, lecturers and researchers from outside Scotland. England was likely to be by far the biggest supplier of this external academic talent.

Third, two of the key drivers of the new economy were oil and gas production, centred in Aberdeen, and financial services concentrated in Edinburgh and, to a lesser extent, Glasgow. By the late 1990s, Scotland was reckoned to be fourth in Europe in the provision of financial services after London, Frankfurt and Paris, with a labour force of over 220,000.[16] As a result, Edinburgh in particular became a major focal point for professional service-class migration. Indeed, so compelling was the capital as a magnet for expertise that between 1991 and 2001 even some Scots who held managerial and professional posts in London and the South East were beginning to return to the Scottish capital to live and work.[17] Over that period the Scots-born population in South East England fell by 19 per cent, while in 2000–1 alone 14,539 returned to Scotland from the same area, the vast majority of working age and with degree-level qualifications. Most of these returnees settled in Edinburgh and its environs, with its vibrant financial services and expanding government functions after devolution. But Aberdeen and Glasgow also proved attractive for many others.[18]

Fourth, inward migration from other parts of the UK peaked twice, at nearly 62,000 per annum between 1988/9 and 1991/2 and again from 2003/4 to 2004/5. The first of the upturns coincided with a sudden and significant rise in unemployment in the South East of England which led to the narrowing of the differential in unemployment opportunities north and south of the border. It has been suggested that the second was triggered by professionals and executives moving from first jobs in the London headquarters of large firms to take up posts in branch offices of the same or other companies in Scotland.[19]

However, survey results suggest that while employment was a necessary precondition for migration to Scottish cities, the search for what was judged a better quality of life was not irrelevant.[20] In the 1960s and 1970s, English civil servants had famously and vociferously resisted dispersal to Scottish centres. Yet more recently Scotland seems to have become decidedly more attractive to migrants from England.[21] Fewer professional or skilled workers settled in the older industrial areas in the hinterland of Glasgow in the west or Dundee in the east, but Aberdeen's profile rose not only because of its new status as 'the oil capital of Europe' but by its promotion as an attractive place to live on the sea coast with access to hill country of unspoilt natural beauty.

The centre of Glasgow was also reinvented over the last forty years or so. The city now prided itself on being the second-biggest shopping centre in the UK after London, the streets in and around the 'Merchant City' district crammed with new restaurants, bistros and pubs. It was even lauded at one point as Europe's 'Capital of Cool' by *National Geographic* magazine.[22] Edinburgh, however, has lured more English professional migrants than any other Scottish city. In terms of 'quality of life' the capital frequently scores very highly in international surveys. In 2016, for example, the City RepTrak international index ranked Edinburgh sixth in the list of the 'most reputable cities' among all G8 countries by measures of aesthetic quality, environment, technology and financial stability. Scotland's capital was placed ahead of London, Paris, Berlin, Rome, Madrid and Dublin in that particular league table.[23]

II

A key difference between the English and the other migrant groups considered in this book is that they never became a compact or recognisable ethnic community, probably because most consider themselves to have 'relocated' within the UK, rather than 'migrated'. English migrants do not come together to celebrate St George's Day, nor do they gather in clubs or societies which draw on a specific English membership or seek to establish English-only political pressure groups. This is one reason which enables them to be considered an 'invisible minority'.[24] Their historical experience differs from the first-generation Irish, Italians, Chinese, Indians, Pakistanis, Poles and others who all, to a greater or lesser extent, either in the past or in the present, have tended to concentrate for a time in particular occupations like manual labour, catering and shopkeeping. These other ethnicities could also often be defined as 'different' in cultural or religious terms from most native-born Scots.[25] Moreover, while more middle-class opportunities may have helped to boost an increase in English movement to Scotland, a broad occupational diversity remained key to their employment profile. In concluding his consideration of their job patterns in the early twentieth century, Murray Watson noted:

> Although there was a marginal bias towards the public services, the English were also working in professional and scientific services, chemicals and allied industries, miscellaneous services, other manufacturing industries, insurance, banking and finance, and gas, electricity and water. Equally there was a diverse spread of occupational categories from unskilled to semi-skilled technical, professional and managerial.[26]

His analysis suggests that the common stereotype of the English in Scotland as emphatically middle class and over-represented in managerial positions may be something of an exaggeration. In another examination of occupational structures, Malcolm B. Dickson observed, 'In many respects the most significant comparisons are in the similarity between the English and Scot-born populations.'[27] Data drawn from the censuses of 2001 and 2011 suggest that this pattern has been maintained into the new millennium.

A similar diversity is at first apparent when the range of English settlement patterns in Scotland is considered. English people can be found in most parts of the central Lowlands, Highlands and Islands and the border counties. That said, detailed examination reveals a more uneven pattern, with some areas of concentration and other places where few English have settled. As already noted, the vast majority live in the urban central belt. Yet here some changes over time should be noted. So far as can be judged, the west-central districts of heavy industry concentration attracted most English people before the 1970s. But that focus changed with deindustrialisation. The east, with Edinburgh and

Aberdeen as the twin poles of the new economy, then experienced a considerable increase in English migration. The oil-rich North East, for instance, where there were 36,365 English-born in 1961, had over 92,333 by 2001. On the other hand, west-central Scotland, outside the city of Glasgow, became the least attractive area for English migrants. The smallest proportions of English-born in Scotland in 2001 were to be found in North Lanarkshire, Renfrewshire, Inverclyde and West Dunbartonshire. Even Glasgow, which remained an important economic hub, was the most 'Scottish' of the four major cities, with almost 90 per cent born in Scotland and only 4.2 per cent in England. In Edinburgh, on the other hand, 77 per cent were Scots while 12 per cent were born in England, around three times the proportions for Glasgow.

When, however, the proportion of English in relation to Scots is considered further, it becomes apparent they have a much higher profile in some places than others. In a general sense they are more visible in several rural areas and in a few middle-class enclaves in the Scottish cities. Of the larger towns and cities, Edinburgh, Stirling, Dunfermline, Inverness, Livingston and Aberdeen, in that order, had most English-born in 2001 as a proportion of their total populations. The high ranking of Dunfermline and Livingston clearly reflected the significance of the 'Edinburgh effect' in their functions as commuter towns for the capital.[28] Edinburgh localities with relatively high proportions of English-born included the middle-class residential districts of the New Town and the southern suburbs of Morningside, Colinton and Grange, as well as commuter towns and villages to the south of the capital such as East Linton, Gullane, Musselburgh and North Berwick.[29]

The Borders and Dumfries and Galloway, the two Scottish local authorities closest to England, also have high ratios of English migrants. These areas combine easy access from northern England with a position across the two countries as a single housing and labour market. Military and naval bases in Scotland, such as Lossiemouth, Gairloch and Leuchars, have significant concentrations of English-born, as do the university towns of St Andrews and Stirling and the village of Bridge of Allan.[30] Nor can visitors to the Highlands fail to notice the numbers of English people in some remote mainland and island localities. In absolute terms, their numbers might be slight but in sparsely populated districts they often have a high profile. Indeed, one study suggested that 30 per cent of the increase in population in the Highlands and Islands between 1977 and 1981 was caused by an influx of people born in England.[31] Again, however, this generalisation does not apply to all areas. Inward migration has been more common in the Inner Hebrides than the Western Isles and is less significant in the northern counties of Caithness and Sutherland than in Argyll and Highland Perthshire to the south. In some parts the concentrations can be especially marked. On the island of Mull, for example, the 2001 census showed that a fifth of the population in all its postcode districts had been born in England.[32]

III

The increasing volume of movement from England since the 1970s and the fact that the English are by far Scotland's largest migrant group of recent times begs the question of the Scottish response to the newcomers. Before the evidence on that issue itself is reviewed in detail, it is possible to suggest some reasons why it might be assumed the English influx could have caused some local tensions in specific localities north of the border.

For over three hundred years, the Scots and English have been partners in a political union which has brought undeniable material benefits to Scotland for much of that long period. Nevertheless, in 2015, 85 per cent of the UK population lived in England, which has always been the dominant partner within the union state.[33] The imbalanced nature of the relationship inevitably tended to produce sensitivity in the junior partner about any perceived threat of further English hegemony. Indeed, England has been described as 'the significant other', with a key role to play in the defining of Scottish identity: 'English people represent a constant foil against which Scottish identity is reinforced and difference asserted.'[34] That feeling is a well-recognised response when a smaller nation has a land border with a much more powerful neighbour. In the Scottish case, identity is in part defined by not being 'the other', that is, not being English. It has also been suggested that 'When the neighbour starts living among you, then these notions of distinctions rise further to the fore.'[35]

Concerns have indeed been raised from time to time about the 'Englishing' of some Scottish cultural institutions, especially universities, galleries, museums and arts organisations. The supposed negative impact of the movement of English people into fragile rural communities has also attracted some comment. In 1968 the distinguished Scottish historian William Ferguson voiced anxieties about the increasing number of English students in Scottish universities and the threat this might pose to the 'democratic' tradition in Scottish higher education.[36] A few years later, an academic from Stirling University, in a letter to *The Scotsman*, condemned the effect 'over-inflated graduate schools of Oxford and

Cambridge' would have on staff recruitment to Scottish universities: 'they are bound to reinforce the already excessive grip on the English universities on the whole structure of Scottish life'.[37] The 1986 television film *The Englishing of Scotland* went further in a message that English migrants were successfully securing many of Scotland's top jobs and that the native-born were experiencing discrimination at the higher end of the labour market.

Particularly in the 1980s and 1990s, complaints also surfaced in the press and elsewhere about the alleged 'colonialism' of English 'white settlers' in the Highlands and Islands. It was said that wealthy southerners were outbidding locals for homes in rural areas; young Scots were losing out on places to live and were being forced to move away as a result; and English incomers were accused of opposing local economic developments because they might impinge on the scenic beauty and tranquillity of life which had attracted them to move to Scotland in the first place.[38]

From the 1970s, three important political developments also warrant consideration when exploring the context of Scottish attitudes to English migrants over that period. First, the explicit southern 'Englishness' of Margaret Thatcher's image and style were reckoned to be a factor in the hostility shown her and her governments by a majority of Scots soon after she assumed power as prime minister in 1979. The Scottish novelist William McIlvanney, who was prominent in the nationalist political movements of the 1980s, declared to huge acclaim at the SNP Conference in 1987 in the course of his lecture 'Stands Scotland where it did?': 'Margaret Thatcher is not just a perpetrator of bad policies. She is a cultural vandal. She takes the axe of her own simplicity to the complexities of Scottish life ... if we allow her to continue she will remove from the word "Scottish" any meaning other than geographical'.[39] A very long compendium of similar critiques from political and civic Scotland could easily be compiled that were much more abusive than these opinions. The sociologist Tony Dickson tried to summarise the roots of the Scottish loathing for Thatcher in an essay published a year after McIlvanney's speech:

> The public person of Mrs Thatcher appears to many Scots to capture all the worst elements of their caricature of the detested English – uncaring, arrogant, always convinced of their own rightness ('there is no alternative'), possessed of an accent that grates on Scottish ears, and affluent enough to afford a retirement home costing around £500,000. She is also associated with the conspicuously 'yuppie'/affluent South-East and the City. These are bitter images for Scots well aware of such stark contrasts offered in Scotland by high unemployment, pockets of appalling social deprivation in the major

urban areas, and reared in a culture where Scottish Protestantism, while not denigrating the accumulation of wealth, has always emphasised distaste for the flouting of its manifestations.[40]

Sir Malcolm Rifkind, her one-time colleague in the UK Cabinet, talked about Margaret Thatcher as a woman who fell victim to the strongly masculine, if not misogynist, culture of Scottish politics at the time: 'She was a woman; she was an English woman; she was a bossy English woman. Combined with the cut-glass voice and an apparently patronizing manner, they were lethal [together].'[41] The combination of popular revulsion at several of the policies of the Westminster governments, the undeniably 'English' persona of the prime minister and the supposed 'colonialist' threat to Scottish values at the time, might have brought concerns about 'the other' to a new and higher level.

Second, the later twentieth century saw a considerable strengthening of Scottish identity. The Scots had long developed a dual or hybrid identity within the Union, a mix of Scottishness and Britishness, which grew out of the new political relationship between England and Scotland after 1707. For most of the three centuries of the Union, Britishness had been dominant within this duality, with British nationalism reaching a high point during the Second World War and the immediate post-war decades when the Welfare State came into being. However, from the 1970s the majority of Scots began increasingly to see themselves either as Scottish, not British, or mainly Scottish and only partly British. Survey evidence suggests the figure on both measures combined was as high as two-thirds in 1974, fell back to just over a half after the failure of the devolution proposals of 1979, but then returned to a new peak in 1997 when the referendum of that year resulted in an overwhelming vote to establish a Scottish Parliament. In electoral terms, the Thatcher years, when there was a sharp erosion of the unionist vote, were a crucial influence. The old Scottish Unionist Party (renamed in 1964 as the Scottish Conservative Party) had always combined loyalty to Britain with concern for Scottish issues and traditional rights. The eighteen years of Thatcherite policies, however, redefined that 'unionist nationalism' as British nationalism, which despite being decisively and continuously rejected at the polls in Scotland led nonetheless to policies which were consistently imposed north of the border. As the political scientist W. L. Miller argued: 'This allowed the SNP to depict unionist nationalism as not merely "British nationalist" but as essentially "English nationalist". At least in party terms that was the "death of unionism" in its historic form; and the assassin was Thatcher, not the Scottish public.'[42]

Third, in parallel with identity changes, there came historic political developments: the opening of the Scottish Parliament in 1999, the election of a SNP majority government in 2011, a referendum on Scottish independence in 2014, and then a landslide victory for the SNP in Scotland in the general election of May 2015. The evidence suggests that devolution *per se* was not feared by most of the English-born in Scotland. Indeed, many seem to have welcomed the granting of devolved powers as a route to better governance of the country. But on the issue of Scottish independence hostility did come more to the fore. YouGov reported after the referendum of September 2014 that 26 per cent of those born in England, Wales or Northern Ireland had voted Yes, little more than half the equivalent figure of 49 per cent among those of Scottish birth. Further research carried out by political scientists at the University of Edinburgh then confirmed that nearly 75 per cent of the more than 420,000 Britons from the rest of the UK (who were overwhelmingly English) voted against independence. These findings might suggest, therefore, that the majority of the English-born in Scotland may now feel alarmed or even threatened by the current popularity of nationalism.[43]

References to incidents of overt anti-English behaviour in Scotland have indeed occurred from time to time and have been highlighted in the national press. One attempt to survey them, published in 2008, noted fourteen public cases ranging from verbal abuse to physical assault which were recorded in *The Herald*, *The Scotsman* and *Daily Record* between 1993 and 2004. The authors of the analysis acknowledged that these results were highly impressionistic, prone both to possible media exaggeration on the one hand and under-recording on the other. The researchers noted that those which did surface occurred mainly in small town and rural settings. Perhaps it may have been of some significance, however, that on the list no incidents were featured before 1994 or between 2004 and 2008, when the findings were published. The fact that only fourteen were reported between 1993 and 2004 was also telling. If press reports provide any guide at all, public abuse against English people can hardly be considered common in Scotland.[44]

Media observers also picked up a few militant organisations, some with violent aspirations, such as the Army for Freeing Scotland, the Scottish Citizen's Army, the Scottish Republican Army and the Scottish National Liberation Army. But these were tiny, fringe groups on the periphery and they seem to have faded from the scene altogether after the 1980s. Indeed, it may be relevant to note that they and the incidents reported above took place mainly in that decade and in the early 1990s, when Scottish alienation from the Tory governments in Westminster was at its peak. It seems also that the attacks and hoaxes associated with these organisations were carried out against 'symbols of English rule', such as political parties and military bases, rather than English people in Scotland. Also, unlike Wales, no reports surfaced of the fire-bombing of English-owned homes in Scotland.[45]

Certainly strong feelings were present in the 1980s and early 1990s as a result of what was widely regarded as anti-Scottish policies emanating from a government in London which Scots had strongly opposed in successive general elections. One opinion poll in 1998, for instance, reported that 43 per cent of Scots believed that anti-English feelings were indeed on the increase north of the border.[46] A year later, the question was pressing enough to be raised in the Scottish Parliament in December 1999, when one SNP MSP argued that anti-English discrimination should be included as an issue during the Parliament's debate on inequality.[47] The intervention of Digby Jones, the then Head of the Confederation of British Industry, when he asserted in 2002 that anti-English hostility was damaging the ability of Scottish companies to recruit south of the border, also triggered a short-term media storm, although the row quickly vanished from the headlines.[48]

Yet these alarmist claims seemed to be in conflict with the increased migration of English workers to Scotland over the same period. Indeed, the press as a whole lost interest in the subject after the Digby Jones controversy calmed down. A survey of the *Scotsman* archive between 2004 and 2016 reveals little of significance reported on Anglophobia. Indeed, for what it is worth, the evidence cited above suggests that most significant anti-English incidents recorded in the media occurred mainly during the Thatcher years. They were rare before that period and equally uncommon after it. One intervention which did elicit some attention was that of the novelist and artist Alasdair Gray in an essay of 2012 with the title *Settlers and Colonists*. Gray suggested that English arts administrators in Scotland could be described either as long-term 'settlers', who were a force for good, or short-term 'colonists', who came north simply to advance their careers before returning south. He claimed that the same phenomenon could be found in other spheres of Scottish life and was not confined to the arts alone. The piece provoked some comment but was soon forgotten.

More systematic data on attitudes to English incomers can be assembled from a useful series of social science studies completed between 1997 and 2008. Geographers, political scientists, sociologists and a historian produced several scholarly articles and books over that period.[49]

In addition, quantitative data compiled by the Commission for Racial Equality (CRE) and the Centre for Education and Research on Racial Equality in Scotland (CERES) can add a further dimension to their conclusions.

Between 1993 and 1999, the CRE received twenty-two complaints of anti-English 'racism' in Scotland, a figure around 5 per cent of its Scottish case load. Not surprisingly, the Commission commented, 'Given that the English outnumbered all other migrant groups and ethnic minorities by a factor of two to one, this was an insignificant number.'[50] CERES also conducted an audit of studies on racial equality the following year. It did encounter some examples of 'anti-Englishness' but the English correspondents who were interviewed did not see them as 'racist' in intent.[51] Commenting on this finding, Murray Watson, author of *Being English in Scotland* (2003), noted that in his own sample of interviewees, 94 per cent considered 'that anti-Englishness was not a serious problem'.[52] More recently in 2013, a Glasgow University Law professor turned Conservative MSP, Adam Tomkins, offered his observations on the prevalence or not of anti-Englishness north of the border. Tomkins was born, raised and educated in England before moving to the west of Scotland in 2003. He admitted to having lived happily there ever since, and though being involved in the rough and tumble of nationalist versus unionist politics said that his experience of anti-English behaviour was rare:

> Of course, anti-Englishness rears its head in Scotland from time to time, and anyone who chooses to go looking for it can find it on extremist websites, for example. But my day-to-day experience of living as an Englishman in Glasgow has been that I meet anti-Englishness only exceptionally. Even when I am targeted by some of the more aggressive Nationalist websites, the reason seems to be not my English ethnicity but my Unionist politics.[53]

IV

The belief that Scotland has traditionally been a welcoming country to strangers is in conflict with some historical realities. The extent of discrimination in the labour market practised against the Catholic Irish and their descendants is now historical orthodoxy. Only from the 1970s did those abuses start to go into decline.[54] It is now hostility to black and Asian people which is the most reported form of racial criminality. Scottish Crown Office data for 2015/16 confirmed that racial offences were the most commonly reported hate crimes, 3,712 charges in all, a figure six times the number for religiously aggravated cases of breach of the peace. It is, of course, a commonplace of criminological research that reported crimes of that nature were likely to be only a fraction of the actual offences committed.[55]

On this evidence, therefore, Scotland has not been immune from racial phobias. Yet the incidence of Anglophobia is much less common compared to other kinds. The evidence collected from interviews with English migrants by Asifa Hussain and William L. Miller suggests it was not widespread and when encountered usually took only the form of some 'resentments', Scots supporting other national sporting teams against England and anti-English badinage. They admit that some Scots often have negative stereotypes of the English, especially some from the southern counties, who according to their interviews can sometimes be seen as arrogant, 'superior' and haughty. But the authors conclude that such perceptions are more likely to be based on class responses to 'superior' upper-class accents rather than anti-English prejudice *per se*.

The researchers found that Islamophobia was much more widespread and potent. Only 5 per cent of Scots interviewed said they would be 'unhappy to have a close relative form a long-term relationship with an English immigrant [sic]', a figure which contrasted sharply with attitudes towards relationships with Muslims (32 per cent being unhappy). Nor did the onset of devolution and the associated strengthening of Scottish identity seem to have posed any increased threat in the view of English interviewees. Most felt at ease living in Scotland and thought that the Scottish Parliament had made little difference in this respect. Indeed, the small number who did detect a difference, agreed – by a margin of two to one – that the effect had been a positive one. Eighty-nine per cent of the sample agreed that their future lay in Scotland.[56]

It is probably too early to determine, however, whether the resounding No vote by most of the English-born living in Scotland in the 2014 referendum will affect attitudes to them of Scots who are committed to independence.[57] Ailsa Henderson and colleagues provide a detailed analysis *inter alia* in Chapter 10 on how UK citizens not born in Scotland voted in the referendum. But, as this is written, no academic research has yet been published on the question of the Scottish response to the overwhelming English-born vote against independence. Certainly, little evidence of any backlash has surfaced in either the print, broadcast or even social media, and Scottish Government sources have been silent on the issue. This is in sharp contrast to the reaction of the Parti Québécois to the result of the Quebec referendum of 1995. Incomers from the rest of Canada were condemned in no uncertain terms by the party leadership for the failure to achieve a vote for the independence of

Quebec. The difference may be because for some time the SNP has jettisoned ethnic nationalism of the exclusive 'blood and soil' type in favour of civic nationalism. This has been described by the political scientist James Kellas as inclusive in the sense that anyone may adopt the majority culture and in so doing 'join the nation'.[58] Thus, in the 2014 referendum, residence in Scotland rather than birth in Scotland was the criterion for being able to vote. As the date in September approached, *The Scotsman* published a feature headed 'English voters living in Scotland could swing the independence referendum towards NO'. The paper reported on a PanelBase poll which had shown about two-thirds (66 per cent) of English people living in Scotland intended to vote against independence. This triggered a robust response from the then SNP leader in Westminster, Angus Robertson MP, who is half-German and was born in Wimbledon. He rejected what he described as a 'concentrated attempt to foster division in Scotland' by linking voting intentions to national identity. Robertson went on to stress that 'At all levels of politics the SNP is represented by those either born in England or with strong connections to England.'[59] It was an overt attempt not only to reassure the English in Scotland but to insist once again on the paramount importance of the SNP's inclusive civic nationalism agenda.

V

The purpose of this section is to present short case-studies of the English-born in two quite different Scottish settings: their experience in a small Hebridean community on the island of Mull and a consideration of their impact on Scottish higher education, a sector which has attracted significant numbers of academic staff from England in recent years and where there was some controversy a few years ago about the likely impact of that migration on the traditional character of Scottish universities.

The English-born people in the Ross of Mull

The Ross of Mull (*An Ros Mhuileach*) is a peninsula of 28 kilometres in the south-west of the island bounded on the north by Loch Scridain and to the south by the Firth of Lorne. It is an area of exceptional scenic beauty which, after a century or more of depopulation, has attracted incomers over the last fifty years or so.[60] Of the current 568 permanent inhabitants, 60 per cent are Scots-born and 37 per cent are defined as 'white-other British'.[61] Few communities in Scotland have a higher proportion of English-born residents in relation to total population.

In November 2016 the author of this chapter contacted a married couple who were both English-born and educated and had lived in the Ross for over forty years. They are very knowledgeable about the community, have long been involved in a number of local organisations and are aware of the subtleties of community relations and how they have developed over time. Both of them were asked to respond to the four questions set out below. The answers given then follow without any editorial changes or comment. The responses are meant to speak for themselves. They represent a brief yet finely grained appraisal of the impact of English incomers on a small community in the Inner Hebrides. Whether the insights they provide are typical or not of other places in that region, only further studies can confirm.[62]

1. In economic, social and cultural terms, have the English-born mainly been an asset to the area or not?
Overall EBs[63] are an asset in economic terms contributing significantly to the turnover albeit principally through tourism and increasing the 'spend' factor in local shops and services. A mixture of buying homes 'with potential' and new developments they have, in the main, used local tradesmen and suppliers. EBs have often brought entrepreneurism [sic] to the area – a necessity given the limited resources e.g. land, that are available. There is a majority of EBs in provision of accommodation and wildlife tours – self-employed initiatives that do not seem to have reached saturation.

Fishing – local shellfish merchants are now into the second generation. In turn this helped with viability of fishing together with government incentives. There has been a steady turnover of EB fishermen passing throughout. If they are not of, or married into a local family, there is a tendency to follow the market and leave when markets fall or at retirement age.

Tourism – many houses are bought by couples at early retirement age – 50s. These EBs will often move away after 15–20 years to be closer to their families and sometimes for additional facilities.

Agriculture – many of the larger farms are an amalgamation of crofts from the time of greatest depopulation – generally owned by indigenous families (some of which do not obviously have another generation to pass them onto). Freehold landed estates are predominantly owned by Europeans. Argyll Estates still holds a considerable area of common grazings land, burdened by Crofting Law, but they are able to sell off plots to developers whose customers are a mixture of EBs and other incomers. Recently efforts by the Crofting Commission to make crofts more available have resulted in purchases of several crofts by EBs with the capital to build on and stock the land. Generally they are warmly welcomed and integrate well into the sharing culture of existing crofters and farmers – livestock farming not being locally competitive other than at the Bunessan Show!

Skilled incomers, some of whom are EB, are welcomed depending on the gaps in the market and complementary to existing businesses.

2. Do they normally integrate well or not?

Socially, EBs make great efforts to integrate into the local social scene – perhaps gravitate naturally towards other EBs for advice and introductions if wanted. Many EB retirees are core to local groups such as the Historical Centre, Gardening group, RNLI, Castaways, with fundraising and voluntary work. Many of these groups would probably have difficulty functioning without them. Scottish/local accents are in a minority in many of these groups (excluding the Pipe Band). Singers on the Ross, including those who belong to the Mull Gaelic Choir, are in the main EB. Most of the Gaelic learners in local classes are EB. Other interest groups have arisen from professional retirees e.g. Bridge Club, U4A. Where EBs do not integrate well is because of differences in social and cultural expectations when they might try to 'improve' the way things are run. Differences are more noticeable in those from further south. Many seem to move here to remove themselves from perceived selfish/ arrogant excesses of the urban south. A considerable number voted for Scottish independence.

3. Have they encountered any hostility or prejudice from the local community?

It would be interesting to know the proportion of EBs to Others but generally EBs are well received. The older local families tend to be the most courteous and welcoming – a Gaelic trait. A few locals may be concerned for the future of their culture and resent the influx of EBs in spite of economic benefits. Hostilities are reserved for a minority (usually in their cups!). Interestingly there can be prejudice from the offspring of mixed marriages i.e. indigenous marrying an EB – perhaps sensitivity of origins combined with other factors.

Particular local action groups such as the Mull and Iona Health & Care and the South West Mull and Iona Development Group are pivotal in everyone working together and important forums of mutual understanding.

4. How in general are they perceived by the indigenous community?
Generally viewed as potentially useful members of the local community, be that for their skills, their time, or as customers.

5. Has the buying of permanent or holiday homes by incomers created any perceived problems for young potential house buyers from the existing community or given rise to local controversy?
In the 80s and 90s there was more grumbling about the buying of houses by EBs even though there was little real competition for the mostly old and often run-down existing properties that became available. A number of local housing initiatives has provided a stepping stone to modern affordable housing for young people. Several skilled self-employed young local people have built new houses – in many ways preferable to older buildings in terms of running costs thereafter.

In the last decade Argyll Estates also made land available to young local families at half the market price which perhaps alleviated some resentment towards EBs who have paid over the locally affordable price for housing. Looking round at ownership of new houses, developments, crofts alongside the buying of second homes (many by Scots these days) and accommodation businesses – a majority run by EBs – there seems to be a reasonable balance at the moment.

Scotland's universities: English-born academic staff

The Scottish universities have been key institutions in the history of the nation since the four 'ancient' foundations in the medieval and early modern periods. By the eighteenth century, Scotland had six compared with England's two at Oxford and Cambridge.[64] They were at the heart of the great intellectual and cultural flowering of the Scottish Enlightenment and by the early nineteenth century Scotland had probably a higher ratio of university places to population size than anywhere in Europe. The universities stood at the pinnacle of the 'national' system of education, which also included the parish and burgh schools. All were central to Scotland's sense of identity.[65] By the Victorian era they also embodied distinctive values as public institutions which differed from the more 'private' and clerical traditions of Oxford and Cambridge. In Scotland, academic work was deemed a public service, with access to 'useful learning' made available to a much larger section of the population than was the case south of the border. By the twentieth century this distinctive character had come to be described as 'democratic intellectualism'.[66]

From the 1970s, as the university sector was transformed from an elite to a mass system of higher education, some fears were expressed that the essential features of the old tradition would come under serious threat. In part this was due to the utilitarianism and instrumentalism of some of the new ideas on higher education.[67] But of even greater concern was that the 'Scottishness' of the system was likely to be eroded as academic staff from England were recruited on a very significant scale to enable the expansion in student places to take place. It was claimed that Scottish academic values were being diluted by English scholars who were more committed to research than teaching, disinterested in civic engagement and hostile to the fundamental 'democratic' nature of the Scottish institutions.[68] The controversy about this 'Englishing' of the universities had mainly died out by 2000, but as late as 2013 an Edinburgh-based academic claimed that the universities were being 'swamped' by staff from elsewhere and especially from England. Scots, it was asserted, were a 'rapidly diminishing species' in many departments and as a result the old values of Scottish higher education were vanishing rapidly.[69]

The central problem with this debate was that much depended on assertion, rhetoric, claim and counter-claim. Systematic evidence to support the 'Englishing' thesis, for or against, was usually notable by its absence. Certainly, the huge expansion of the universities in the 1960s and 1970s did draw in large numbers of academics from outside Scotland. Between 1950 and 1970 the staff in the nation's universities rose three-fold[70] and migration from south of the border was indeed substantial. One estimate suggests that, in 1964, 53 per cent of staff in Scottish higher education had taken their first degree in England. By 2001 the figure was 46 per cent.[71] The vast majority of these would not have been Scots-born. Yet this was not an entirely new phenomenon. In the 1880s a third of professors in Scottish universities were recruited from outside the country and this was a trend which persisted until at least the Second World War.[72]

Detailed research by Lindsay Paterson and Ross Bond published in 2003 and 2005 has helped to resolve some aspects of the question of the supposed 'English effect'.[73] First, they note the research culture in some disciplines north of the border, notably in humanities and social sciences, was internationally weak in the 1950s and that recruitment of research-active scholars from England soon did much to strengthen it. The present writer experienced the impact, first as an undergraduate in History and then in the early stages of his career as a university teacher at Strathclyde University. In the 1960s there were eleven staff in the

Department of Economic History in that institution, of which nine were born and educated in England. Their interest in Scottish historical topics developed rapidly after appointment and subsequently their pioneering research on subjects as varied as the industrial, maritime, labour and political history of Scotland became firmly embedded in their advanced teaching at Honours level.[74] Modern Scottish historiography owes a great debt to that generation of historians from south of the border, especially in the area of economic and social history, not simply at Strathclyde but also in Aberdeen, Edinburgh and Glasgow.

Post-1707 Scottish history had long been neglected by Scots-born scholars in favour of studies of the independent kingdom before the Union. Historians born and educated in England, notably T. C. Smout, Rosalind Mitchison, Michael Flinn, John Butt, Edgar Lythe, Peter Payne, Michael Anderson and several others, together with some leading Scottish scholars, transformed the historiography of modern Scotland in the 1960s and 1970s. They were also enthusiastically involved in the training of a new generation of Scots-born historians, several of whom have now taken over the role of academic leaders in the subject.[75] This is but a single example from one discipline of the English-born impact on the humanities and social sciences north of the border. Significantly, these have been the very subjects where research on Scottish themes has flourished as never before during the last quarter of the twentieth century and beyond.[76]

Second, far from playing the role of colonisers, academic incomers from England appear to have 'gone native' after acquiring a post in a Scottish university. Survey evidence suggests they hardly differed from their Scottish counterparts on such issues as the civic role of universities, public engagement, collaboration between institutions and learning as a public good; in other words, they have fitted easily into the Scottish tradition of democratic intellectualism.[77] In that sense, they resemble other English migrants considered in this chapter who often come to adopt attitudes which mirror those of the Scots among whom they live and work.

Third, Scottish distinctiveness seems not to have drained away but has instead been strengthened in the universities since the 1990s by key changes made at both funding and political levels. Since 1992 the universities have been resourced by a Scottish-based funding agency, now known as the Scottish Funding Council, rather than by a UK body. Moreover, since 1999 and the foundation of the Scottish Parliament, political responsibility for higher education has been devolved to Scottish ministers. In recent years the removal of tuition fees for Scottish-based undergraduates could be seen as the assertion of the tradition of learning as a public good, in contrast to the marketisation of much of higher education in England.

As this is written in 2017, it is beyond doubt that several Scottish universities have established a formidable international reputation over the last four decades or so. Indeed, not since the heady days of the eighteenth-century Enlightenment have they achieved such high global standing. Scotland now has five universities in the world's top 200, a remarkable achievement for a country with a population of just over five million. Ireland, with broadly similar numbers, has one.[78] As the prestigious scientific journal *Nature* pointed out in 2011, Scotland produced more research citations per unit of gross domestic product than any country in the world and was second only to Switzerland globally in citations per head of population.[79] The country's reputation among international students is also exceptionally high. In 2013 'overall learning satisfaction of international students in Scotland's universities was better than both the rest of the UK and other European study destinations'. The sector also managed to attract high-quality graduate students from abroad at a rate which surpassed the rest of Britain.[80] It is reasonable to conclude, therefore, that the recruitment of highly talented non-Scottish-born academic staff, most of whom are from the rest of the UK, has much to do with these achievements.

VI

Some press and other public comment in the 1980s and 1990s presented a negative view of English migration to Scotland, associating it with so-called 'white settlement' having an adverse cultural and demographic impact on some rural communities. This chapter for the most part rejects that perspective as mainly based on myth and exaggeration rather than on ascertainable fact. On the whole, English people in Scotland have integrated well in their new environment. In cities and towns they have contributed high-quality skills and professional expertise, helping to enable financial services, science-based industry and higher education in particular to excel internationally. Moreover, in some rural areas they, and indeed also many urban Scots, have often brought fresh blood, capital and business acumen to several communities which have suffered from long-term population decline and the continued haemorrhage of young people, especially when they reach the age for university entry.[81] Like other immigrants surveyed in this book who have come in rising numbers to Scotland over the last half century or so, they have also added more cultural diversity to the country as a whole.

Self-evidently, the fact that the English-born are mainly white, British and have inhabited the same island as Scots since time immemorial has helped to ensure their relatively easy acceptance north of the border compared to some other migrants. For instance, a sampling of Scottish opinion carried out in February 2014 by the Migration Observatory at Oxford University concluded *inter alia* that only one in ten Scots thought that those moving into the country from the rest of the UK could really be described as 'immigrants'.[82] English integration into Scottish society was also facilitated by their gradual and usually unobtrusive growth rather than by any sudden inrush of large numbers.

Further, Scots today seem to regard immigration more positively than the rest of mainland UK. The Migration Observatory found that in 2014 around three-quarters of the sample of interviewees in England and Wales supported a reduction in immigration compared to just over half north of the border. The same survey concluded that most of the Scots questioned thought immigration a good thing.[83] This may in part be because the scale of inward movement, despite recent increases, still remains far below the influx into England. The fact also that the current Scottish Government strongly supports more immigration, the nation's long history of loss of young and active people through centuries of emigration and the fear of the economic consequences of an ageing population, are some of the additional factors which have probably helped to shape these more positive opinions.

England might indeed have been seen in Scottish tradition as 'the other' or 'the Auld Enemy'. But there are some other historical factors to be set in the balance against that clichéd perception, including the close mutual partnership of over 250 years in the governance and administration of the British empire, the collective blood sacrifices of the two world wars in the twentieth century and, by no means least, the age-old movement of Scots to England which have developed and embedded countless family connections north and south of the border. After long periods of hostility, violence and war in medieval times, both countries have for many centuries managed to live together in relative harmony within the same small land mass.

Crucially, too, twenty-first-century Scottish nationalism, possibly uniquely now in Europe, projects itself as civic, inclusive and social democratic rather than ethnic. The current SNP government also takes a positive view of immigration and is keen to encourage more migrants to settle in Scotland. If you live in Scotland, then you are recognised as a Scottish citizen. The criterion for inclusion is territorial rather than tribal. In the 2014 independence referendum, those of Scots descent living outside Scotland were denied a vote, while those who were not, but who lived in Scotland, were able to take part.

That background helps to explain why English people in modern Scotland do not feel the need to see themselves like some ethnicities do as an 'immigrant community' or 'strangers in a strange land'. They have little need to construct defensive solidarity against real or imagined external threats in their new homeland, despite some predictable frissons and occasional tensions derived from the long and complex set of relationships between the two nations. It also helped, of course, that, unlike the Catholic Irish, the English never posed a threat to traditional Scottish religious values or were thought to seriously threaten the jobs or wages levels of Scottish workers.

In consequence of all this, the English in Scotland have tended to fall below the research radar until very recently, despite their increasing numbers and demographic ranking as the country's largest migrant group by far since the 1920s. Only in the last two decades or so have they begun to attract the kind of serious scholarly investigation which has helped to make the writing of this chapter possible.

NOTES

1. Murray Watson, *Being English in Scotland* (Edinburgh: Edinburgh University Press, 2003), p. 1. See, for example, T. M. Devine, *The Scottish Nation: A Modern History* (London: Penguin Books, 2006). Throughout the chapter, the English will be described as 'migrants' rather than 'immigrants'. As the Migration Observatory at Oxford University has noted, 'a person who moves from England to Scotland, or vice versa, despite travelling between two areas that are recognised as "nations" is still not an international migrant in migration statistics'. See The Migration Observatory, 'Commentary: Who counts as a migrant in Scotland?', 2 April 2014.
2. Ian McIntosh, Douglas Robertson and Duncan Sim, *English People in Scotland* (Lampeter: Edwin Mellen Press, 2008), p. 15.
3. Roger Swift and Sheridan Gilley (eds), *The Irish in the Victorian City* (London: Croom Helm, 1985), p. 187.
4. Ibid., p. 16.
5. Michael Anderson, 'Migrants in Scotland's population histories since 1850', in *Scotland's Population – The Registrar General's Annual Review of Demographic Trends 2015* (Edinburgh: National Records of Scotland, 2016), pp. 79–106.
6. M. Dickson, 'Should auld acquaintance be forgot? A comparison of the Scots and English in Scotland', *Scottish Affairs*, 7 (1994), pp. 112–34.
7. www.scotlandcensus.gov.uk

8. Watson, *Being English*, p. 29.
9. For example, see Allan M. Findlay, Aileen Stockdale, Caroline Hoy and Cassie Higgins, 'The structuring of service-class migration: English migration to Scotties cities', *Urban Studies*, 40:10 (2003), pp. 2067–81.
10. This and the paragraphs which immediately follow are based on Devine, *Scottish Nation*, pp. 631–55; G. C. Peden, 'A new Scotland? The economy', in T. M. Devine and Jenny Wormald (eds), *The Oxford Handbook of Modern Scottish History* (Oxford: Oxford University Press, 2012), pp. 652–71; and T. M. Devine, Clive Lee and George Peden (eds), *The Transformation of Scotland: The Economy since 1700* (Edinburgh: Edinburgh University Press, 2005), pp. 233–65.
11. Devine, *Scottish Nation*, p. 645.
12. Findlay et al., 'Structuring of service-class migration', pp. 2067–81.
13. J. Firn, 'External control and regional development: The case of Scotland', *Environment and Planning* A, 7 (1975), p. 403; S. Boyle, M. Burns et al., *Scotland's Economy: Claiming the Future* (London: Croom Helm, 1989), p. 43.
14. T. G. K. Bryce and W. M. Humes (eds), *Scottish Education* (Edinburgh: Edinburgh University Press, 1999), pp. 63–72.
15. http://www.sfc.ac.uk/web/FILES/Statistical_publications_SFCST052016_HigherEducationStudentsandQualifiersatS/SFCST052016_HE_Students_and_Qualifiers_2014-15.pdf
16. Devine, *Scottish Nation*, pp. 595–6.
17. Allan Findlay, Colin Mason, Richard Harrison, Donald Houston and David McCollum, 'Getting off the escalator? A study of Scots out-migration from a global city region', *Environment and Planning* A, 40:9 (2008), pp. 2169–85.
18. Ibid.
19. Information provided by Michael Anderson from his forthcoming major study of Scottish demographic history. I am most grateful to Professor Anderson for this point. See also Findlay et al., 'Getting off the escalator', pp. 2169–85.
20. Ibid., p. 2181.
21. Richard Parry, 'The rise and fall of civil service dispersal to Scotland', http://www.scottishgovernmentyearbooks.ed.ac.uk/record/22840/1/1981/6 rise and fall of civil service dispersal.pdf, accessed 4 November 2016.
22. Devine, *Scottish Nation*, p. 647.
23. City Rep Trak, Top Cities by Reputation 2016, https://reputationinstitute.com/thought-leadership/city-reptrak, accessed 4 November 2016.
24. This is the subtitle of McIntosh, Robertson and Sim, *English People in Scotland*.
25. A recent overview is by Ben Braber, 'Immigrants', in Devine and Wormald (eds), *Oxford Handbook of Modern Scottish History*, pp. 491–509.
26. Watson, *Being English in Scotland*, p. 99.

27. Dickson, 'Should auld acquaintance be forgot?', pp. 112–34.
28. Ibid.
29. McIntosh et al., *English People in Scotland*, p. 21.
30. Ibid., pp. 20–2.
31. H. Jones, 'Incomers to peripheral areas in northern Scotland: Some housing considerations', in B. McGregor, D. Robertson and M. Schucksmith (eds), *Rural Housing in Scotland: Recent Research and Policy* (Aberdeen: Aberdeen University Press, 1981), p. 126; Sean Damer, 'Scotland in miniature? Second homes on Arran', *Scottish Affairs*, 31 (2000), pp. 37–54.
32. McIntosh et al., *English People in Scotland*, p. 22.
33. T. M. Devine (ed.), *Scotland and the Union 1707–2007* (Edinburgh: Edinburgh University Press, 2008).
34. Asifa Hussain and William L. Miller, 'The auld enemy in the new Scotland', in William L. Miller (ed.), *Anglo-Scottish Relations from 1900 to Devolution* (Oxford: Oxford University Press, 2005), p. 185.
35. Douglas Robertson, Ian McIntosh and Duncan Sim, 'The English in Scotland: Focusing on an invisible minority', in John Beech, Owen Hand, Mark A. Mulhern and Jeremy Weston (eds), *Scottish Life and Society. A Compendium of Scottish Ethnology. Volume 9: The Individual and Community Life* (Edinburgh: John Donald, 2005), pp. 575–603.
36. W. Ferguson, *Scotland: 1689 to the Present* (Edinburgh: Oliver & Boyd, 1968), p. 408.
37. *The Scotsman*, 20 September 1974.
38. Some examples are collected in Paul Boyle, 'Contrasting English and Scottish residents in the Scottish Highlands and Islands', *Scottish Geographical Magazine*, 113:2 (1997), pp. 98–104.
39. William McIlvanney, *Surviving the Shipwreck* (Edinburgh: Mainstream, 1991), p. 240.
40. A. D. R. Dickson, 'The peculiarities of the Scottish nation, culture and political action', *Political Quarterly*, 59:3 (1988), p. 3.
41. Sir Malcolm Rifkind, 'Foreword', in David Torrance, *We in Scotland? Thatcherism in a Cold Climate* (Edinburgh: Birlinn, 2009), p. xv.
42. W. L. Miller, 'The death of Unionism?', in Devine (ed.), *Scotland and the Union*, p. 179. For changes in national identity over this period more generally, see David McCrone, *The New Sociology of Scotland* (London: Sage, 2017), pp. 738–57.
43. John Curtice, 'So who voted Yes and who voted No?', 26 September 2014, http://blog.whatscotlandthinks.org/2014/09/voted-yes-voted, downloaded 8 November 2016; Ailsa Henderson, 'Why Scotland voted No', http://centreonconstitutionalchange.ac.uk/sites/default/files/Scottish%20Referendum%20Study%2027%20March%202015.pdf, 27 March, 2015, downloaded 8 November 2016. See also Ailsa Henderson's chapter later in this book.
44. McIntosh et al., *English People in Scotland*, pp. 62–7.

45. Watson, *Being English in Scotland*, p. 13.
46. *The Sunday Times*, 12 June 1998.
47. McIntosh et al., *English People in Scotland*, pp. 61-2.
48. *Sunday Herald*, 24 February 2002.
49. In chronological order they are: Isobel Lindsay, 'The uses and abuses of national stereotypes', *Scottish Affairs*, 20 (1997), pp. 133–47; Watson, *Being English in Scotland*; Ian McIntosh, Duncan Sim and Douglas Robertson, '"It's as if you're some alien . . .": Exploring anti-English attitudes in Scotland', *Sociological Research Online*, 9:2 (2004), pp. 1-15, http://www.socresonline.org.uk/9/2/mcintosh.html, accessed 3 September 2016; Allan M. Findlay, Caroline Hoy and Aileen Stockdale, 'In what sense English? An exploration of English migrant identities and identification', *Journal of Ethnic and Migration Studies*, 30:1 (2004), pp. 52–79; Asifa Hussain and William Miller, *Multicultural Nationalism: Islamophobia, Anglophobia and Devolution* (Oxford: Oxford University Press, 2006); McIntosh et al., *English People in Scotland*.
50. 'Attacks blamed on Scots' racism', *Guardian Unlimited Special Reports*, 24 March 1999; Watson, *Being English in Scotland*, pp. 17–18.
51. Scottish Social Work Inspectorate, Race Equality Audit; ceres.ed.ac.uk, summer 2000.
52. Watson, *Being English in Scotland*, p. 127.
53. Adam Tomkins, 'On the nature of Scottish nationalism', *Notes from North Britain*, 2 October 2013, https://notesfromnorthbritain.wordpress.com/2013/10/02/on-the-nature-of-scottish-nationalism.
54. T. M. Devine, 'The end of disadvantage? Descendants of Irish-Catholic immigrants in modern Scotland since 1945', in Martin J. Mitchell (ed.), *The Irish in Scotland: New Perspectives* (Edinburgh: John Donald, 2008), pp. 191–207; T. M. Devine (ed.), *Scotland's Shame? Bigotry and Sectarianism in Modern Scotland* (Edinburgh: Mainstream, 2000); Steve Bruce, *Scottish Gods: Religion in Modern Scotland* (Edinburgh: Edinburgh University Press, 2014), pp. 41–79.
55. http://www.copfs.gov.uk/media-site/media-releases/1329-hate-crime-in-scotland-2015-16, downloaded 3 December 2016.
56. Hussain and Miller, *Multicultural Nationalism*, p. 75.
57. Hussain and Miller, 'Auld enemy in the new "Scotland"', pp. 197, 199.
58. James Kellas, *The Politics of Nationalism and Ethnicity* (2nd edn, Basingstoke: Macmillan, 1998), p. 65.
59. http://www.scotsman.com/news/politics/scottish-independence-english-could-swing-vote-1-3414714, accessed 2 November 2016.
60. J. Stewart Cameron, *A History of the Ross of Mull* (Bunessan: Ross of Mull Historical Centre, 2013).
61. http://cos.churchofscotland.org.uk/resources/statistics_for_mission/parish_profiles/211306.pdf, accessed 3 December 2016.

62. The answers to questions were sent to the author by email attachment on 20 November 2016. The couple wish to preserve their anonymity.

63. English-born incomers.

64. Edinburgh, St Andrews, Glasgow, King's College and Marischal College, both in Aberdeen, and the Andersonian University in Glasgow which was founded in 1796 and after several iterations became the University of Strathclyde in 1964.

65. Devine, *Scottish Nation*, pp. 77–8.

66. G. E. Davie, *The Democratic Intellect* (Edinburgh: Edinburgh University Press, 1961) and *The Crisis of the Democratic Intellect* (Edinburgh: Polygon Press, 1986).

67. Lindsay Paterson and Ross Bond, 'Have Scottish academic values been eroded?', *Scottish Affairs*, 52 (2005), p. 15. I am most grateful to Professor Paterson for drawing my attention to his important research and that of his colleague, Ross Bond.

68. See, for example, Paul Scott, 'Scottish Higher Education regained: Accident or design?', *Scottish Affairs*, 7 (1994), pp. 68–85.

69. 'Claim universities swamped with non-Scottish staff', *The Herald*, 14 February 2013.

70. Paterson and Bond, 'Scottish academic values', p. 17.

71. Ibid., p. 16.

72. R. D. Anderson, 'Scottish university professors, 1800–1939: The emergence of an elite', *Scottish Economic and Social History*, 7 (1987), pp. 27–54.

73. Paterson and Bond, 'Scottish academic values', pp. 14–15; Lindsay Paterson, 'The survival of the democratic intellect: Academic values in Scotland and England', *Higher Education Quarterly*, 57:1 (2003), pp. 67–93.

74. Some of the exceptions among Scottish-born historians of the modern period included such distinguished figures as R. H. Campbell, Malcolm Gray, William Ferguson, Henry Hamilton and W. H. Marwick.

75. Devine and Wormald, 'Introduction: The study of modern Scottish history', in Devine and Wormald (eds), *Oxford Handbook of Modern Scottish History*, pp. 1–18.

76. Paterson and Bond, 'Scottish academic values', p. 29.

77. Ibid., pp. 35–6.

78. www.timeshighereducation.com/world-/univesrity rankings/2016, accessed 17 November 2016.

79. *Nature*, 472:5, 7 April 2011. See also the Scottish Government Report, International Comparative Performance of Scotland's Research Base, November 2009.

80. Neil Kemp and William Lawton, *A Strategic Analysis of the Scottish Higher Education Sector's Distinctive Assets*, The British Council, April 2013, p. 3.

81. David Short and Aileen Stockdale, 'English migrants in the Scottish countryside: Opportunities for rural Scotland?', *Scottish Geographical Journal*,

115:3 (1999), pp. 177–92; Lynn Jamieson and Leslie Groves, 'Drivers of youth out-migration from rural Scotland: Key issues and annotated bibliography', *Scottish Government Social Research* (2008), online at http://www. research.ed.ac.uk/portal/files/12692769/Drivers_of_Youth_Out_Migrat ion_from_Rural_Scotland.pdf.
82. Migration Observatory Scottish Public Opinion, 10 February 2014, www. migration observatory.ox.ac.uk/resources/reports/scottish-public-opinion, downloaded 20 November 2016.
83. Ibid.

3

'New' Jews in Scotland since 1945*

Nicholas J. Evans and Angela McCarthy

Unlike other migrant groups examined in this book who predominantly arrived in Scotland after 1945, the influx of the Jews, like that of the English, has a longer history. Studies of their experiences in the nineteenth and early twentieth centuries focus overwhelmingly on Glasgow, especially around the Gorbals area where more than 90 per cent of Scotland's Jewish community lived in the late Victorian and Edwardian periods.[1] Yet scholarly studies of Jewish migration to Scotland after 1945 are notable by their virtual absence,[2] a feature which mirrors British Jewish Studies more widely.[3] When they are considered within broader British Jewry Studies, the Scottish experience appears as an afterthought despite Jews historically forming the third-largest minority ethnic group in Scotland and the numeric significance of Glasgow Jewry placing it among the five largest UK Jewish communities after the Second World War.[4] Such neglect seems surprising since, in the aftermath of the Second World War, so many displaced persons, including Jews who had survived the Holocaust, found their way to Britain and were 'the last significant Jewish migration to Scotland'.[5] Moreover, the research that has been published depicts those arriving as a homogeneous group specifically fleeing from the Holocaust and then maintaining a strong attachment to their faith after their migration.[6] Therefore, despite claims to the contrary, historical studies of the Jewish migrant experience in Britain remain chronologically and spatially biased – as studies of the south of England have preoccupied the vast majority of Anglo-Jewish scholars.[7]

In order to partially redress this imbalance, this chapter offers a preliminary overview of the Jewish migrant experience in Scotland since

* Acknowledgement: We would like to thank Harvey Kaplan for his advice during the research and writing of this chapter.

1945 set in a brief comparative context with the pre-1945 period. It draws primarily upon unpublished and online personal testimonies gathered by the Scottish Jewish Archives Centre (formed in 1987), together with those collected by the authors. These are supplemented with published reports from the Scottish Council of Jewish Communities (SCoJeC), established in 1999 as a single communal voice for Scottish Jewry, and both Scottish Executive and British Parliamentary groups tasked with enquiring into the state of contemporary prejudice in devolved Scotland and Britain more generally. Throughout, the digitised newspapers of the *Jewish Chronicle* (1841 to the present) provide important insights into what different parts of the Jewish community felt about the changing nature of life in Scotland between the Second World War and Brexit.[8]

Our aims are two-fold. First, we outline how those we describe as 'New' Jewish migrants differed both from those who came to Scotland before the 1940s and the multigenerational descent group (descendants of earlier migrants). This approach is important as many studies frequently conflate these different groups, rendering 'New' Jews arriving after 1945 as marginalised in the making of contemporary Scottish Jewry. Where possible, we try also to identify the ethnic range of Jewish newcomers to Scotland and their discernible contribution to one of Scotland's most visible Black, Asian and Minority Ethnic (BAME) groups. Earlier substantial waves of Jewish migration to Scotland were dominated by working-class Eastern European migrants from imperial Russia,[9] while more recent Jewish 'migrants' have come from England, Europe, Israel and North America, and have tended to be more highly educated sojourners not always intent on permanently settling in Scotland.[10] Furthermore, our exploration encompasses cultural as well as religious, political and social dimensions of Jewishness in Scotland. This is key, for those settling after the Second World War often were highly skilled individuals, including Orthodox Ashkenazi Jews (a group which preoccupies Scottish Jewish scholarship), Reform Jews and a small number of Sephardim.[11] Scottish Jewry therefore changed significantly after 1945 and is more diverse than the limited scholarship suggests.[12] Moreover, unlike the earlier, integrated Jews who settled in the Lowlands, often over several generations, 'New' Jews moved across all areas of Scotland and appear to have had a different experience of life to their co-religionists living in cities, including difficulties in being able to maintain a 'Jewish' lifestyle.

Our second aim is to examine the perception of anti-Semitism in Scotland and the extent to which it has become prevalent in recent times, who it is directed against, and the factors that might influence it. This is important, for while Scotland remains the only part of the four nations of the UK never to experience sustained forms of virulent anti-Semitism, anti-Israeli sentiment has gained traction within certain areas of Scotland in recent years. This, according to both communal and official reports, has become of particular concern for all Jews living in the country.[13]

MOTIVATIONS, NUMBERS AND SETTLEMENT

Scotland's Jewish migrants during much of the nineteenth century were principally drawn from England, Germany and Poland.[14] By the 1870s around 1,000 resided in Glasgow and Edinburgh, most of them manufacturers and retailers, jewellers and tailors.[15] They comprised a relatively secure and mainly middle-class group, which then changed from the later nineteenth century as immigration altered the scale and character of Scottish Jewry. Political persecution in the Russian empire prompted around 2.5 million Jews to leave their homes in Russia, Poland, Romania, Austria-Hungary and other parts of Eastern Europe between 1881 and 1914 to seek religious and political freedom abroad.[16] Around 150,000 settled in Britain during this period, helping the total Jewish population reach almost 300,000, of whom only a small proportion chose to settle in Glasgow.[17] Although statistics are patchy, by the time of the 1911 census there were almost 12,000 Jews in Scotland, three-fifths of whom were foreign-born, with around 7,000 in Glasgow and a further 1,600 in Edinburgh.[18] Unlike the established Jewish community, most of these newcomers were working class and engaged in the clothing and furniture trades or eked out a meagre living by hawking.[19] Glasgow proved especially attractive as a destination because of its burgeoning industrialisation and the availability of cheap housing in the Gorbals. To maintain an orthodox Jewish lifestyle, even those working outside the Scottish cities returned to Glasgow or Edinburgh for the Sabbath each week.[20]

The statistics for Jews in Scotland are highly unreliable and recovering accurate figures of the scale of early Scottish Jewry is challenging, as many Jews were only in the country for a short period of time, their transmigration taking them to other destinations, especially the United States and Canada.[21] Indeed, an estimated 10,000 Jews were said to have passed through Glasgow for America in just one year, 1908.[22] Nevertheless, more permanent settlement in Glasgow was still substantial enough for ten synagogues to have been established there by the early 1900s.[23] After 1910, however, large-scale transit through Scotland became rare, as those journeying through the UK now favoured movement through English rather than Scottish ports.[24] During the interwar period, large-scale Jewish migration came to a virtual halt, with the US Quota Acts of 1921 and 1924 restricting the number of Eastern Europeans allowed to settle in the United States – and thus transiting through Scottish ports. Jews did, however, continue to migrate north from England, thereby extending the working-class Jewish community of Glasgow and the more educated Jewish group in Edinburgh. The scale and character of Scottish Jewry eventually stabilised with most Jews resident in Glasgow, while smaller communities could be found in Edinburgh, Dundee, Aberdeen, Dunfermline, Inverness, Ayr, Falkirk and Greenock.[25] Natural increase meant that by 1939 Scotland had around 20,000 Jews, with an estimated 15,000 in Glasgow, though many of the affluent were now migrating to the more respectable districts of Newton Mearns and Giffnock.[26]

The occupations of Jews also began to change, with hawking later becoming dominated by Asian migrants and male Jews increasingly entering managerial or professional occupations.[27] Medicine became a particular favourite.[28] Scottish Jews therefore mirrored the occupational profile of sizeable Jewish communities across northern Britain, especially Hull, Leeds, Manchester and Liverpool, where their professional duties in law and medicine were also combined with involvement in civic life.[29] Crucially, most Jews quickly assimilated and visible signs of ultra-orthodoxy (or Charedi Judaism) were absent, which helped to prevent the sort of anti-Semitic attacks towards Jews who could be visibly identified as conservative in English communities at Gateshead, North Manchester, and Stamford Hill in London.[30] The upward mobility of Jews and suburbanisation also enabled them to break free from the Gorbals heartlands, and enabled them to have more positive encounters with the host population than Irish Catholics did.[31]

During and after the Holocaust, Jewish and non-Jewish communities across the length and breadth of Scotland became home to Jewish refugees.[32] They brought about a significant change in the distribution of Jewish settlement, with an impact on towns and villages with little experience of Judaism. Like their counterparts south of the border, often highly skilled adult refugees arrived in Britain on work permits for menial roles or were children entering as part of the Kindertransport. All came from Central rather than Eastern Europe and often from large cities. Having predominantly lived liberal Jewish lifestyles, they differed from the 'traditional' Jewish settler as often not being involved in the Orthodox way of life.[33] They were thus willing, indeed often happy, to live 'beyond the pale' – geographically, religiously or socially.

The fortunate were able to enrol as university students in Aberdeen, Glasgow and Edinburgh, and so lived outside the existing immigrant ghettos of Scotland's Jewish past. Others found themselves living in isolation in the Highlands and Islands.[34] They did not long for Jewish companionship and kosher food, but rather enjoyed a peaceful life in remote areas where, as David Daiches recalled in his autobiography, solitary Jewish pedlars would visit customers in faraway places.[35] Jewish and non-Jewish charities consciously supported this broad dispersal of refugees, to reduce the incidence of anti-Jewish feeling which sometimes prevailed in other parts of the UK. Non-Jewish organisations and individual families were also active in providing refuge for the victims of Nazism.[36] The extent of Scottish charity towards Jews reaffirmed the belief that the country was a very tolerant place. Though Henry Maitles reminds us of the flirtation of some Scots with interwar Fascism, this was an ugly moment in an otherwise unblemished tradition of refuge for those fleeing religious persecution.[37]

Because of the combination of natural increase, migration from England and these new refugee arrivals, Scotland's Jewish community reached its numerical peak of approximately 20,000 on the eve of the First World War.[38] This high point lasted until the late 1960s, distinguishing Scotland from Jewish settlements elsewhere in the UK which began to decline several decades earlier.[39] Some of Scotland's 'New' Jews were doubtless attracted by employment opportunities during the post-war economic boom. It may also be that Scotland had established something of a reputation as a safe place for Jews. Certainly Scottish toleration was frequently highlighted in both Jewish and non-Jewish newspapers.[40] Yet it seems to have been mainly the lure of the country's universities and sizeable population centres of Glasgow and Edinburgh which attracted refugees arriving in Britain to settle in Scotland rather than in the large Jewish communities south of the border at Leeds, Manchester and London. This, however, often went hand-in-hand with escaping persecution, and Jewish refugees continued to be drawn to Scotland during the Cold War.[41]

Marianne Lazlo, for instance, left Hungary in 1956. At the British Embassy she learned of a need for miners, teachers and doctors. She and her husband were selected and travelled to Dover. While he initially pursued a PhD at St Thomas' Hospital in London, Marianne worked at Stoke Mandeville Hospital as an auxiliary nurse. Her lack of English, she felt, meant 'the nurses hated me . . . and they asked me always to do all the dirty jobs that I wasn't supposed to be doing, that was supposed to be her job, their job . . . So it wasn't a very nice experience.'

Eventually, her husband secured a post at Edinburgh University and the family moved to the city in 1959.[42] It was therefore the lure of higher education and not just religious freedom that drew some of those fleeing post-war Europe to settle in Edinburgh. Meanwhile, Veronika Keczkes also arrived from Hungary with her husband who became a physician. She moved to Glasgow in 1957 and yet consciously avoided Glasgow's synagogues, as she married 'out' after hiding during the Holocaust and was then forced to flee with her Catholic fiancé after the Hungarian rising of 1956. Knowing how important his religion was, she chose to bring up her own Scottish-born family as Catholics. She recalled, after settling in Glasgow, 'unfortunately I wasn't interested at all and I had no connection at all [with] the Jewish community. And when we came down from Scotland . . . in 1966 I was still not interested [in Judaism]. If you marry in a Catholic church, erm, then you are obliged to bring up the children as Catholics and this is what I did . . . My husband was much stronger in the religion than me – he was a very good Catholic. I was a very poor Jew, bad Jew and so he really won the day. I supported him and I wasn't interested at all quite frankly.'[43] For those fleeing political and religious persecution from the other side of the Iron Curtain, Scotland was not a fabled *goldene medina* ('golden land') described as the reason for earlier Jewish settlement.[44] Instead, escaping persecution by reaching Britain was the main concern, and settlement in Scotland was an economic or educational afterthought once the refugees had attained asylum.

By contrast with the earlier migrations, more recent 'New' Jews in Scotland came from a greater range of countries than earlier Jewish settlers, especially England, the USA and Israel. Their recorded numbers, however, stayed small so that by the time of the 2001 census, 6,580 migrants and Scots-born self-identified as being of the Jewish religion.[45] Yet attempts by the community or the state to appraise the scale and character of post-war Scottish Jewish life often excluded both those raised as Jewish but who were no longer identified as such, as well as those who were reluctant to publicly identify themselves in this way.[46] Among those who did choose to admit their Jewish identity in the 2001 census, 70 per cent were born in Scotland, 16 per cent in England, 3 per cent each in the USA and Middle East, and under 2 per cent from EU countries, with only 1 per cent from Eastern Europe.[47] A decade later, the Scottish census recorded 400 Israeli-born migrants in Scotland, of whom 177 identified as Jewish.[48] Some researchers estimate, however, that the number was probably closer to 1,000.[49] Despite these recent influxes from abroad, Scotland's Jewish community still largely consists of the Scottish-born, prompting one commentator to observe, 'Scottish Jews are no longer an immigrant community'.[50]

The absence of a numerically strong immigrant presence among Scotland's Jewish community is one factor in the community's demographic decline since the late 1960s. Though both the 2001 and 2011 censuses reveal every local authority in Scotland had some Jews – confirming how dispersed the community had become – the numbers in Glasgow had fallen by 20 per cent but had risen in the rest of Scotland by 16 per cent, with the largest increases in Aberdeen and Fife.[51] Deaths among an ageing cohort and intermarriage with non-Jews also help explain the statistical decline of Scottish Jewry.[52] But also relevant is the emigration of members of the younger generation to England or Israel seeking the company of other Jews in their age group, including potential spouses.[53] As one male respondent to a survey living in Edinburgh put it, 'If my children want to marry someone who's Jewish, they can't stay here, because there's not enough critical mass amongst the Jewish population. Essentially young people tend to be drawn to Manchester, Israel sometimes of course, mainly London.'[54] That pattern in Scotland is similar to other parts of the Jewish diaspora at home and abroad. These factors also help to explain the unwillingness of 'New' Jews to settle in Scotland, which contributes to the decline of the existing community. For those who did go north, the demand for highly qualified positions, often in the universities or energy industries, or a desire to escape urban life in the remote Highlands and Islands, seem to be the most relevant influences for settling in Scotland after the Second World War.

LIVING A 'JEWISH' LIFESTYLE

One distinctive feature of 'New' Jews, by contrast to earlier settlers, is their reported difficulties in living a 'Jewish' lifestyle. In the earlier period, 'There were Yiddish posters on the hoardings, Hebrew lettering on the shops, Jewish faces, Jewish butchers, Jewish bakers with Jewish bread, and Jewish grocers with barrels of herring in the doorway . . . One heard Yiddish in the streets, more so in fact than English.'[55] As well as language, a Jewish identity was initially maintained through after-school or weekend Hebrew classes, though Jewish children received their education in state schools.[56] Synagogues were a vital medium through which to maintain a Jewish identity. Jewish welfare and philanthropic societies were also established to aid Jews in need as well as to provide social support.[57] Literary societies were formed along with Yiddish newspapers.[58] However, all were located in the Jewish heartland in Glasgow, explaining why it continued to lure waves of immigrants.

Earlier aspects of a cohesive Jewish identity relied on the continual arrival of Orthodox families. Once the inward migration of Orthodox Jews dwindled, some structures of Jewish life in Scotland began to wilt. The largest synagogues began to close, though some of the middle-sized ones survived. Smaller synagogues, at Aberdeen and Dundee, resorted to monthly meetings to try to preserve some form of Jewish life. Smaller purpose-built synagogues on the edges of Scotland's largest two cities arose to cater for the growing suburbanisation of the increasingly affluent middle- class Jews. Crucially, the 'New' Jews considered here quickly established homes in emerging suburban Jewish communities such as the Glasgow suburbs of Giffnock and Newton Mearns in East Renfrewshire, as well as places further away from the traditional places of Scottish settlement, including Ayrshire and Argyll, but also as far distant as Orkney and Shetland.[59] Moreover, Scottish Jews were the only community by the beginning of the twenty-first century who were disproportionately recorded as living outside the Glasgow and Edinburgh local authority areas. More than 49 per cent of Scottish Jews resided in East Renfrewshire, showing the rapid pace of their suburbanisation.[60]

Among the challenges that these 'New' Jews confronted were difficulties accessing kosher food and other religious items, particularly in locations beyond the Lowland belt.[61] More generally, those seeking circumcision of their youth encountered complications, since no mohel (someone trained in circumcisions) lives in Scotland.[62] Burials were also problematic in areas with no established Jewish cemeteries. In the Highlands, one couple recounted how a council worker had investigated Jewish burial customs and gave 'permission to be buried with white bricks around our graves to demarcate the "Jewish section"'.[63] Despite challenges in maintaining a Jewish identity, in certain places like the Highlands, where some are choosing to settle, 'New' Jews stood out: 'I grew up in New York City in the midst of many ethnic groups. When I lived in the central belt there were enough Jewish people around so that being Jewish was not a complete oddity. This is not the case in the Highlands.'[64] As one American in Edinburgh put it: 'When I lived in the US, I wouldn't have to seek Jews out, because they're in the environment. You find them through work, through neighbours, through friends – I get invited to holiday dinners, the local gift shop will have a menorah in the window or gift cards, there's Jewish culture around me. When you come here, there's a mono-culture that's non-Jewish – that made me kind of look harder for it.'[65] Even if in a more limited fashion to what they were accustomed to, 'New Jews' endeavoured to maintain aspects of their identity, including attending the nearest synagogue: 'We lived in Houston where there were five synagogues – and no one knew who you are. But here the community immediately took us in! There was ONE shul, and only one place to go. It felt very welcoming, they said, "Yay, we're so glad you're here – now we have more Jews!"'[66] Another Israeli-born Jew was surprised to learn many years after settling in the North East of Scotland that a small Jewish community functioned near her home.[67]

Some 'New' Jews also met with difficulties in their dealings with the established Jewish community. Critical here is the assorted branches of Judaism, which did not always lead to solidarity. '[T]here should be more tolerance between different branches of Judaism, instead of sometimes hostility', one female living in rural Scotland remarked. Others suggested that synagogues should cater beyond the purely religious dimension, to facilitate social activities. 'After all', according to one female in her sixties living in Glasgow, 'synagogues were designed not only to be Houses of Prayer but Houses of Assembly.' Another man in his fifties recollected, 'I tried for nearly one year to join one congregation.'[68] However, some 'New' Jews may have seen emigration to Scotland as an escape from Judaism – temporarily or permanently.[69]

Still others professed an avoidance or ignorance of their Jewish identity as a result of the Holocaust. One female, aged in her fifties and living in the central belt, revealed:

> Four of my dad's cousins, his grandfather and his step grandmother had died in Auschwitz, and my dad had a deep seated fear of any of that happening to his children. He changed his name, he became a devout Catholic, and pretended to people that he was Welsh rather than foreign. There were big family secrets that I didn't know anything about till my teens, when my dad's family decided I should know all this. So that's why I had no experience of being Jewish as a child, and certainly not a lot of being Jewish as an adult.[70]

Another male in his fifties living in rural Scotland recalled:

> My mum and dad were holocaust survivors, they came over to England to escape Hitler and to escape from being Jewish to some extent. To them, being Jewish was a very traumatic thing, and to my mum at any rate her family had been killed for being Jewish, so they brought me up in what they thought was safety. The first I knew I was Jewish was when my cousin moved in over the road and said 'Do you want to come to shul?'[71]

National identities could also be problematic. Born in Hamburg, Germany, to Polish parents, and having spent time in England, Ike

Gibson did not identify 'as German weirdly enough, despite having been there. I think I have always thought of myself as English in Scotland but as you can see I'm not really English.'[72] For others, hybrid identities became part of their new life in Scotland. For instance, Marianne Lazlo perceived similarities between Scottish and Hungarian customs: 'They had the haggis and we also had the haggis.' She later learned of historical connections between the two lands and generally found the Scots friendly, although some were 'very clannish'. Her attraction to Scotland included providing her son with a kilt when he undertook a school exchange to France. He appeared in a French newspaper donning the kilt: 'So that was my son with a Hungarian name with a kilt representing Scotland in France.'[73] These remarks suggest that various factors prevent both 'New' Jews and the multigenerational descent group from being visible and vocal about their identity. A further factor to consider is the response, including allegations of anti-Semitism, of the host society towards 'New' Jews.

RESPONSES OF THE HOST SOCIETY TOWARDS JEWS

The overarching narrative of Scotland's pre-1945 Jewish migrants and multigenerational descent group is of a coherent community that largely experienced a tolerant reception from the host population. In Glasgow, Kenneth Collins found 'There was little serious anti-Semitism and the community was well tolerated, even in the Gorbals where the Jews formed a significant and visible minority.'[74] Some scholars have attempted to qualify this generalisation to suggest a more negative interpretation but their evidence tends to be based on isolated episodes of discrimination reported in the *Jewish Chronicle* rather than anything more substantially corroborated.[75] Others have used autobiographies to show that anti-Semitism in the Gorbals was not 'particularly pronounced' and perceptions of anti-Semitic attacks could be due to factors other than Jewishness.[76] While prejudice was pervasive and could emerge anywhere, including Scotland, it needs to be placed in a broader context. As Tony Kushner explains:

> In wartime Britain, over 1,200 Jewish servicemen and women and many other Jewish civilians lost their lives as a result of the conflict, but no Jew was killed by his fellow citizens. Violence was not absent in the British scene – fascists and organised antisemites were responsible for physical attacks on Jews and their property in the phoney war period, and later Jewish evacuees and even occasionally Jewish ex-servicemen were beaten up . . . Yet, taken together, such incidents pale into near total insignificance compared with the

enormity of Nazi barbarism towards Jews. 'Physical' antisemitism in Britain during the Second World War, when set against the riots of the earlier conflict, appears meagre. Unlike even its greatest ally, the United States, Britain was free from 1939 to 1945 of major anti-Jewish disturbances.[77]

Ben Braber attributes this lack of serious prejudice towards early Jews in Scotland primarily to the relatively small size of the community. Yet small numbers did not prevent some other ethnicities from experiencing discrimination and antagonism.[78] More significant were other factors in explaining the lack of prejudice towards Scottish Jews. First, early Jewish migrants could draw upon their own welfare agencies rather than the public purse.[79] Second, Jewish schoolchildren attended non-denominational schools, so facilitating integration into Scottish society, which later led in some cases to intermarriage outside Judaism.[80] The Irish Catholic community, by contrast, maintained its separate schooling supported by the state after 1918. The antagonism between Catholics and Protestants was a further factor making for a relatively smooth settlement for Jews in the nineteenth and early twentieth centuries. Such tension meant the Irish and Jews generally co-existed peacefully, as did the Jews and Scottish Protestants.[81]

Some 'New' Jews arriving in Scotland after 1945 likewise believed they encountered a more tolerant atmosphere as an outcome of Catholic–Protestant sectarian tensions. In the words of Bob Kutner, who arrived in Glasgow in 1949, the city was 'grimy but great ... And the people were wonderful. I didn't meet much racism. In fact I found none. But I did, I was aware of the hatred that the Catholics and Protestants carried for each other and of the effect it had.' Such conflict, Kutner reckoned, meant they 'took no notice of me being Jewish'.[82] Others made similar comments. 'The Protestants and Catholics fight each other and ignore us', one man in his sixties in Glasgow admitted.[83]

Catholic–Protestant tensions may indeed have been one factor curbing hostility towards the Jewish community. But some 'New' Jews also pointed to perceived parallels between the Scots and the Jewish people. According to one female in her sixties, 'There was [in the past] an affinity between the Jews and the Scots, the Scots have a greater appreciation of the Old Testament than the English, respect for the Jews who were learned in that book, and a long history of oppression by those people to the south [laughs]. I think that played into it, there was an identification with the Jew, the underdog.'[84] Such perceived parallels between Jews and other peoples who claim to be oppressed can be found among Jews elsewhere in the world.[85] Others, like Ernest Levy, attributed an easy settlement to the Jewish community's ability to blend with the general community and the Scots not being 'poisoned by prejudices' nor possessing 'that fear of the stranger which you will find in central Europe'.[86]

Since the early twenty-first century, however, there has been a heightened sense among some within the Jewish community in Scotland that anti-Semitism (being targeted simply for being Jewish) is on the rise. Reports from within the community point to forms of malice such as the vandalism of synagogues and cemeteries, the graffiti of Nazi symbols and slogans, Hitler salutes and verbal abuse.[87] But were such actions anti-Semitic or anti-Israeli sentiment? For the SCoJeC Director Ephraim Borowski and former SCoJeC Chair Kenneth Collins there was no doubt. In a 2010 report for the Institute for Global Jewish Affairs they noted, 'There has been historically little antisemitism in Scotland, and in particular good relations with the churches. Recently there has been a significant increase [in anti-Semitism], much of it associated with events in the Middle East.'[88] How has this new assessment arisen and is the increase as significant as they suggest?

Data gathered by numerous agencies indicates that in 2006 there were 594 reported incidents of anti-Semitism in Britain, with 16 in Scotland, including violent assaults and destruction of property.[89] By 2011, with the growth of conflict in the Middle East, 20 anti-Semitic incidents were reported in Scotland. Half were assaults or damage to Jewish property, while the remainder were abusive behaviour.[90] In comparative terms, 16 prosecutions were made in relation to religious aggravation against Judaism, 15 connected to Islam and 400 connected to Catholicism. Considering these figures per head of population, however, the Jewish community has stated that 1 in 465 Jews were subjected to a religious hate crime compared with 1 in over 2,000 for Catholics and Muslims.[91] An Antisemitic Incidents Report for the year 2014 noted 31 incidents (21 in Glasgow alone) compared with 14 in 2013 and 7 in 2012.[92] Another report conducted by the SCoJeC in 2015 further suggested that such activity had intensified. In the single month of August 2014, 12 anti-Semitic incidents were reported to the Council. While seemingly low, that monthly total matched almost all reports for the entire previous year.[93] The latest report for 2016, prepared by the Jewish-run Community Security Trust (CST) about the nature of anti-Semitism in Britain, referred to 15 incidents of anti-Semitism in Scotland.[94] Compared with other areas of the UK with a similar sized Jewish population, this was remarkably small.[95]

Qualitative data have also been used to suggest rising anti-Semitism. As one twenty-one-year-old female in the North East of Scotland reported, she found 'antisemitic symbols and writing drawn on the front door in chalk, and nearly being assaulted during a Scottish referendum rally for being a "Jew fucker"'.[96] A 2011 report also claimed that half of Jewish Scottish students 'experienced some form of antisemitism'.[97] Among the evidence supplied was a medical student taking Jewish holidays who claimed to have been told by her Dean, 'because this is a secular university, we don't need to take any account of students' religion', while one of her professors told her she was 'not doing your people any favours as we'll think twice about taking anyone with a Jewish name in future'.[98] Students also reported anti-Semitic attacks in student residences, on campus and in public places. Despite reporting them, university authorities took little action.[99] This apparently transformed environment was also noted by the SCoJeC, which claimed that enquiries from foreigners about pursuing an education in Scotland had changed from 2007, when knowledge was sought about religious facilities, and 2012, when enquiries focused on security and anti-Semitism.[100] While this may reflect increased concerns relating to Jewishness in their own communities, it could also reflect the concentration of foreign-born Jews attending Scotland's leading universities. Analysis of data from the most recent census highlights that the places where anti-Semitic attacks were most likely to occur were also those containing the largest proportion identified as either non-UK nationals or having one parent who was a non-UK national. It was therefore the local authority comprising the University of St Andrews (Fife) that had one of the largest proportions (43 per cent) that fell into either of these categories, followed by Aberdeen and Stirling (both on 37 per cent), and then the city of Edinburgh (33 per cent) and Dundee (25 per cent). Meanwhile, the largest Jewish community, located in East Renfrewshire, had only 2 per cent who were foreign-born Jews.[101]

Such quantitative information arguably explains why so many of the respondents to communal reports about growing Scottish prejudice in Scotland were foreign-born Jews. Every Israeli who responded to the 2012 inquiry from the Jewish community reported feeling threatened or uncomfortable.[102] The examples they provided, however, do not contain any evidence of anti-Semitism. Instead, one Israeli man in his forties living in Edinburgh noted, 'As far as the children are concerned we are telling them to be less open about being Israelis.'[103] Another female in her forties in Edinburgh disclosed, 'You are always a bit wary about saying you're Israeli.'[104] One male Israeli aged in his twenties in Edinburgh told how 'I met a group of people in a bar, and after around 30 minutes of talking they finally asked me where I'm from. When I said I was from Israel, they started shouting at me loudly, and other people joined. They yelled that they feel disgusted by my country, and things like that.'[105] In the Highlands, a man in his fifties described his decision to '**keep my mouth shut and keep my Jewish and Israeli identity in a sealed box and hidden from view**'.[106] Other Israelis decided not to speak Hebrew in public: 'I feel scared to speak in my language or tell people I'm Jewish or from Israel . . . I try to hide anything about being Jewish when I'm outside my house.'[107] Others stopped going to religious services.[108] Reflecting on the situation, a female in her sixties living in Glasgow stated, 'When I arrived here 30 something years ago I was not aware of antisemitism and Israelis were held in high esteem. Years later when my son attended secondary school he was bullied by some boys for being Jewish . . . **I do not feel as safe as I used to feel here**.'[109] An inquiry into incidents between 2012 and 2014 further revealed that 32 per cent of survey respondents felt anxious and vulnerable and almost one-fifth kept their Jewish identity secret.[110]

All these examples, however, are problematic. First, the quantitative data on which to base conclusions is slim. Second, qualitative data show little evidence of explicit anti-Semitism, but rather a sense of people feeling more uncomfortable. Third, much of the evidence emerges from questionnaires conducted by the Jewish community with the Jewish community, but their published summaries only provide brief descriptions of respondents (for example, male, thirties, Edinburgh). Crucially, therefore, it might be that many of the examples have come from just a few individuals. Fourth, by contrast with Israelis, several other foreign-born Jews note that the level of anti-Semitism in Scotland was not widespread. Some recalled only a couple of instances in their lives where they had been targeted for their Jewish identity. Others perceived anti-Semitism in Scotland as less alarming than elsewhere. An American Jewish man in Glasgow had encountered a more sinister environment in New York: 'in Scotland, at least people don't use guns as part of their argument with people from different backgrounds'.[111] His remark, however, does not specifically identify attacks against Jews, and may be more of an indictment about other 'race' crimes in the United States. Another, a female in her sixties, noted, 'I know there's an undercurrent of antizionism and little bits of antisemitism peeking through but apart from that, it's an easy place to live compared with other parts of Great Britain.'[112]

Of course, as the CST notes in its annual report for 2016, both qualitative and quantitative data seldom reveal how widespread such prejudice is due to a presumed under-reporting of anti-Semitic incidents.[113] Nor can we fully know the context in which each incident arose. It appears, however, that evidence for what is perceived as anti-Semitism in contemporary Scotland may more convincingly reflect Scottish opposition to Israel and its policies against Palestine. Rather than religious hatred, then, politically motivated anti-Zionism was the strongest variant of anti-Jewish feeling that respondents encountered, and that included hostility to events in the Middle East and particularly to the war in Gaza. More recently, other explanations for alleged anti-Semitism included the Paris and Copenhagen terrorist attacks of 2015, which targeted Jews among others, and the perceived lack of support since the establishment of Police Scotland.[114] Such linkages are not surprising given the ties, both historically and contemporary, of Jews in Scotland to Israel and the strong support for Zionism within Scotland's largest Jewish community. As Kenneth Collins explains:

> The foundation of the State of Israel in 1948 led to a further wave of *Aliya* [religious emigration to Israel]. This continued during the following years, though some found conditions in the new State harsh and returned to Glasgow. Fundraising for Israel became a core communal activity . . . Fundraising, political support and the further development of the Zionist youth movements, which came to dominate local youth activity, continued enhanced after the drama of the Six Day War in June 1967 which saw a rapid expansion in community action for Israel . . . In recent years Zionism has remained a powerful ideology within the community with Aliya and fundraising still high on the agenda . . . The waves of Aliya over the years have ensured that there are few Jewish families who do not have close friends and family in Israel. Glasgow support for Israel has been strong and unwavering but has not always been uncritical.[115]

The conflation of attitudes towards Jews and Israel concerned many, prompting one respondent to remark that it 'has created a sense that the Scottish Jewish community is somehow accountable for Israeli responses in the Middle East'.[116] Another, in similar words, stated: 'being Jewish seems to have become as much a statement of my perceived political views and affiliation as it is the culture of my birth'.[117] Another commented that 'Israelis living in Scotland cannot make a separation between being Jewish and being Israeli in the same way that other Jewish people can.'[118] Students at Scotland's universities were not immune to such dilemmas. In 2012 members of the University of Edinburgh's Jewish Society felt the need to distance themselves from publicly supporting Israel. The week after a report on 7 December 2012 in the *Jewish Chronicle* headlined 'Students quit "toxic" Edinburgh', the newspaper announced that the campus' Jewish Society had taken the decision to distance itself from Israel to protect members' religious and political affiliations.[119] In a letter to the newspaper, Keziah Berelson, the President of the Edinburgh Jewish Society, revealed the challenges faced by Scottish Jewish students with regard to the Middle East. Berelson wrote, 'At Edinburgh University Jewish Society we were disappointed to read your article. The Jsoc has not been divided over this issue. The Jewish experience on campus has been for the most part hugely positive. Jewish students are proud to be Jewish in Edinburgh and have never been afraid to be so on campus. We are a pluralist and apolitical society, and we wish to ensure that all members feel welcome and at ease, in both their religious and political affiliations. This resulted in a unanimous decision to create a separate Israel Society.'[120]

The example of Dundee in the 1980s provides further evidence that what we are dealing with is growing anti-Israeli sentiment that shapes anti-Semitism and, even then, this is spatially restricted to Scotland's larger cities, principally Glasgow, Edinburgh, Dundee and Aberdeen.[121] In his study of Jewish Dundee, Nathan Abrams has argued that the Jewish community there faced an unusually high degree of prejudice, even arguing that the dramatic decline in the city's Jewish population was due to anti-Zionist and anti-Semitic activity. Tensions were said to have developed in the community due to the support which Arab and Muslim students at Dundee University gave to the Palestinian cause, coupled with the city council proposals in the early 1980s to twin Dundee with the West Bank town of Nablus and Dundee Labour Party's condemnation of Israeli policy. The synagogue at Dundee became a target for graffiti and swastikas, gravestones were vandalised and some Jews even received death threats. The incidents were, however, sporadic, and Abrams notes that throughout the 1990s there were no reported incidents of anti-Semitism. Even so, the experience of the 1980s was said to have encouraged many Jews to move away from Dundee and cause a decline in Jewish settlement in the city. By 2011 the Jewish community in Dundee numbered only 22. According to Abrams, they stayed on due to the presence of Jews among staff and students at the city's universities, professional employment opportunities and the resilience of a few individuals and families.[122] In 1960, the population had been 89, falling to 12 in the 1980s. Even so, death and departures for elsewhere were likely to have been the key reasons for these small numbers.

Yet at least one reader of Abram's work has challenged his analysis and argues that his representation of modern Dundee cannot go uncontested. Sarah Glynn asserts that it is not, and has never been, a city scarred by anti-Semitism. The public support for the Palestinian cause was the product of a strong left – and anti-racist – movement rather than one founded on anti-Semitism: 'the activities of a few isolated neo-Nazis should never be elevated by presenting them as representative of wider society'.[123] Glynn's additional point about the welcome refuge which Dundee provided for Jews was supported in a recent study by Kirk Hansen.[124] Glynn asserts, 'While there was a sprinkling of far-right activists in Dundee, even some of the Nazi graffiti may have been the relatively mindless actions of youth gangs, and other ethnic minorities were also targeted. Abrams records that "individual Jews received death threats"; but the only actual damage was to property, albeit this included property with deep emotional significance such as the synagogue and cemetery.'[125] Certainly, the city was a frequent promoter of Palestine at personal and civic levels and some individuals did scrawl racist graffiti on the houses of post-Second World War Jewish residents and religious buildings connected with their Jewish identity. Yet in the Scottish context, Dundee remained unusual. The general pattern of the absence of much prejudice to Jews in Scotland attracted little media interest and that tended to give a high profile to the actions of the few who did engage in it.

Whatever the reasons for the blurring between anti-Jewish and anti-Israeli sentiment, such prejudice reveals that Scots have become more rather than less sympathetic to the Middle East since the 1980s. Even within the Jewish community, as Suzanne Audrey reminds us, 'Jewish support has not been uncritical and the Glasgow Friends of Peace Now have held meetings with Palestinian representatives.'[126] Most Scottish Jews, whether old or new, appear to support Harvey Kaplan's summary that 'historically, the most pressing religious tension in the lives of people in Glasgow and the west of Scotland was the Catholic/Protestant and Celtic/Rangers tension – but much less so now. However, the issue for Jews nowadays is less likely to be classic anti-Semitism, but rather anti-Zionism, sometimes spilling over into anti-Semitism.'[127] The problem remains in identifying the dividing line between the two.

European legislation sets forth definitions for anti-Semitism, though on rare occasions where successful prosecutions for prejudice have taken place in Scotland, such as when a vile act was committed towards an Israeli student on the University of St Andrews Campus in 2011, Scots law provided a more accommodating legislative structure for prosecuting hatred than elsewhere in the UK. As the CST report on *Antisemitic Discourse in Britain in 2011* observed, 'In Scotland, the conviction of Paul Donnachie on criminal and racist charges showed that anti-Israel behaviour can be prosecuted under legislation relating to race, colour, nationality or ethnicity.'[128] Section 50A of the Criminal Law (Consolidation) (Scotland) Act 1995 clearly states that '"racial group" means a group of persons defined by reference to race, colour, nationality (including citizenship) or ethnic or national origins' and thereby Donnachie's 'anti-Israel behaviour is deemed both criminal and racist'.[129] Crucially, 'Sheriff Charlie Macnair, who heard the case, made it clear that Donnachie broke the law specifically because of his anti-Israel abuse, rather than for antisemitism.'[130]

CONCLUSION

Since the arrival of refugees from Nazism and then Soviet aggression towards surrounding countries during the middle of the twentieth century, Scotland's Jewish population has declined. Though migrants from England, elsewhere in Europe, the United States and Israel have all diversified Scottish Jewry, they have failed to halt the declining statistical and proportional significance of one of Scotland's oldest BAME communities. They have also faced forms of prejudice because of the close links between Scottish Jewry and its support for Zionism. After a century and a half of limited anti-Semitism in Scotland, unlike the other three nations of the UK, anti-Israeli sentiment has caused unease among both established and 'New' Jewish communities. Though 'New' Jewish communities, especially those temporarily dwelling in Scotland while studying or working in the nation's four largest cities, have observed prejudice more than the established Jews, after 1948 the fears of the Jewish community have grown steadily. Such concerns appear to have been associated with the rise of pro-Palestinian support. Rather than sweeping the prejudice under the proverbial carpet, Jewish communal leaders have instead turned to investigating, reporting and promoting awareness of prejudice when it does occur. Yet all point to the growth of anti-Israeli feeling rather than anti-Semitism. Even so, the relative absence of popular prejudice towards the Jewish population remains a defining feature of Scotland's past that differentiates it from other parts of the UK.

NOTES

1. Kenneth Collins, *Second City Jewry* (Glasgow: Scottish Jewish Archives Centre, 1990); Kenneth Collins (ed.), *Aspects of Scottish Jewry* (Glasgow: Scottish Jewish Archives Centre, 1987), pp. 1–34; Ben Braber, *Jews in Glasgow, 1879–1939: Immigration and Integration* (Edgware: Vallentine Mitchell, 2007). A rare comparative study by Suzanne Audrey,

Multiculturalism in Practice: Irish, Jewish, Indian and Pakistani Migration to Scotland (Aldershot: Ashgate, 2000), pp. 46–60, also focuses upon Glasgow Jewry.

2. Some studies explore Jewish migrants to Scotland immediately before 1945: Frances Williams, *The Forgotten Kindertransportees: The Scottish Experience* (London: Bloomsbury, 2014); Rosa Sacharin, *Recollections of Child Refugees from 1938 to the Present* (Glasgow: Scottish Annual Reunion of Kinder – SAROK, 1999); Rosa Sacharin, *SAROK – A History of the Kindertransport – Scotland* (Glasgow: SAROK, 2008); Paula Cowan, 'Auld lang syne: The experiences of the *Kinder* in Scotland', *Prism*, 5 (2013), pp. 24–9; and Rainer Koelmel, 'Die Geschichte Deutsch-Judaische Refugees in Schottland', PhD, University of Heidelberg, 1979. Only *Jewish Glasgow* has sought to integrate the earlier and later periods of the city's Jewish past more fully. See Kenneth Collins, Harvey Kaplan and Stephen Kliner, *Jewish Glasgow: An Illustrated History* (Glasgow: Scottish Jewish Archives Centre, 2013).

3. A few rare studies of Jewish migrants in Britain after 1945 include: Tony Kushner, 'Holocaust survivors in Britain: An overview and research agenda', *Journal of Holocaust Education*, 4:2 (Winter 1995) pp. 147–66; Tony Kushner and Katherine Knox, *Refugees in an Age of Genocide* (London: Frank Cass, 1999); David Cesarani, *Justice Delayed: How Britain Became a Refuge for Nazi War Criminals* (London: Heinemann, 1992); Louise London, *Whitehall and the Jews, 1933–1948: British Immigration Policy, Jewish Refugees and the Holocaust* (Cambridge: Cambridge University Press, 2001). Recent studies of the suburbanisation of Anglo-Jewry have sought to explain the dispersal of second- and third-generation immigrants. See Mark Clapson, 'The suburban aspiration in England since 1919', *Contemporary British History*, 14:1 (2000), pp. 160–2.

4. Hannah Ewence's recent studies are rare examples of a scholar including reference to Jewish suburbanisation from the Gorbals in broader studies of Jewish Britain. See Hannah Ewence, 'The Jew in the eruv, the Jew in the suburb: Contesting the public face and the private space of British Jewry', *Jewish Culture and History*, 12:3 (2012), p. 479; Hannah Ewence, 'Re-negotiating Jewish identity and belonging in post-war suburban Britain', in Maria Diemling and Larry Ray (eds), *Boundaries, Identity and Belonging in Modern Judaism* (London: Routledge Jewish Studies Series, 2015), p. 152.

5. Audrey, *Multiculturalism in Practice*, p. 48.

6. One of the few studies to even mention Reform Judaism in Scotland is Audrey, *Multiculturalism in Practice*, p. 58.

7. Louise London, *Whitehall and the Jews, 1933–1948: British Immigration Policy, Jewish Refugees and the Holocaust* (Cambridge: Cambridge University Press, 2001) and the many works by Tony Kushner, especially *Anglo-Jewry Since 1066: Place, Locality and Memory* (Manchester:

Manchester University Press, 2008) and (with Knox), *Refugees in an Age of Genocide.*

8. *The Jewish Chronicle*, online at www.thejc.com/archive.

9. Harvey Kaplan, *The Gorbals Jewish Community in 1901* (Glasgow: Scottish Jewish Archives Centre, 2006). The exception is early studies of Dundee Jewry by A. Levy, 'The origins of Scottish Jewry', *Transactions of the Jewish Historical Society of England*, 19 (1955–9), pp. 129–62.

10. Fiona Frank, Ephraim Borowski and Leah Granat, 'Being Jewish in Scotland: Project Findings, 2013' (Glasgow: Scottish Council of Jewish Communities, 2013), p. 8.

11. Sephardim Jews are of Iberian, Mediterranean, Arabian and North African origin, while Ashkenazim Jews connect to Central and Eastern Europe and Russia. See Kenneth Collins, *Scotland's Jews: A Guide to the History and Community of the Jews in Scotland* (Glasgow: Scottish Council of Jewish Communities, 2008), p. 39. References to Sephardim residing in Scotland are difficult to find. However, Tova Benski's study of the Jewish community in Scotland, based on fieldwork between 1973 and 1974, suggests a useful profile for the nature of Jewish life after the Second World War. She states, 'Only 5 per cent held no synagogue affiliation, while 89 per cent were members of an Orthodox synagogue, and 6 per cent were affiliated to the Reform stream.' See Tova Benski, 'Identification, group survival and inter-group relations: The case of a middle-class Jewish community in Scotland', *Ethnic and Racial Studies*, 4:3 (July 1981), p. 308. Also see Harvey L. Kaplan, 'Sephardi Jews in Scotland', *Scottish Jewish Archives Centre Newsletter*, 19:2 (2007), p. 3.

12. Even scholars such as Nathan Abrams who have sought to broaden Scottish Jewish Studies beyond the tale of two cities (Glasgow and Edinburgh) do not fully engage with the post-1945 period because of the tendency of smaller communities to close. See Nathan Abrams, *Caledonian Jews: A Study of Seven Small Communities in Scotland* (Jefferson, NC and London: McFarland & Co. Inc., 2009).

13. This extreme anti-Jewish sentiment in the four nations has been approached by national historians in each part of the UK. See, for example, Dermot Keogh, *Jews in Twentieth-Century Ireland* (Cork: Cork University Press, 1998); Geoffrey Alderman, 'Anti-Jewish riots of August 1911 in South Wales', *Welsh History Review*, 6 (1972), pp. 190–200; Colin Holmes, 'The Tredegar riots of 1911', *Welsh History Review*, 11 (1982), pp. 214–25; W. D. Rubinstein, 'The Anti Jewish riots of 1911 in South Wales: A re-examination', *Welsh History Review*, 18 (1997), pp. 667–99; Ben Braber, 'The trial of Oscar Slater (1909) and anti-Jewish prejudices in Edwardian Glasgow', *History*, 88:290 (2003), pp. 262–79; Henry Maitles, 'Blackshirts across the border: The British union of fascists in Scotland', *Scottish Historical Review*, 82:1 (2003), pp. 92–100; Nathan Abrams, 'Jute, journalism, jam and Jews: The anomalous survival of the Dundee

Hebrew congregation', *Northern Scotland*, 3:1 (2012), pp. 86–97. Broader studies of prejudice that have sought a holistic approach include Tony Kushner, *The Persistence of Prejudice: Anti-Semitism in British Society during the Second World War* (Manchester: Manchester University Press, 1989) and Geoffrey Alderman, *Modern British Jewry* (Oxford: Clarendon Press, 1998, rev. edn).

14. Tova Benski, 'Glasgow', in Aubrey Newman (ed.), *Provincial Jewry in Victorian Britain* (London: Jewish Historical Society of England, 1975), pp. 2–3; Alan M. Tigay, 'The Jewish traveller – Glasgow and Edinburgh: Jews have prospered in Scotland's two largest cities for over 200 years, building a strong religious tradition while becoming devout Scots', *Hadassah Magazine* (October 2008), p. 61.

15. Braber, *Jews in Glasgow*, p. 79; T. M. Devine, *The Scottish Nation, 1700–2000* (London: Penguin, 1999), p. 518.

16. Braber, *Jews in Glasgow*, p. 4.

17. Ibid.

18. Collins, *The Jewish Experience in Scotland*, p. 30.

19. Braber, *Jews in Glasgow*, p. 192.

20. Abrams, *Caledonian Jews*, p. 25.

21. Nicholas Evans, 'Commerce, state and anti-alienism: Balancing Britain's interests in the late Victorian period', in Eitan Bar-Josef and Nadia Valman (eds), *The 'Jew' in Late-Victorian and Edwardian Culture: Between the East End and East Africa* (Basingstoke: Palgrave, 2009), pp. 80–97.

22. Collins, *Scotland's Jews*, p. 16.

23. Avram Taylor, '"In Glasgow but not quite of it"? Eastern European Jewish immigrants in a provincial Jewish community from c. 1890 to c. 1945', *Continuity and Change*, 28:3 (2013), p. 452.

24. Evans, 'Commerce, state and anti-alienism', p. 89.

25. Frank et al., 'Being Jewish in Scotland: Project Findings, 2013', p. 8.

26. Braber, *Jews in Glasgow*, p. 4; Avram Taylor, '"Remembering spring through Gorbals voices": Autobiography and the memory of a community', *Immigrants and Minorities*, 28:1 (2010), p. 7.

27. Benski suggests those men living in Newton Mearns in the 1970s were typically in managerial or professional occupations (55 per cent), while 18 per cent were in professional occupations. See Benski, 'Identification, group survival and inter-group relations', p. 308.

28. Kenneth Collins, *Go and Learn: The International Story of Jews and Medicine in Scotland* (Aberdeen: Aberdeen University Press, 1988), pp. 81–97.

29. See, for example, the socio-economic profile of Leeds Jewry in 2001: Stanley Waterman, *The Jews of Leeds in 2001: Portrait of a Community* (London: Institute for Jewish Policy Research, 2003), pp. 20–1.

30. See, for example, 'Revealed: Shocking rise in anti-Semitic attacks in London', *The Evening Standard*, 11 October 2016; 'Charedi teenager

who was victim of assault released from hospital', *Jewish Chronicle*, 11 September 2015; 'Reports of anti-Semitism in Gateshead's Jewish community rocket', *Newcastle Chronicle*, 27 July 2017.

31. Oliver Valins, 'Stubborn identities and the construction of socio-spatial boundaries: Ultra-orthodox Jews living in contemporary Britain', *Transactions of the Institute of British Geographers*, 28:2 (June 2003), pp. 158–75; Billy Kenefick, 'The Jews and Irish in modern Scotland: Anti-Semitism, sectarianism and social mobility', *Immigrants and Minorities*, 31:2 (2013), pp. 189–213.

32. Henry Maitles, 'Blackshirts across the border', pp. 92–100.

33. Williams, *The Forgotten Kindertransportees*, p. 84.

34. Ethel G. Hoffman, *Mackerel at Midnight: Growing Up Jewish on the Shetland Isles* (Edinburgh: Mercat Press, rev. edn, 2006).

35. David Daiches, *Two Worlds: An Edinburgh Jewish Childhood* (London: Macmillan, 1957), p. 121.

36. Harvey Kaplan, in his review of Frances Williams, *The Forgotten Kindertransportees*, points out that 66 per cent of Scottish Kindertransportees were placed in Jewish homes compared to just 30 per cent in Britain as a whole. See Harvey Kaplan, 'Book reviews – Frances Williams, The Forgotten Kindertransportees – The Scottish experience', *Holocaust Studies: A Journal of Culture and History*, 20:3 (2014), p. 183.

37. Maitles, 'Blackshirts across the border', pp. 92–100.

38. Tigay, 'The Jewish traveller', p. 61; Kenneth Collins, *The Jewish Experience in Scotland: From Immigration to Integration* (Glasgow: Scottish Jewish Archives Centre, 2016), p. 144.

39. Kenefick, 'The Jews and Irish in modern Scotland', pp. 189–213.

40. See, for example, Anshel Pfeffer, 'Does Scotland manage to be anti-Israel without being anti-Semitic?', *Haaretz*, 2 November 2012; Douglas Murray, 'Why is the SNP endorsing Israel haters', *New Statesman* blog, 13 August 2014. Accessed at https://blogs.spectator.co.uk/2014/08/why-is-the-snp-endorsing-israel-haters/.

41. For a detailed analysis of the refugees arriving in Scotland, see the work of Frances Williams.

42. Interview with Marianne Lazlo, Gathering the Voices project, http://www.gatheringthevoices.com/testimonials/marianne-lazlo/

43. Nicholas Evans, interview with Veronika Keczkes, 12 November 2014.

44. The *Goldene Medina* is a Yiddish term meaning 'golden land' and was used for a number of Western countries during the late nineteenth and early twentieth centuries.

45. Marlena Schmool, 'Jews in Scotland: The 2001 census', in Collins et al. (eds), *Scotland's Jews*, p. 56.

46. 'Being Jewish in Scotland', p. 8.

47. Analysis of religion in the 2001 census reveals the country of birth of Scottish people reporting to be Jews was: Scotland (70 per cent), England

(16.2 per cent), USA (3.1 per cent), Middle East (2.7 per cent), other EU countries (1.9 per cent) and the Republic of Ireland (0.5 per cent). See Table A.3.6: 'Country of birth of all people reporting their current religion to be JEWISH – All People', Office of the Chief Statistician, *Analysis of Religion in the 2001 Census: Summary Report* (Edinburgh: Scottish Executive, 2005), p. 69.

48. Fiona Frank, Ephraim Borowski and Leah Granat, with Rebecca Hounsom, 'What's changed about being Jewish in Scotland: 2015 Project Findings' (Glasgow: Scottish Council of Jewish Communities, 2015), p. 10.
49. Ibid., p. 22.
50. Schmool, 'Jews in Scotland', p. 57.
51. Frank et al., 'What's changed', p. 25.
52. Collins, *Scotland's Jews*, p. 31.
53. Frank et al., 'Being Jewish in Scotland', p. 14.
54. Ibid., p. 14.
55. Chaim Bermant, *Coming Home* (London: Allen & Unwin, 1976), p. 52.
56. Braber, *Jews in Glasgow*, p. 49.
57. Collins, *Scotland's Jews*, p. 17.
58. Ibid., pp. 28–9.
59. See the discussion of the places connected with Holocaust-era, post-war and modern Scottish Jewish artists in Collins et al., *Jewish Glasgow*, pp. 175–85.
60. 'Proportion of each religion group living in each local authority by current religion – all people', Office of the Chief Statistician, *Analysis of Religion*, Table 1.17, p. 32.
61. Frank et al., 'What's changed', p. 24.
62. Frank et al., 'Being Jewish in Scotland', p. 15.
63. Ibid., p. 28.
64. Frank et al., 'What's changed', p. 25.
65. Frank et al., 'Being Jewish in Scotland', p. 12.
66. Frank et al., 'What's changed', p. 24.
67. Frank et al., 'Being Jewish in Scotland', p. 11.
68. Ibid., p. 15.
69. Collins, *Scotland's Jews*, p. 22.
70. Frank et al., 'Being Jewish in Scotland', p. 16.
71. Ibid., p. 16.
72. Interview with Ike Gibson, Scottish Jewish Archives Centre.
73. Interview with Marianne Lazlo, Gathering the Voices project, http://www.gatheringthevoices.com/testimonials/marianne-lazlo
74. Collins, *Aspects of Scottish Jewry*, p. 52.
75. For example, Abrams, *Caledonian Jews*; Abrams, 'Jute, journalism, jam and Jews', pp. 86–97.
76. Taylor, '"Remembering spring through Gorbals voices"', pp. 1–30.
77. Kushner, *The Persistence of Prejudice*, p. 188.

78. See, for instance, hostility levied at Lithuanians and Italians in Devine, *The Scottish Nation*, pp. 507–18.

79. Devine, *The Scottish Nation*, pp. 520–1; Braber, 'Immigrants', p. 503.

80. Kenefick, 'The Jews and Irish in modern Scotland', pp. 202, 203.

81. Ibid., p. 196.

82. Interview with Bob Kutner, Gathering the Voices project, http://www.gatheringthevoices.com/testimonials/bob-kutner

83. Frank et al., 'Being Jewish in Scotland', p. 22.

84. Ibid., p. 16.

85. In New Zealand, for instance, some parallels were made between Jewish refugees from Nazism and Maori, including similarities between cultures, and experiences of loss and social marginalisation. See Leonard Bell, 'Introduction', in Leonard Bell and Diana Morrow (eds), *Jewish Lives in New Zealand: A History* (Auckland: Godwit, 2012), p. 17. Jews are not alone in this regard, however, with Scottish Highlanders and Irish Catholics also drawing parallels with indigenous peoples. See Angela McCarthy, *Scottishness and Irishness in New Zealand since 1840* (Manchester: Manchester University Press, 2011), ch. 7.

86. Interviews with Ernest Levy, 9 July 1990, and 14 July 1994, p. 5, Scottish Jewish Archives Centre.

87. Frank et al., 'Being Jewish in Scotland', p. 20.

88. Cited in 'Forced to take the high road', *The Jewish Chronicle*, 19 March 2010, p. 4.

89. The Community Security Trust, *Antisemitic Incidents Report 2006* (London: The Community Security Trust, 2007), pp. 7, 14.

90. Frank et al., 'Being Jewish in Scotland', p. 19.

91. Ibid., p. 22.

92. 'A Jewish Manifesto for the Scottish Parliament' (Glasgow: Scottish Council of Jewish Communities, [n.d.]), p. 6.

93. Frank et al., 'What's changed', p. 6.

94. Community Service Trust, *Antisemitic Incidents Report 2016* (London: Community Service Trust, 2017), p. 29. See also https://cst.org.uk/data/file/b/e/Incidents%20Report%202016.1486376547.pdf.

95. 'Antisemitic incidents in UK leap by 30 percent', *The Jewish Chronicle*, 28 July 2017, pp. 4–5.

96. Frank et al., 'What's changed', p. 20.

97. Frank et al., 'Being Jewish in Scotland', p. 21.

98. Ibid., p. 21.

99. Frank et al., 'What's changed', p. 19.

100. Frank et al., 'Being Jewish in Scotland', p. 22.

101. 'Table DC2204SC – National identity by religion – all people', National Records of Scotland, *Scotland's Census 2011*, www.scotlandscensus.gov.uk (accessed 3 August 2017). Data based on information for the following local authorities: Fife (106 non-UK-born Jews out of 245), Aberdeen city

(58 non-UK Jews out of 155), Stirling (23 non-UK Jews out of 63), city of Edinburgh (285 non-UK Jews out of 855) and East Renfrewshire (37 non-UK Jews out of 2,399).

102. Frank et al., 'What's changed', p. 8.
103. Ibid., p. 12.
104. Frank et al., 'Being Jewish in Scotland', p. 24.
105. Frank et al., 'What's changed', p. 19.
106. Ibid., p. 12. Bold in original.
107. Ibid., p. 22.
108. Ibid., p. 7.
109. Ibid., p. 22. Bold in original.
110. Ibid., p. 5.
111. Frank et al., 'Being Jewish in Scotland', p. 19.
112. Frank et al., 'What's changed', p. 23.
113. Community Security Trust, *Antisemitic Incidents Report 2016* (London: Community Security Trust, 2017), p. 5.
114. Frank et al., 'What's changed', pp. 14, 21.
115. Collins et al., *Jewish Glasgow*, pp. 91, 94.
116. Frank et al., 'What's changed', p. 16.
117. Ibid., p. 18.
118. Ibid., p. 22.
119. 'Students quit "toxic" Edinburgh', *The Jewish Chronicle*, 7 December 2012, p. 5.
120. 'Jewish life in the Scottish capital', *The Jewish Chronicle*, 12 December 2012, p. 24.
121. Beyond the larger cities, pro-Israeli events have taken place, such as that held in Inverness in June 2017.
122. Abrams, 'Jute, journalism, jam and Jews', pp. 86–97.
123. Sarah Glynn, 'Dundee responds: A reply to Nathan Abrams' article on the history of Dundee's Jewish community, published in the last issue of this journal, and to his earlier book chapter, on which that article was based', *Northern Scotland*, 4:1 (April 2013), pp. 78–86.
124. Kirk Hansen, *Jewish Identity and Attitudes Toward Militarism in Scotland c. 1898 to the 1920s*, PhD, University of Dundee, 2015.
125. Glynn, 'Dundee responds', p. 79.
126. Audrey, *Multiculturalism in Practice*, p. 60.
127. Interview with Harvey Kaplan by Nicholas Evans, 24 July 2017.
128. Community Security Trust, *Antisemitic Discourse in Britain in 2011* (London: CST, 2011), p. 3.
129. Ibid., p. 36.
130. Ibid., p. 36.

4

The Migration and Settlement of Pakistanis and Indians[1]

Stefano Bonino

The migration and settlement of Pakistanis and Indians in Scotland became particularly sustained after the Second World War in a context of a labour shortage that brought numerous people from the former British empire (1858–1947) to settle in the United Kingdom, including Scotland. But these migratory and settlement processes were intimately linked to the development of the empire in the past. Previously, the role of Scotland in the empire has been downplayed, but recent historiography has cast more light on the key military, administrative and missionary Scottish presence in British colonies.[2] This included involvement in India and Africa. Indeed, between one-quarter and one-third of the members of the East India Company civil service elite grade were Scottish, at a time when Scots comprised one in ten of the British population.[3] Scots could also be found as merchants and agents in the coffee, tea, jute and indigo industries.[4] This chapter begins with a brief overview of this earlier migration stream before turning to examine the post-1945 period.

SOME HISTORICAL CONNECTIONS

Historical contact between Scottish elites and Indian people was significant and it is therefore not surprising that even today the Scottish tartan remains a feature in the formal regalia of the Indian military.[5] The deep connection between South Asia and Scotland was further illustrated by the involvement of Indians alongside British and Scottish regiments during the two world wars.[6] Indeed, India raised the world's largest volunteer armies, about 2.5 million people during the Second World War, fighting in all theatres of conflict.[7] Yet the flow to Scotland from India largely comprised three distinct streams: seamen, students and pedlars.

Between the mid-eighteenth century and the mid-nineteenth century, a steady, although numerically unknown, flow of Indian seamen (also known as 'lascars') and servants reached Scotland for both short-term and permanent employment.[8] By the end of the nineteenth century, Indian seamen had developed small colonies in the main Scottish port cities, especially Glasgow but also Edinburgh and Dundee. The latter had become an important centre for both the import of jute and the export of jute products. The industry attracted Indian seamen from Bengal, a flow that would continue into the 1920s and early 1930s.[9] However, it is Glasgow, the so-called 'Second City of Empire',[10] that became (and still remains) the key host urban centre of South Asian migrants in Scotland. Notably, Glasgow hosted a branch of the All-India Union of Seamen (AIUS), which also had branches in London and Liverpool, the latter opening in 1943. Alongside other trade unions, such as the All-India Seamen's Federation (AISF), the AIUS helped colonial workers, mostly people of Indian origin, to become more aware of their rights and to openly voice their economic demands.[11] Indian seamen were, however, primarily sojourners and mostly returned to India to prepare the way for more sustained settlement in the future.

Students were a second key stream among the early migrant flow from India to Scotland. An inflow of middle- and upper-middle-class students coming from India had been recorded in the 1840s and 'Scottish universities were especially popular, perhaps because of the disproportionately large numbers of Scottish teachers in India'.[12] By the beginning of the twentieth century, membership of the Edinburgh Indian Students' Association, which had originally been set up by six students in 1883, reached 200.[13] In 1911 the Glasgow Indian Union was also established.[14] Indian students reached Scotland in relatively large numbers both before and after 1945, due to the colonial and post-colonial connections between Scottish and Indian universities.

In the early to mid-1920s, alongside a minority of Indians who found jobs as wage labourers, mostly in the iron and steel industries in Lanarkshire, many Indians worked as itinerant pedlars. While peddling largely catered for the poorer elements of Scottish society, especially in Glasgow and rural areas,[15] it soon became a decent source of income for those Indians who could not find work and had to create their own jobs. When others realised that peddling could be a profitable activity, the number of Indians increased and the market soon became saturated. This situation forced the community to disperse to Aberdeen, Dundee and Edinburgh and also, during the economic depression of the early 1930s, to remote villages across the country.[16] From 1933 onwards, a modest economic recovery helped the community to prosper and the improved economic situation towards the end of the 1930s enticed more migrants to seek Scotland's shores. By 1939 approximately 30 per cent (about 190) of pedlar certificates in Glasgow were issued to South Asians.[17]

The inflow of Indians to Scotland in the period before 1945 also resulted in a unique event to mark the cultural and religious formal establishment of the Muslim community in Scotland, many of whose members were and still are Pakistani, as two-thirds of today's Muslims are of Pakistani origin or heritage. In 1933 the first Muslim-branded organisation in Scotland, a branch of the Muslim Association, was established in Glasgow, the only Scottish city to have a local Muslim organisation. The Muslim Association and a splinter group set up in 1943 called the Union of Muslims later merged into a single organisation, the Muslim Mission.[18] The efforts of the organisation and local community members enabled the acquisition of a building at 27–29 Oxford Street (Gorbals) in Glasgow in 1944. This building was converted into the first Scottish mosque later that year, around the same time as the first burial plot for Muslims was acquired in the Sandymount Cemetery in Glasgow.[19] The first mosque and the first Muslim burial plot in Scotland were just two of the early symbols of what would become a strongly visible Pakistani and Muslim settlement in the country.

Despite these three streams of migrants, the limited migration of South Asians to Scotland throughout the nineteenth century and, later on, in the twentieth century was contemporaneous with the immigration of other foreign communities, especially those of English, Irish, Italian, Lithuanian, Jewish and Polish origin.[20] In contrast to these migrant communities, however, the number of South Asians remained very low until after the Second World War. Thereafter, the migration and settlement of Indians and Pakistanis became both more numerous and more visible. The next four sections of the chapter will consider the development of these two communities in Scotland from 1945 until the present day, with a focus on migration flows, settlement and occupational patterns, culture and religion, and racism.

THE MIGRATION FLOW

Partition between India and Pakistan in 1947 pushed Indians from Punjab and Gujarat to relocate to the United Kingdom, including Scotland. While some Indians migrated directly to Scotland from the subcontinent, most relocated having first arrived in England. In terms of geographical origin, most of the [Indian] immigrants arriving in Scotland before the Second World War had their origins in the Jallandhar and Ludhiana districts of the Punjab which, although mainly Muslim, were incorporated into India after the 1947 Partition of the sub-continent.[21]

The Indian community is divided along religious and cultural lines represented by Hindus and Sikhs. The first Indian Sikhs were Bhatra pedlars and traders who arrived in small numbers during the 1920s and 1930s. Bhatras are a 'trading' caste (*jati/biradari*) in Punjab and earn their living by peddling, market trading, running businesses and so on. They are a low-status caste and a minority community compared to the main Sikhs in the United Kingdom, namely Jats, Ramgarhias and, to a minor extent, Khattris. Scottish Bhatras encouraged other Bhatras to migrate from Punjab to Scotland. Later on, Sikhs arrived in large numbers in the 1950s as part of a chain migration. Unlike Hindus, Sikhs tended to be a more homogeneous community due to their common origins and outlook.[22]

Hindus mostly migrated to Scotland from Punjab and Gujarat. Similar to other New Commonwealth migrants, they arrived in the country a little later than most migrant groups. Distinguishable Hindu signifiers are clothes (for example, *sari*, *shalwar kameez* and so on), marks (*tilak*, *tikka* or *bindi*, which is a mark on the forehead), skin colour and so on. Important kinship networks are, for example, the Lohana and Patidar communities. Hinduism brings together Punjabis, Gujaratis and other Indians, but there are distinct cultural traditions in terms of language, food, style of dress and religious outlook that prevent these different factions from mixing with one another. The major cleavage within the Indian community was not just between Punjabis and Gujaratis, but also between direct Punjabi migrants and East African Gujaratis.[23]

On 14 August 1947 India separated into two states and Pakistan appeared on the world map. The following day, India obtained independence from Great Britain. As a result of Partition, many Indians in Scotland unwittingly became Pakistanis and celebrated the occasion.[24] Pakistanis comprised the largest chunk of the post-Second World War migration from the subcontinent to Scotland and were mostly Muslims from the Lyallpur area.[25] High unemployment, increasing contact between Scotland and Pakistan and family reunification sped up the population movement and the chain migration from the subcontinent to Scottish shores. Pakistanis maintained strong national connections with their homeland, often exemplified by community gatherings, the use of the Urdu language and the annual celebration of Pakistan Independence

Day. At the same time, their clothing demonstrated their attempts to adapt to wider society. The Pakistani national two-piece dress, a long shirt and loose trousers known as *shalwar kameez*, or the one-piece loose sarong (*dhotti*), was often replaced by suits with ties and, in some instances, overcoats and hats.[26]

Once the process of mass population movement between India and Pakistan ended, by late 1948, migration from the subcontinent to Scotland started to gather pace and 'the 1950s saw many more coming from Pakistan and a few also from India'.[27] As the British industrial boom of the early 1950s turned into recession by 1955, many factories, particularly textile mills, closed down or reduced their work-force. Several South Asian workers lost their jobs in Yorkshire and the Midlands and redundant immigrants from Birmingham and Bradford made their way to Glasgow, Edinburgh and Dundee, where jobs were available. Their relatives and friends also migrated from Pakistan to join Scottish transport departments, bakeries or chemical factories. Moreover, around the mid-1950s South Asian settlers started bringing their families from Pakistan and India, after realising that they would stay in Scotland permanently rather than work for a few years, make money and return home.[28]

Similar to the situation in England, the Commonwealth Immigrants Act 1962 brought a fresh wave of South Asians to Scotland. Many Pakistanis and Indians had already moved to the country in 1961 as part of a 'beat the ban' strategy, when the Act was under consideration. But after 1962 and throughout the 1960s and 1970s, family members of earlier South Asian migrants joined the developing community in Scotland as part of the chain migration.[29] Direct Indian migrants arrived in large numbers in the early to mid-1960s and Indians from East Africa reached Scotland during the late 1960s and early 1970s, particularly after the expulsion of the entire Asian population from Uganda in 1972.[30] The flow stopped during the period of decolonialisation and nationalisation, when Kenya, Uganda and Tanzania became independent.[31] This was not an exclusively Scottish phenomenon, as a similar pattern can be found in the experience of South Asian migration to England.[32]

The South Asian migration of the 1950s and 1960s was dominated by single males who had come to work and then send remittances back to their extended families. As such, they were often non-English-speaking, lived in multi-occupied housing – often as a *biraderi* (brotherhood or clan) group – and were employed in gangs rather than as individu-als (which was generally the case with West Indian immigrants). Such work was to be found in the metal-bashing industries of the West

Midlands, the woollen textile mills of West Yorkshire and the cotton mills of Lancashire. Sikhs and Pakistanis were concentrated in the West Midlands, and Pakistani and Indian Muslims in the northern mill towns. While London had, in general, the most cosmopolitan population of South Asians, the area north of Birmingham and into Scotland became more exclusively Pakistani.[33]

But the labour shortage in Scotland was not as serious as in much of England, as the Scottish economy had not grown and transformed to the same extent as the English economy during the same period.[34] Nonetheless, the mid-1940s and the mid-1950s had brought historical changes in the welfare of the Scottish people. There were several factors behind their increasing affluence and positive changes in their employment, health and living standards. These included the Marshall Plan, providing aid from the United States to Europe, which opened up new markets for exports from English and Scottish industries; strong socio-economic state intervention in agriculture and rural society; the nationalisation of coal, railways, electricity, iron and steel; the Beveridge Plan, requiring compulsory national insurance; the creation of the National Health Service; the mechanisation of agriculture; and the growing availability of new housing, particularly council houses.[35]

Better times and the need to fill menial jobs brought a new wave of South Asians to Scotland,[36] especially because Irish migration and the low-cost labour it brought had slowed down by this period. The 1970s and 1980s saw the expansion, dispersal and consolidation of the Scottish South Asian community, mostly due to the arrival of the wives and children of settlers from Pakistan but also through the internal migration of a few hundred Indian and Pakistani families from England to Scotland. This movement of people differed from previous ones in quantity and speed, as the pioneering pedlars had already demonstrated a spirit of entrepreneurship that would be developed and applied by new migrants. By the early 1970s, many had become successful shop and restaurant owners north of the border, where increasing numbers of Asian-owned businesses were prospering.[37] Indeed, 'when the news of the successes of the Scottish Asian entrepreneurs spread to England around 1970, many of their aspiring compatriots there sold their homes and headed north with all their savings to acquire or start a business'.[38]

This migration was driven not only by commercial opportunities, family connections and the relative prosperity of the Scottish South Asian community but also by the perception of a tolerant and pleasant Scottish environment.[39] A slow but steady migration from England to Scotland gathered pace around the mid-1970s and continued at that speed until the mid-1980s.[40] Between 1991 and the early 2010s, Scotland registered increasing numbers of both Indian and Pakistani migrants. Indian migration increased from 9,000 people in 1991 to 10,500 people in 2001 and up to 23,500 people in 2011, becoming today's second-largest non-UK source of migrants and the most popular non-EU country. Meanwhile, Pakistani migration rose from 9,400 in 1991 to 12,600 in 2001 and up to 20,000 in 2011.[41] The settlement patterns of the South Asian community have therefore changed over the past seventy years, and differences have emerged between the Indian and the Pakistani experiences, as will be outlined in the next section.

SETTLEMENT AND OCCUPATIONAL PATTERNS

More than 400 Indians had settled in Scotland by 1940, particularly in the Gorbals district of Glasgow, and in the Highlands, Islands and North East.[42] This concentration in the Gorbals area by the early 1950s, and particularly in Nicholson Street, was shown by the northern end of the street being termed 'Burma Road'. This revealed 'a certain vagueness in the Glaswegians' image of the Indian sub-continent, for the majority of Asians at that time had come from the Punjab'.[43]

Between the mid-1940s and the mid-1950s, South Asians could be found working in unskilled and semi-skilled professions in jute mills, the building industry, transport departments and bakeries.[44] They also worked as waiters and as dishwashers in restaurants in central Glasgow and these occupations taught them the skills they would later need to open various Indian restaurants in the city.[45] Cheap rented accommodation and easy access to the workplace encouraged the settlement of South Asians in the central business district of Glasgow. At the same time, while the East End was the main area of settlement in other cities, in Glasgow it did not receive a large South Asian population, possibly due to a lack of vacant housing in what was an overcrowded working-class area.[46]

During the 1960s, South Asian migrants and settlers began to climb the economic labour ladder by opening small businesses that would slowly replace peddling.[47] While 50 per cent (about 330) of pedlar certificates in Glasgow were issued to South Asians by the end of the 1950s,[48] by 1965 they had more than halved in number. The chief constable of the City of Glasgow Police granted peddling certificates to 120 Indians and 188 Pakistanis in 1955, to 72 Indians and 116 Pakistanis in 1960, and to 51 Indians and 80 Pakistanis in 1965.[49] Compared to earlier arrivals, then, South Asian migrants and settlers at this time held better economic and educational backgrounds, and 'a new occupational structure began to emerge, with a shift from fairly menial employment towards the establishment of small family businesses'.[50] South Asian grocery shops and newspaper shops opened in Scottish cities and, in order to survive, they often cut prices and stayed open after midnight.[51] At the same time, small factory workshops began to emerge, trading as cash-and-carry warehouses.[52]

In Glasgow, South Asians dispersed beyond the Gorbals to new tenement housing in Pollokshields and Govanhill.[53] The Scottish population showed some initial prejudice towards the more visible presence of Asians at a time when, by contrast, hostility towards descendants of Irish Catholic migrants was in decline. Even so, 'racial tensions north of the border never reached the acute levels of some English cities, though this may have been mainly due to the relatively small number of coloured immigrants to Scotland in these years'.[54] Instead, little by little, 'Pakistani corner-shops became as much a part of the Scottish retail scene as the Italian ice-cream parlour established many decades before'.[55] The spread of grocery shops followed a more general move to petit bourgeois activities, which helped the South Asian community establish itself and penetrate the Scottish socio-economic system as small entrepreneurs.[56] This process was facilitated by the fact that

> the Asian migration to Scotland was not as centrally related to the demands of the capitalist economy as in the instance of New Commonwealth migration to England in the same period and in the case of the Irish migration to Scotland in the nineteenth century.[57]

The South Asian community grew substantially by 1966. At that time, 8,000 South Asians were living in Glasgow alone. Many of them were children who had travelled in family groups. While by the 1970s the rate of growth in the community had declined, thereafter numbers increased.[58] By 1983, for instance, Indians and Pakistanis numbered 12,000 in Glasgow, 2,100 in Edinburgh and 1,500 in Dundee.[59] During the decade 1961–71, 'the Gorbals were more or less evacuated, partly through voluntary migration and partly because of the extensive demolition then going on in the transformation of the Gorbals/Hutchesontown Comprehensive Development Area'.[60] Therefore, South Asians moved to Pollokshields East, while Govanhill provided a second nucleus and proved to be particularly attractive to the Pakistani community. Notably, 'the decline of the traditional shipbuilding and dockland industries in Govan had led to vacant accommodation in this area, and, as in the North, some of this [was] taken up by Asians'.[61] By 1983 there was also a considerable presence of Pakistanis in the owner-occupied Glasgow suburbs of Bearsden, Milngavie, Bishopbriggs and Eastwood, and a comparatively lower presence in areas of local authority housing. This process of suburbanisation brought Pakistanis from their traditional settlement areas.[62]

Yet the South Asian group was far from monolithic and there was much variation that reflected ethnic and social class differences. Indians adopted more traditional British middle-class residential goals and chose suburbs of high environmental quality,[63] while Pakistanis still clung to their old areas of settlement and occupied poorer-quality houses.[64] The academic literature remains divided on the post-Second World War integration of South Asians in Scotland. For some authors, the South Asian experience in Scotland is similar to that of the Jewish community, insofar as both communities

> began in retailing, particularly in the clothing trade, before beginning to enter 'white collar' employment and the professions and were initially concentrated in the inner cities, such as the Gorbals area of Glasgow, before moving outwards to more affluent suburbs.[65]

However, others argue that in the first part of the 1970s Asians remained conscious of their vastly different cultural background and appeared to regard Britain as a place of work where they might settle for a while and whence they remitted substantial sums of money to families to whom they intended ultimately to return. Living in self-segregated communities, they tended to retain as much of their way of life as possible, and not to value social integration. The prediction of patterns of spatial evolution is further complicated by the fact that the Asian population was itself sharply differentiated along national, religious and class lines, each subgroup of which was capable of exhibiting an individual environmental response.[66]

This diversification can be seen in occupational trends, particularly with the expansion of businesses, including new sectors such as motor repair, the service industry, property, do-it-yourself shops, catering and computer technology. At the same time, young, educated, Scottish-born Pakistanis were entering a range of professions that allowed a certain degree of social mobility. In the early 1990s, around 22,000 Pakistanis and 10,000 Indians were living all over Scotland.[67] Sixty-five per cent of South Asians owned a business,[68] forming a visible presence in the main urban areas as shop, restaurant and takeaway owners, as well as through a growing participation in global and local political affairs.

By 2001 the census recorded around 32,000 Pakistanis and 15,000 Indians in Scotland and further demonstrated the differing features of the two communities.[69] At that time, both communities had high self-employment rates: 32 per cent for Pakistanis and 22 per cent for Indians. One reason alleged for this distinctive pattern was their difficulty in competing with white people in the labour market.[70] But while Pakistanis were low on the wealth distribution scale, Indians were close to the middle and had no substantial disadvantage compared to the wider population. Indians and Pakistanis also recorded high levels of owner-occupation caused by 'the inability of social rented housing adequately to meet their housing needs'.[71] Indian women had a slightly higher than average hourly pay compared to white British women, while Pakistani women suffered substantial gaps in pay. Indian school pupils performed better than white pupils. Both Indians and Pakistanis had the lowest rates of participation in sport among ethnic minorities (31 per cent and 21 per cent respectively) and the highest incidence of diabetes (14 per cent and 18 per cent respectively), and were, alongside Chinese households, the ethnic groups with the highest proportion of cars.[72]

At present, 49,000 Pakistanis and 33,000 Indians reside in Scotland.[73] The two communities have different social and economic profiles that demonstrate their differing experiences of settlement and integration. On the one hand, Indians are the group most likely to be highly qualified (62 per cent are educated to degree level and above), to work in top professions (37 per cent are 'professionals' and 11 per cent are 'managers, directors and senior officials') and to have the highest social status (36 per cent compared to 19 per cent for the population as a whole). Thirty-three per cent of Indians work in public administration, education and health, and 30 per cent are in the distribution, hotel and restaurant industries. They are also a young community, clustering around 20 to 39 years of age, and have relatively low numbers of children and retired people.[74]

On the other hand, Pakistanis are the group most likely to be self-employed (14 per cent), to be 'managers, directors and senior officials' (20 per cent), to work in 'sales and customer service occupations' (22 per cent) and to have relatively high proportions of economically inactive people who look after home or family (13 per cent). Fifty per cent of Pakistanis work in the distribution, hotel and restaurant industries, and 17 per cent in public administration, education and health. Alongside gypsies, travellers, other British and Irish people, Pakistanis have the highest proportion of people (16 per cent) who work 49 or more hours per week. Thirty-five per cent of them are in the lowest social grades

(D and E). Pakistanis also have a younger than average age profile, but this differs from that of Indians due to a higher proportion of children and teenagers.[75]

CULTURE AND RELIGION

While the number of South Asians living in Scotland increased over time, community members began to realise that their interests often differed from those of the white Scottish majority. At the time of Partition, a splinter group of the Edinburgh Indian Students' Association called the Edinburgh Pakistani Association was established to act as a religious organisation for Muslims. Later, in 1955, a group of young Pakistanis founded the Pakistan Social and Cultural Society in Glasgow, which operated under the aegis of the Muslim Mission and catered for the social, cultural and recreational needs of the settled community. The Pakistan Society and the Muslim Mission later operated as the two wings of the Pakistan Association when this was founded in 1962,[76] while twenty years afterwards, in 1982, the Scottish Pakistani Association was founded to promote cultural and social activities that could develop better understanding between the Pakistani community and other Scottish people.[77]

The 1960s saw a more visibly Muslim, and not simply South Asian, presence across the main Scottish cities. This element is important because many Pakistanis in Scotland are Muslim (91 per cent) and Muslim-ness would slowly become their core public identity following the changes in public attitudes towards Muslims after the Rushdie Affair in 1988–9 and the terrorist attacks on the United States in 2001. The 1960s also saw more tense relationships between Indians and Pakistanis over both the Kashmiri conflict and the different faiths of the two communities. Indians, for instance, cluster around three main religions: Hinduism (41 per cent), Sikhism (23 per cent) and Christianity (18 per cent). Muslims considered Hindus to be idol worshippers and polytheists, while Hindus regarded Muslims as followers of an intolerant religion (Islam).[78] In 1962 the second Scottish mosque opened in Edinburgh. Dundee followed the trend in the late 1960s. Nineteen-seventy marked an important year in the history of Pakistani settlement in the country. In that year Bashir Maan, who had arrived in Scotland from Pakistan in 1953 and had already been appointed as the first-ever Muslim Justice of the Peace in Scotland in 1968, became the first Muslim city councillor (Glasgow) to be elected in the United Kingdom.

Bashir Maan played a key role as a political pioneer for the Scottish

Pakistani community. Throughout his career he was deeply involved in Scottish–Pakistani relations, both domestically and abroad. Between the 1950s and the 1990s, acting in various professional capacities and at times with support from the Muslim Mission and the Pakistan Social and Cultural Society of Glasgow, he welcomed to Scotland several major Pakistani political and religious figures.[79] Among them were General Yusuf Khan, Pakistan's high commissioner to the United Kingdom, during the Pakistan Independence Day celebrations in 1959 and 1960; Sir Muhammad Zafarullah Khan, the first foreign minister of Pakistan and the first Muslim and only Pakistani to preside over the United Nations General Assembly and the International Court of Justice, at a panel for the Pakistan Independence Day celebrations at Kingston Halls in Glasgow in 1965; and President Ayub Khan, the second president of Pakistan (1958–69), during the presidential state visit to the United Kingdom at Holyrood in 1966.[80] Furthermore, Maan engaged in high-profile visits to Pakistan with the Royal Family, Lord Provost William Gray, President Zia-ul-Haq, President Ayub Khan, Prime Minister Junejo and others.[81] He also met several members of the Royal Family (Queen Elizabeth, Prince Charles, Princess Anne and so on) on numerous public occasions and was extremely involved in public events and political action, such as rallying in support of the Kashmiri cause and anti-racist campaigns, speaking at the Islamic Society of Britain and at numerous mosques and setting up the Pakistan 50th Anniversary Scholarship, which was funded by a donation from Yaqub Ali through the Scottish Pakistani Association to Strathclyde University.[82]

Meanwhile, the social welfare of the Indian community, particularly of labourers, pedlars, sailors and factory workers and some middle-class people, was served by the Indian Workers' Association, which had been founded in Coventry in 1937 and had branches across the United Kingdom. While being primarily intended to improve Indian workers' conditions, it also connected with the wider British labour movement.[83] The organisation opened its Scottish branch in Glasgow in 1971 and was an exception to the largely apolitical character of South Asian associations in the country. Indeed, it was the first overtly political migrant organisation in Scotland. Its Marxist and Marxist-Leninist political outlook emerged from the involvement of many of its original members in the Indian Communist Party and the independence movement in India.[84]

Within the Indian community, Hindus and Sikhs have experienced different settlement outcomes from each other and have strong political, ideological, ethnic, economic and class differences. On the one hand, the Hindu population was and still is mostly composed of professional and middle-class people, resembling the white middle-class community. On the other hand, the Sikh Indian community remains working class in character. Although they are both Punjabi, Hindus and Sikhs tend to remain separate and to attend their own temples. Even within the British Hindu community, there are differences between Scottish and English Hindu people, insofar as the former are a smaller and more isolated aggregate of people with a higher chance of having non-Hindu friends.[85] The community in the Scottish capital, Edinburgh, is fairly heterogeneous and similar to the ones in Leeds and Bristol but different from the ones in London and the Midlands, where the communities are larger and more homogeneous.[86]

The first Sikh temple in Edinburgh, called the Gurdwara, was built in 1958 in a converted house in Hopefield Terrace. It moved to another house in Academy Street in 1971. Due to growing numbers, in 1976 the temple moved to the site of an old church in Mill Lane. During that period, the Indian community had access to an unknown number of Sikh and Hindu temples in Scotland (one in Edinburgh). The temple in Edinburgh, called the Hindu Mandir and Sanskriti Kendra, was formed in 1981 for small groups of Indians and mostly through the efforts of a Kenyan Gujarati woman. There were two types of worship: (1) regular meetings (*satsangs*) on the second day of every month; and (2) annual Hindu festivals. There were also various festivities: Diwali; Nawratri; Krishna; Janamasthami; and Ram Nawmi.[87]

During the 1970s and the 1980s, community structures based on 'Indian-ness' attempted to encourage cooperation between different Indian groups in town. In 1974 the Edinburgh Indian Students' Association was replaced by the Edinburgh Indian Association (EIA), a secular but Hindu-oriented organisation founded by recently arrived East African Indians. The EIA aimed to 'promote' Indian culture and represented the idea of a pan-Indian community. It included among its members Hindus, Sikhs, Muslims, Christians and Buddhists, although it primarily celebrated Hindu festivals, such as Holi and Diwali, rather than Muslim and Sikh festivals. Its membership ranged between 50 and 100 families, with some variation from year to year. The meetings of the Association were arranged as social functions, such as small gatherings of Indians and concerts in large halls. The activities of the EIA decreased in number, and general interest in the Association declined in the early 1990s. But while the Edinburgh Hindu Mandir and Sanskriti Kendra and the EIA reinforced the idea of 'Indian-ness' (Hindu/Indian community), each of them had their own orientation: one geared towards the Hindu community and based on a shared religious tradition; and the other geared towards the Indian community and with a secular, inclusive and pan-Indian outlook based on a shared ethnic/cultural/national identity.[88] In other words,

> the EIA puts a great deal of emphasis on being a meeting place, where cultural diversity can be subsumed, but not forgotten, within the notion of the rich tapestry of 'Indian culture'. [...] The Mandir, on the other hand, certainly attempts to be a meeting place also, but it is primarily a place for Hindus to come into contact with their gods, as well as with each other.[89]

In terms of educational and economic backgrounds, the temple leaders were more petit bourgeois in nature, running businesses as shopkeepers (their families were occupied in middle-ranking professions) and aspiring to achieve values similar to those of the British lower-middle class.[90] In contrast, the EIA leaders were of a higher and wealthier status, running prestigious restaurant projects and having offspring working in upper-middle-class occupations such as law. However, the two groups' membership was not markedly different. While styles of religious practice were based on regional traditions, worship was designed to appeal mostly to Hindus. Given this, a hybrid of traditions came from the dominant Punjabi and Gujarati factions.[91] In the same decade, the election of Mohammad Sarwar as Member of Parliament (MP) for Glasgow Govan in 1997, the first Muslim MP in the United Kingdom, bestowed another 'first' on Scottish politics and signalled the emergence of a visible Muslim presence within the country's public sphere.

In the 1980s, the number of Indians and Pakistanis in Scotland was around 25,000.[92] Yet in 1984, the conflict between the Indian army and Punjabi Sikhs reverberated within the Scottish community, insofar as the trauma of Indian troops invading the sacred Sikh shrine of Amritsar led many Edinburgh Sikhs to sympathise with the demands for a separate Sikh state of Khalistan and to lose their Indian identity.[93] Scotland also experienced an increase in the number of mosques – nine by the early 1980s: four in Glasgow, two in Edinburgh and one each in Aberdeen, Dundee and Motherwell.[94]

RACISM

The perception of a more tolerant Scotland might derive from the apparent lack of an adverse reaction to the post-1945 South Asian immigration compared to the hostility shown to Irish Catholics and their descendants until relatively recent times. But that contrast does not necessarily confirm the absence of racism. Robert Miles and Anne Dunlop argue that 'there has not been a racialization of the political process in Scotland since 1945'[95] but that racism is present both in the political consciousness and in the everyday experiences of people of South Asian origin.[96] Moreover, Scotland should not take all the credit for its successes, as it is socially and politically located within a larger multinational state, the United Kingdom, which has played an important role in welcoming ethnic minorities. Despite experiencing a smoother settlement in Scotland, compared to England, racism and discrimination have not been absent from the life of South Asians in the country.[97]

The British National Party, the National Front and neo-fascist organisations were historically involved in the printing of neo-fascist newspapers and the organisation of political rallies. In the 1980s their activities 'link[ed] the much longer tradition of anti-Catholicism with a racism which focuses on the [South] Asian presence'.[98] In response, South Asians started uniting in more self-conscious political organisations, such as the Scottish Asian Action Committee and the Minority Ethnic Teachers Association. However, there was 'no sustained campaign of political resistance on the part of people of Indian and Pakistani origin in Scotland'[99] due to the relatively small presence of the British National Party and the National Front in Scotland. The ever-burning fires of sectarianism further blocked the fascist advance in Scotland. The attempts of fascists, for example the Scottish Fascist Democratic Party, to plant their roots in the country were very short-lived. In this way, 'militant Protestantism [institutionalised by the Scottish Protestant League and by Protestant Action] became an effective substitute in the context of a distinct political process in Scotland'.[100] Nowadays, more or less intense sectarian divisions between Celtic and Rangers football clubs and anti-racist political statements have acted as a prophylactic against the creation of mass support for the Scottish Defence League (SDL), which fails to draw many members from the typical targets for recruitment of the Defence Leagues – that is, football casuals.[101]

A measure of presumed Scottish egalitarianism can be found in a large-scale survey of majority attitudes towards Pakistani and English migrants in Scotland, as well as majority attitudes towards Muslims in both Scotland and England.[102] Despite the fact that Scottish people score higher on Islamophobia than Anglophobia in relative terms, 42 per cent of Scots consider conflicts between Muslims and non-Muslims to be at least 'fairly serious', as opposed to 61 per cent of English people in

England. More broadly, Scotland is perceived to be less Islamophobic than England. Among the explanations proposed by the study's authors are factors related to the particular settlement and development of Muslim communities in Scotland (many of whose members are Pakistani) and the specific features of Scottish geographies and socio-political attitudes towards diversity, notably the following:

- the smaller Muslim population in Scotland
- the fact that many Muslims in Scotland are self-employed and work in business, while a good number of Muslims in England are unskilled labourers
- higher levels of segregation within English Muslim communities
- higher levels of racism in England, possibly due to the fact that Islamophobia is 'much more closely tied to English nationalism within England than Scottish nationalism within Scotland'.[103]

Overall, racism in Scotland is declining, while prejudicial attitudes have also fallen in Great Britain since the 1980s.[104] More than seven in ten British people now hold positive views of Muslims.[105] It is true that statistics recorded by the police in Scotland in 2013/14 show a 4 per cent increase in racist incidents (4,807) compared to 2012/13 (4,628).[106] But much of this is due to the higher number of incidents involving white British victims and complainers (1,423 in 2013/14 compared to 1,139 in 2012/13). These figures must also be contextualised within an overall trend of decreasing numbers of racist incidents recorded by the police between 2006/7 and 2013/14,[107] although unreported hate crimes[108] and a climate of fear of new Islamist terrorist attacks[109] might disrupt this trend. Similarly, racism should not be underestimated, as Pakistanis (20 per cent – that is, 1,107) and Indians (6 per cent – that is, 340) still constitute 26 per cent (1,447) of victims and complainers of racist incidents (5,626). They also contribute towards 35 per cent of the total population of Asian origin (Bangladeshi, Chinese, Indian, Pakistani and other Asian) who are victimised and complain about racism across the country.[110]

THE COMMUNITIES TODAY

To understand how ethnic minorities settle in a host country and how they perceive themselves within the nation state where they live, identity provides a useful and important marker of cultural retention. The identity of Indians has a strong ethnic component, as 44 per cent of community members consider themselves to be Indian only.[111] This follows a UK-wide trend that found that Indian Hindus, who represent a large section of the Indian community, were likely to maintain exclusive identities within the first generation.[112] On the other hand, Pakistanis are a largely Muslim (91 per cent) community. About 87 per cent of Pakistanis in Scotland feel either Scottish (about 31 per cent) or British, or a combination of identities including Scottish, British and Pakistani. Only 13 per cent define their identity as solely Pakistani.[113] This divergence in identities between Pakistanis and Indians can be partly explained by the younger nature of the Pakistani community compared to the Indian community. In fact, 30 per cent of Pakistanis in Scotland are aged 0–15, compared to 20 per cent of Indians, who also have a larger component (30 per cent) of people aged 25–34,[114] some of whom are also likely to be students who are in Scotland to pursue education and will subsequently leave the country.

The Pakistani community undeniably faces some challenges. Pakistanis (and Bangladeshis) are among the most segregated ethnic groups in Glasgow, although their levels of segregation have been falling and are lower than in major cities in England and Wales, for example Bradford, Manchester and Cardiff.[115] In Glasgow, many Pakistanis live in Govanhill and East Pollokshields. East Pollokshields is a sociologically distinctive area, where 53 per cent of the population are from minority ethnic groups – a very high figure compared to the Glaswegian average of 12 per cent and a Scottish average of 4 per cent.[116] Of those belonging to minority ethnic groups, 43 per cent are Muslim, and almost 35 per cent of residents speak a language other than English as their main language, compared to a Glaswegian average of fewer than 15 per cent and a Scottish average of fewer than 10 per cent.[117]

The area suffers from overcrowding,[118] is burdened with serious problems of discrimination and racism,[119] and has become a distinctively Pakistani and Muslim district: shops have dual signs (English and Urdu), South Asian clothes shops display mannequins dressed in *shalvar kameez*, and there are beauty salons that are for women only.[120] However, it remains a 'reasonably affluent area, with almost a third of the population belonging to the professional/managerial class'.[121]

Pakistanis (and Bangladeshis) often live in deprived areas, although to a much lesser extent than fellow countrymen in England.[122] Indeed, data from the Scottish Index of Multiple Deprivation 2012 demonstrates that only 2 per cent of Pakistanis live in the most deprived 10 per cent of datazones in Glasgow. This is a percentage lower than for any other group, including white Scottish people (11 per cent).[123] Pakistanis are also less likely to live in the 15 per cent most deprived areas across

Scotland when compared to the national average.[124] In Edinburgh there are pockets of economic disadvantage and there remains some ethnic clustering among older Pakistanis through mosques, community centres, socio-cultural gatherings and family visits. But there are no predominantly 'Pakistani' neighbourhoods, unlike in major English conurbations.[125] It is true that many older members of the Pakistani migrant community live in Leith (East Edinburgh), Gorgie (West Edinburgh) and Broughton (North Edinburgh). But the community is fairly widespread and this encourages interaction between young Pakistanis and other Scottish people.[126]

The community is dispersed throughout Scotland and today Pakistanis can be found in East Dunbartonshire, East Renfrewshire, Falkirk, Fife, North Lanarkshire and South Lanarkshire. Scotland hosts seventy-six locations for prayer[127] consisting of mosques, temporary spaces for prayers, prayer rooms managed by university Islamic societies, Muslim community centres and cultural associations. An element that makes Scotland quite different from England is that, despite high rates of unemployment, a larger proportion of people of Pakistani origin or heritage work in higher-status occupations in Scotland than in England. Scottish Pakistanis have higher employment rates than Pakistanis in London, North West England and the East of England, and Scottish Indians have higher employment rates than Indians in London and the North West.[128] Pakistanis also have the highest proportion of self-employed people among all minority ethnic groups in Scotland.[129]

In addition, younger generations are increasingly entering the higher education system, to the extent that not only are young Pakistanis more educated than their parents[130] but they also pursue further education more than native Scots.[131] They are moving up the socio-economic ladder at a steady pace. This is part of a wider process that has also been identified in England and Wales, where the second and third generations of most minority ethnic groups have made significant progress and where Pakistanis have an ambition to be university-educated and strive for upward social mobility.[132] But it is important to note that the baseline financial condition of Pakistanis in Scotland was originally better compared to that of the community in England. This is largely due to the fact that members of the Pakistani community who migrated and settled in Scotland originated from the relatively well-off area of Faisalabad in the Punjab, unlike their fellow Pakistanis who live south of the border. These migrants to England had instead left rural Mirpur for Bradford, Birmingham and other major English cities to offer cheap guest labour to the British economy, which was recovering after the

Second World War, after the displacement of over 100,000 people following the construction of the Mangla Dam.[133]

Nowadays, Scottish Pakistanis are formally represented in government by MSPs Humza Yousaf, also Minister for Transport and the Islands, and Anas Sarwar. Former MSPs Hanzala Malik and the late Bashir Ahmad (the first ethnic minority MSP, elected in 2007) also served in the Scottish Government. The connections between Scotland and India and Pakistan remain extremely strong. Patna, a small village in East Ayrshire, was named after the capital of Bihar in eastern India by its founder William Fullarton, the son of a military commander for the East India Company who was born in Bihar.[134] A few years ago, families of nurses from Kerala in India, who now work in Scotland, founded the Malayali Christian community in Edinburgh.[135] Twenty-three Indian films[136] have used Scottish locations in the past two decades, including landmarks such as Edinburgh's Royal Mile, Crossraguel Abbey in Ayrshire and Eilean Donan Castle in the Highlands.[137] Processions to celebrate Baisakhi, the harvest festival of Punjab in India, through the Leith area of Edinburgh, with the wearing of tartan turbans by the Sikh community, demonstrate the symbolic integration of South Asian and Scottish identities.[138] The Pakistani town of Sialkot is one of the world's top manufacturers of bagpipes,[139] while the parliamentary oath made in both Urdu and English by Scottish-born MSP Humza Yousaf in 2016[140] is a reminder of the ever-present linguistic and cultural connections between the two countries. The annual Mela Festival is also an important South Asian festival that is 'an example of how minority cultures can become part of the mainstream ... *without* surrendering the ongoing, parallel evolution of their own separate cultures and identities'.[141] In the years to come

> it can be expected that not only will the forces of transnationalism therefore sustain existing linkages between Scotland, Pakistan and India, but they will produce demands for more frequent travel back and forth as well as the emergence of new international linkages with Indian and Pakistani communities in other parts of the world (and probably especially with those settled in the USA and Canada).[142]

In the past decade, many South Asians, who have historically supported Labour, have switched their support to the Scottish National Party[143] and started advocating for Scottish independence, possibly at even higher levels than the Scottish majority.[144] The independence debate also spurred young people across the ethno-religious spectrum to reflect on the meanings of being Scottish and 'many felt that Scotland was a "fair society" that was "diverse" and "friendly"'.[145] But there are also some challenges that confront the South Asian community in Scotland. The recent struggle between the conservative and liberal sections of the Muslim community for control of Glasgow Central Mosque is a case in point.[146] The tensions between the older and younger generations are about ethnic diversity, the place of women in mosques and the role of Islam. These debates will shape the face and the future of the community.

Historically, the visits to Scotland of leading Islamist Omar Bakri Muhammad in the 1990s were carried out discreetly.[147] Similarly, more recent public opposition to Islamist terrorism from Scottish Muslim organisations and individuals[148] testifies to the fact that the relatively well-off, small, educated and dispersed Scottish Muslim community places a strong emphasis on unity and tolerance. Yet, the ever-present threat posed by violent radicalisation is exemplified by the notable cases of individuals who have joined terrorist organisations: Glaswegian Aqsa Mahmood travelled to Syria and turned into a recruiter for the Islamic State in 2013,[149] while Aberdonian Abdul Rakib Amin joined the Islamic State in 2014 and was later killed in a drone strike.[150] In more recent times (March 2016), a member of the minority Ahmadiyya Muslim community in Glasgow, Asad Shah, was murdered hours after wishing his customers a happy Easter on social media,[151] while his murderer, Tanveer Ahmed, later inspired anti-blasphemy hardliners in Pakistan and beyond.[152] This incident and the security concerns expressed by Asad Shah's family are a reminder of the sectarian lines that divide Scottish Muslims and the rifts that trouble different Islamic denominations.[153] While Indians are divided along religious and cultural lines, Pakistanis share a common religion (Islam), yet one that has the power to promote deeply polarised attitudes from the wider community.

The two communities share similarities that emerge from their common South Asian background. At present, the most troubling cultural aspect concerns forced marriage, which entails a non-consensual wedding and is 'widely recognised at a national and international level as a violation of [men's,] women's and children's human rights and as a form of violence against women and children'.[154] While many cases tend to go unreported to the police, often due to the inward-looking nature of some minority ethnic communities, a recent Scottish Government study found 191 cases of forced marriage reported by survey respondents between 2011 and 2014. Victims were mainly from Pakistani (79 people – that is, 55 per cent) and Indian (13 people – that is, 9 per cent) ethnic backgrounds. In 25 cases (37 per cent) the country of origin was Pakistan, while in 7 cases (10 per cent) it was India.[155] These practices feature nuances and complexities that go beyond the narrow realm of culture and touch upon broader issues of gender discrimination, social justice and human rights. Yet their prevalence within certain communities and their breaching of international human rights standards, contravention of British law and defiance of Islamic and South Asian laws[156] are a reminder that cultural retention within Pakistani and the Indian communities has not come without a cost to their host society.

CONCLUSION

After centuries of slow but continuous migration from the Indian subcontinent to Scotland, the demise of the British Raj and the Partition of India in 1947 gave rise to two distinct communities divided along ethnic, cultural and religious lines: Indians and Pakistanis. This migration gained momentum after 1947 and has continued until the present. Seven decades after Partition, Indians and Pakistanis populate every main Scottish town, bringing a distinctive South Asian flavour to the urban and rural character of the country that is exemplified by ethnic restaurants and grocery shops, mosques, religious celebrations and festivals. The two communities took different educational and economic trajectories that are reflected in their current financial conditions. Nowadays, Indians boast employment rates almost on a par with white people, while Pakistanis' rates are lower than average but still higher than those of Pakistanis in either London or the main English regions. The settlement of the two communities has not been free of obstacles, but the prejudice and discrimination that Pakistanis and Indians have faced have not prevented them from integrating into Scottish society in a relatively successful manner. Nevertheless, hard-line attitudes and the risk of violent radicalisation among some members of the Pakistani community, the polarising views that Islam attracts in a post-9/11 world and the problem of forced marriage that both Pakistanis and Indians share, are reminders that the process of cultural adaptation in Scotland is yet to be fully completed.

NOTES

1. This chapter draws on material from Stefano Bonino, *Muslims in Scotland: The Making of Community in a Post-9/11 World* (Edinburgh: Edinburgh University Press, 2016).

2. T. M. Devine, *The Scottish Nation: A Modern History* (London: Penguin Books, 2012), pp. 622–6.
3. Nasar Meer, 'Looking up in Scotland? Multinationalism, multiculturalism and political elites', *Ethnic and Racial Studies*, 38:9 (2015), p. 1487.
4. Robert Miles and Anne Dunlop, 'Racism in Britain: The Scottish dimension', in Peter Jackson (ed.), *Race and Racism: Essays in Social Geography* (London: Allen & Unwin, 1987), p. 100.
5. Nasar Meer, 'What would independence mean for Scotland's racial minorities?', *The Guardian*, 20 May 2011, http://www.theguardian.com/politics/2011/may/20/independence-scotland-racial-minorities (last accessed 19 December 2016).
6. Robert Hall, 'World War One at home, Perth, Scotland: Diaspora, Indian troops and WW1', *BBC Radio Scotland*, 17 November 2014, http://www.bbc.co.uk/programmes/p02c4kpq (last accessed 19 December 2016).
7. British Library, *World Wars: Asians in Britain*, undated, http://www.bl.uk/learning/histcitizen/asians/worldwars/theworldwars.html (last accessed 21 December 2016); Ian Sumner, *The Indian Army: 1914–1947* (Oxford: Osprey Publishing, 2001), pp. 23–9; Hall, 'World War One at home'. Nowadays there remain thirteen graves of Muslim soldiers (mostly from Punjab in today's Pakistan) from the Royal Indian Army Service Corps in four Scottish cemeteries (Aberdeen, Keith, Dornoch and Kingussie). See Irfan Malik, *These Graves of Indian Muslim Soldiers in Britain Will Surprise You*, 18 October 2016, http://blogs.arynews.tv/the-graves-of-indian-muslim-soldiers-in-britain-will-surprise-you (last accessed 21 December 2016).
8. Bashir Maan, *The Thistle and the Crescent* (Glendaruel: Argyll Publishing, 2008), pp. 185–214.
9. Ibid., pp. 185–214.
10. Humayun Ansari, *The Infidel Within: Muslims in Britain Since 1800* (London: Hurst, 2004), p. 36.
11. Ibid., p. 36.
12. Ibid., p. 32.
13. Ibid., p. 32.
14. Nick Bailey, Alison Bowes and Duncan Sim, 'Pakistanis in Scotland: Census data and research issues', *Scottish Geographical Magazine*, 111:1 (1995), p. 36.
15. Bashir Maan, *Muslims in Scotland* (Glendaruel: Argyll Publishing, 2014), p. 21.
16. Ansari, *The Infidel Within*, pp. 40–51.
17. Bashir Maan, *The New Scots: The Story of Asians in Scotland* (Edinburgh: John Donald Publishers, 1992), pp. 162–5.
18. Maan, *Muslims in Scotland*, p. 30.
19. Ibid., pp. 31–2.
20. Devine, *The Scottish Nation*, pp. 486–522.

21. Bailey, Bowes and Sim, 'Pakistanis in Scotland', p. 36.
22. Malory Nie, *A Place for our Gods: The Construction of an Edinburgh Hindu Temple Community* (Richmond: Curzon Press, 1995).
23. Ibid.
24. Maan, *The New Scots*, pp. 153–65.
25. Ibid., p. 48.
26. Omar Shaikh and Stefano Bonino, 'Feeling Scottish and being Muslim: Findings from the Colourful Heritage Project', in Peter Hopkins (ed.), *Scotland's Muslims: Society, Politics and Identity* (Edinburgh: Edinburgh University Press, 2017).
27. Maan, *The Thistle and the Crescent*, p. 199.
28. Ibid., pp. 185–214.
29. Ali Wardak, *Social Control and Deviance: A South Asian Community in Scotland* (Aldershot: Ashgate, 2000), pp. 20–7.
30. Nie, *A Place for our Gods*, pp. 49–50.
31. Ibid., pp. 49–50.
32. Ansari, *The Infidel Within*, pp. 145–65.
33. Ceri Peach, 'South Asian migration and settlement in Great Britain, 1951–2001', *Contemporary South Asia*, 15:2 (2006), p. 136.
34. Miles and Dunlop, 'Racism in Britain', pp. 100–3.
35. Devine, *The Scottish Nation*, pp. 555–65.
36. Ibid., pp. 555–65.
37. Maan, *The New Scots*, pp. 157–81.
38. Ibid., p. 171.
39. Sue Morrison, *She Settles in the Shields* (Glasgow: Glasgow Women's Library, 2009), pp. 90–107.
40. Maan, *The New Scots*, pp. 171–2.
41. Scottish Government, *Scotland's Diaspora and Overseas-Born Population: Update 2016* (Edinburgh: Scottish Government, 2016); National Records of Scotland, *2011 Census* (Edinburgh: National Records of Scotland, 2013).
42. Bailey, Bowes and Sim, 'Pakistanis in Scotland', p. 48.
43. Geoffrey Kearsley and S. R. Srivastava, 'The spatial evolution of Glasgow's Asian community', *Scottish Geographical Magazine*, 90:2 (1974), p. 112.
44. Maan, *The New Scots*, pp. 149–81.
45. Kearsley and Srivastava, 'The spatial evolution of Glasgow's Asian community', pp. 112–13.
46. Ibid., pp. 112–13.
47. Maan, *The New Scots*, pp. 149–81.
48. Ibid., pp. 162–5.
49. Register of Pedlars' Certificates granted by the Chief Constable of the City of Glasgow Police – Pedlars' Act 1871, 34 and 35 Vict. C. 96, Mitchell Library, Glasgow.

50. Kearsley and Srivastava, 'The spatial evolution of Glasgow's Asian community', p. 114.
51. Maan, *The New Scots*, pp. 182–200.
52. Kearsley and Srivastava, 'The spatial evolution of Glasgow's Asian community', pp. 113–14.
53. Ibid., p. 113.
54. Devine, *The Scottish Nation*, p. 564.
55. Ibid., p. 564.
56. Miles and Dunlop, 'Racism in Britain', p. 103.
57. Ibid., p. 125.
58. Kearsley and Srivastava, 'The spatial evolution of Glasgow's Asian community', pp. 114–15.
59. Huw Jones and Maureen Davenport, 'The Pakistani community in Dundee: A study of its growth and demographic structure', *Scottish Geographical Magazine*, 88:2 (1972), p. 75.
60. Kearsley and Srivastava, 'The spatial evolution of Glasgow's Asian community', p. 115.
61. Ibid., p. 115.
62. Jones and Davenport, 'The Pakistani community in Dundee', p. 75.
63. Kearsley and Srivastava, 'The spatial evolution of Glasgow's Asian community', p. 123.
64. Bailey, Bowes and Sim, 'Pakistanis in Scotland', pp. 37–8.
65. Ibid., p. 37.
66. Kearsley and Srivastava, 'The spatial evolution of Glasgow's Asian community', p. 111.
67. Nie, *A Place for our Gods*, pp. 5–14.
68. Bailey, Bowes and Sim, 'Pakistanis in Scotland', pp. 40–1.
69. Scottish Government, *Scottish Government Equality Outcomes: Ethnicity Evidence Review* (Edinburgh: Scottish Government, 2013), p. 10.
70. Bailey, Bowes and Sim, 'Pakistanis in Scotland', pp. 36–7.
71. Scottish Government, *Scottish Government Equality Outcomes*, p. 30.
72. Ibid.
73. They are the fourth-largest ethnic group after 'other white', 'Polish' and 'Irish'. National Records of Scotland, *The Registrar General's Annual Review of Demographic Trends* (Edinburgh: HM General Register House, 2015).
74. Ibid.
75. Ibid.
76. Maan, *Muslims in Scotland*, pp. 51–2.
77. Shaikh and Bonino, 'Feeling Scottish and being Muslim'.
78. Nie, *A Place for our Gods*, pp. 41–3.
79. The following are only a few examples. The absence of a description in some photographs included in the Bashir Maan Archive makes it impos-

sible to ascertain the political and religious figures involved in the events attended by Bashir Maan.

80. Bashir Maan Archive, T-CH1/1/1/5, Mitchell Library, Glasgow; Bashir Maan Archive, T-CH1/1/2/2, Mitchell Library, Glasgow; Bashir Maan Archive, T-CH1/1/3, Mitchell Library, Glasgow.

81. Bashir Maan Archive, T-CH1/1/1/1, Mitchell Library, Glasgow; Bashir Maan Archive, T-CH1/1/1/2, Mitchell Library, Glasgow.

82. Bashir Maan Archive, T-CH1/1/2/2, Mitchell Library, Glasgow; Bashir Maan Archive, T-CH1/1/2/3, Mitchell Library, Glasgow; Bashir Maan Archive, T-CH1/1/2/5, Mitchell Library, Glasgow.

83. British Library, *Asians in Britain: 1858–1950*, undated, http://www.bl.uk/learning/histcitizen/asians/worldwars/theworldwars.html (last accessed 21 December 2016).

84. Anne Dunlop, 'An united front? Anti-racist political mobilisation in Scotland', *Scottish Affairs*, 3 (1993), p. 94.

85. Nie, *A Place for our Gods*, pp. 36–41.

86. Ibid., pp. 65–6.

87. Ibid., pp. 67–102.

88. Ibid., pp. 175–80.

89. Ibid., pp. 177–8.

90. Ibid., pp. 175–80.

91. Ibid., pp. 175–80.

92. Ibid., pp. 5–14.

93. Ibid., pp. 5–14.

94. Maan, *The Thistle and the Crescent*, p. 203.

95. Robert Miles and Anne Dunlop, 'The racialization of politics in Britain: Why Scotland is different', *Patterns of Prejudice*, 20:1 (1986), p. 26.

96. Ibid., pp. 23–33.

97. Alison Bowes, Jacqui McCluskey and Duncan Sim, 'Racism and harassment of Asians in Glasgow', *Ethnic and Racial Studies*, 13:1 (1990), pp. 71–91; Miles and Dunlop, 'Racism in Britain', pp. 98–116.

98. Miles and Dunlop, 'Racism in Britain', p. 113.

99. Miles and Dunlop, 'The racialization of politics in Britain', p. 26.

100. Miles and Dunlop, 'Racism in Britain', p. 105.

101. Ruari Sutherland, '"The Scottish hate us more than the Muslims . . .": The North/South divide? A comparative analysis of the agenda, activities and development of the English and Scottish Defence Leagues', *Reinvention: A Journal of Undergraduate Research*, British Conference of Undergraduate Research 2012 Special Issue, http://www.warwick.ac.uk/go/reinvention-journal/issues/bcur2012specialissue/Sutherland (last accessed 12 March 2017).

102. Asifa Hussain and William Miller, *Multicultural Nationalism: Islamophobia, Anglophobia, and Devolution* (Oxford: Oxford University Press, 2006).

103. Ibid., p. 65.

104. Robert Ford, 'Is racial prejudice declining in Britain?', *British Journal of Sociology*, 59:4 (2008), pp. 609–36.

105. Pew Global Attitudes Project, *Faith in European Project Reviving* (Washington, DC: Pew Research Centre, 2015).

106. Scottish Government, 'Racist incidents recorded by the police in Scotland, 2012–13', *Statistical Bulletin: Crime and Justice Series*, 2013.

107. Scottish Government, 'Racist incidents recorded by the police in Scotland, 2013–14', *Statistical Bulletin: Crime and Justice Series*, 2015. The decrease in recorded racist incidents follows a wider trend of decreasing crime rates in Scotland, which at the time of writing are at their lowest levels since 1974. See Scottish Government, 'Recorded crime in Scotland 2014–15', *Statistical Bulletin: Crime and Justice Series*, 2015; Scottish Government, 'Recorded crime in Scotland 2015–16', *Statistical Bulletin: Crime and Justice Series*, 2016.

108. Maureen McBride, 'A review of the evidence on hate crime and prejudice: Report for the Independent Advisory Group on hate crime, prejudice and community cohesion', *SCCJR Report 07/2016*, http://www.sccjr.ac.uk/wp-content/uploads/2016/09/A-Review-of-the-Evidence-on-Hate-Crime-and-Prejudice.pdf (last accessed 19 December 2016).

109. Peter Swindon, 'Scots Muslims speak out over racist abuse after terror attacks', *Herald Scotland*, 31 July 2016, http://www.heraldscotland.com/news/14653092.Verbal_abuse__violence_and_suspicion__prominent_Scots_Muslims_speak_out_as_racism_ramps_up_amid_summer_of_terror (last accessed 11 January 2016).

110. Scottish Government, 'Racist incidents recorded by the police in Scotland, 2013–14'.

111. This identity is indicated as 'other only' in the census but tends to indicate the ethnic identity of origin of the group under consideration.

112. National Records of Scotland, *2011 Census: Key Results on Population, Ethnicity, Identity, Language, Religion, Health, Housing and Accommodation in Scotland – Release 24* (Edinburgh: National Records of Scotland, 2013).

113. Ibid.

114. Alita Nandi and Lucinda Platt, 'Britishness and identity assimilation among the UK's minority and majority ethnic groups', *Understanding Society*, Working paper series, no. 2013–08, December 2013, https://www.understandingsociety.ac.uk/research/publications/working-paper/understanding-society/2013-08.pdf (last accessed 19 December 2016).

115. Brian Kelly and Stephen Ashe, 'Ethnic mixing in Glasgow', *Local Dynamics of Diversity: Evidence from the 2011 Census* (Manchester: Centre on Dynamics of Diversity, 2014).

116. 'Understanding Glasgow', *Glasgow Neighbourhood Data Profiles: Pollokshields East*, undated, http://www.understandingglasgow.com/pro

files/2_south_sector/46_pollokshields_east (last accessed 19 December 2016).

117. Brian Kelly and Stephen Ashe, 'Geographies of deprivation and diversity in Glasgow', *Local Dynamics of Diversity: Evidence from the 2011 Census* (Manchester: Centre on Dynamics of Diversity, 2014).

118. 'Understanding Glasgow'.

119. Peter Hopkins, 'Everyday racism in Scotland: A case study of East Pollokshields', *Scottish Affairs*, 49 (2004), pp. 98–9.

120. Asifa Siraj, 'Meanings of modesty and the hijab amongst Muslim women in Glasgow, Scotland', *Gender, Place and Culture: A Journal of Feminist Geography*, 18:6 (2011), pp. 720–2.

121. Hopkins, 'Everyday racism in Scotland', p. 95.

122. Elshayyal, *Scottish Muslims in Numbers*, p. 37.

123. Kelly and Ashe, 'Geographies of deprivation and diversity in Glasgow', p. 3.

124. Elshayyal, *Scottish Muslims in Numbers*, p. 36.

125. Bonino, *Muslims in Scotland*, pp. 24–5.

126. Karen Qureshi, 'Respected and respectable: The centrality of "performance" and "audiences" in the (re)production and potential revision of gendered ethnicities', *Particip@tions: Journal of Audience and Reception Studies*, 1:2 (2004), http://www.participations.org/volume%201/issue%202/1_02_qureshi_article.htm (last accessed 19 December 2016).

127. Mehmood Naqshbandi, *UK Mosque Statistics/Masjid Statistics*, 2015, http://www.muslimsinbritain.org/resources/masjid_report.pdf (last accessed 19 December 2016); Mehmood Naqshbandi, *Muslims in Britain: UK Mosque/Masjid Directory*, 2016, http://mosques.muslimsinbritain.org/index.php (last accessed 19 December 2016).

128. Elisabet Weedon, Sheila Riddell, Gillean McCluskey and Kristina Konstantoni, *Muslim Families' Educational Experiences in England and Scotland* (Edinburgh: University of Edinburgh, Centre for Research in Education Inclusion and Diversity, 2013), p. 5.

129. National Records of Scotland, *2011 Census: Key Results on Population*.

130. Hopkins, 'Everyday racism in Scotland', pp. 96–8.

131. National Records of Scotland, *2011 Census: Key Results on Population, Ethnicity, Identity, Language, Religion, Health, Housing and Accommodation in Scotland*.

132. Tariq Modood, *Multicultural Politics: Racism, Ethnicity and Muslims in Britain* (Minneapolis, MN: University of Minnesota Press, 2005), pp. 92–8.

133. Ansari, *The Infidel Within*, pp. 152–3.

134. Aditi Malhotra, '"Broon Scots" exhibition celebrates Scotland's South Asians', *The Wall Street Journal*, 18 September 2014, http://blogs.wsj.com/indiarealtime/2014/09/18/broon-scots-exhibition-celebrates-scotlands-south-asians (last accessed 21 December 2016).

135. Ibid.
136. The first two were *Main Solah Baras Ki* and *Kuch Kuch Hota Hai* in 1998. See BBC News, 'When Bollywood came to Scotland', *BBC News*, 20 January 2015, http://www.bbc.co.uk/news/uk-scotland-30878983 (last accessed 21 December 2016).
137. Ibid.
138. Ibid.
139. Imtiaz Tyab, 'Fair winds for Pakistan's bagpipe industry', *Al Jazeera*, 13 February 2013, http://www.aljazeera.com/video/asia/2013/02/20132137 1749190628.html (last accessed 5 January 2017).
140. Julie Gilbert, 'Glasgow MSP takes oath in Urdu as Parliament sworn in at Holyrood', *Glasgow Live*, 12 May 2016, http://www.glasgowlive. co.uk/news/glasgow-news/glasgow-msp-takes-oath-urdu-11324660 (last accessed 5 January 2017).
141. Jan Penrose, 'Multiple multiculturalisms: Insights from the Edinburgh Mela', *Social and Cultural Geography*, 14:7 (2013), p. 847 (emphasis in the original).
142. Allan Findlay, *A Migration Research Agenda for Scotland*, paper presented to the ESRC/Scottish Executive seminar on Scottish Population Trends, GRO Scotland, 17 May 2004, p. 15.
143. Neil McGarvey and Gareth Mulvey, 'Identities and politics in the 2014 Scottish independence referendum: The Polish and Pakistani experience', in Roberta Medda-Windischer and Patricia Popelier (eds), *Pro-independence Movements and Immigration: Discourse, Policy and Practice* (Leiden: Brill, 2016), pp. 156–7.
144. Hussain and Miller, *Multicultural Nationalism*, pp. 164–7; *The Economist* (2009), 'Islam in tartan', *The Economist*, 7 May, http://www.economist. com/node/13611699 (last accessed 29 March 2016).
145. Peter Hopkins, Katherine Botterill, Gurchathen Sanghera and Rowena Arshad, *Faith, Ethnicity, Place: Young People's Everyday Geopolitics in Scotland*, Research Report (Swindon: Arts and Humanities Research Council, 2015), p. 21.
146. David Leask, 'Analysis: The new generation of liberal Scottish Muslims taking control of Scotland's biggest mosque', *Herald Scotland*, 19 January 2016, http://www.heraldscotland.com/news/14213213.Analysis_ _the_new_generation_of_liberal_Scottish_Muslims_taking_control_of_ Scotland_s_biggest_mosque (last accessed 13 March 2017).
147. *Herald Scotland*, 'How Scotland's Muslims are fighting the rise of radical Islam at home', *Herald Scotland*, 1 February 2015, http://m.heraldscot-land.com/news/13199694.Revealed__how_Scotland_s_Muslims_are_ fighting_the_rise_of_radical_Islam_at_home (last accessed 10 January 2017).
148. BBC News, 'Hundreds attend anti-terror rally', *BBC News*, 7 July 2007, http://news.bbc.co.uk/1/hi/scotland/glasgow_and_west/6279416.

stm (last accessed 10 January 2017); David O'Leary, 'Scottish Muslims plan rally against Islamic State', *The Scotsman*, 12 October 2014, http://www.scotsman.com/news/scottish-muslims-plan-rally-against-islamic-state-1-3570268 (last accessed 10 January 2017); Victoria Weldon, 'Scottish Muslims condemn "barbaric" murder', *Herald Scotland*, 15 September 2014, http://www.heraldscotland.com/news/13179985.Scottish_Muslims_condemn__barbaric__murder (last accessed 10 January 2017); *Herald Scotland*, 'Muslim groups unite against terrorism', *Herald Scotland*, 2 July 2015, http://www.heraldscotland.com/news/13366460.Muslim_groups_unite_against_terrorism (last accessed 10 January 2017).

149. Ashley Fantz and Atika Shubert, 'From Scottish teen to ISIS bride and recruiter: The Aqsa Mahmood story', *CNN*, 24 February 2015, http://edition.cnn.com/2015/02/23/world/scottish-teen-isis-recruiter (last accessed 10 January 2017).

150. David Maddox, 'Scots jihadist killed by RAF drone strike in Syria', *The Scotsman*, 7 September 2015, http://www.scotsman.com/news/politics/scots-jihadist-killed-by-raf-drone-strike-in-syria-1-3879933 (last accessed 10 January 2017).

151. BBC News, 'Arrest after Glasgow shopkeeper Asad Shah dies in attack', *BBC News*, 26 March 2016, http://www.bbc.com/news/uk-scotland-glasgow-west-3589 8543 (last accessed 10 January 2017).

152. Secunder Kermani and Sajid Iqbal, 'Murderer Tanveer Ahmed inspires Pakistani hardliners from Scottish jail', *BBC News*, 1 March 2017, http://www.bbc.co.uk/news/world-asia-39112840 (last accessed 1 March 2017).

153. Peter Swindon, 'Asad Shah family fear for safety after killing linked to sectarian tensions in Muslim community', *Evening Times*, 27 March 2016, http://m.eveningtimes.co.uk/news/14386376.Asad_Shah_family_fear_for_ safety_after_killing_linked_to_sectarian_tensions_in_Muslim_community (last accessed 10 January 2017).

154. Scottish Government, *Understanding Forced Marriage in Scotland* (Edinburgh: Scottish Government, 2016), p. 8. See also Stefano Bonino, 'Policing forced marriages among Pakistanis in the United Kingdom', in Margaret Malloch and Paul Rigby (eds), *Human Trafficking: The Complexities of Exploitation* (Edinburgh: Edinburgh University Press, 2016), pp. 159–74.

155. Scottish Government, *Understanding Forced Marriage in Scotland*.

156. Bonino, 'Policing forced marriages among Pakistanis in the United Kingdom', pp. 159–60.

5

Immigration to Scotland from Overseas: The Experience of Nurses

Ima Jackson

Migration is a challenging experience, both for new citizens and for their host society. But the migration of nurses and midwives to Scotland from the post-colonial Commonwealth countries in the 1950s was distinctive, not least in the unique intimacy of their engagement with Britain. These Commonwealth citizens felt part of the wider 'family' of British culture and organisations. They did not, however, merely join the UK workforce. Instead, migrant nurses and midwives came to care for members of the host society, and that care was provided when Britons were especially vulnerable through illness, pain, distress or (for midwives) the emotional intensity of childbirth. As immigrant midwives and nurses placed Black hands on the white bodies of their new patients, the power dynamics and authority embedded within the professional/patient relationship disrupted or inverted many of the assumptions and structures held by both parties. The Black nurse was the professional and was in charge. This societal shift occurring for the first time in homes and hospitals in Scotland and the UK, compounded by the level of intimacy which comes with a caring role, gives this particular migrant experience a context and texture different from any other.

This chapter explores the social, political and policy context environment for nurse[1] migration to Scotland since the 1950s and relates the experience of some of these new clinicians. Information from historical sources and more recent empirical data are combined in order to provide insight into the ambitions, hopes and disappointments of midwives and nurses arriving in Scotland from overseas.

From its inception in 1948, the NHS has relied on the recruitment of overseas nurses to meet its staffing needs.[2] The first staff came primarily from the West Indies and Africa, but more recently nurses have been recruited from the Philippines, India and EU countries, especially Spain.[3]

Most of these early newcomers were recruited directly from overseas, but today employers also recruit migrants already in the UK, including nurses who arrived in Scotland as refugees or asylum seekers.[4]

Those nurses who came to Scotland from Commonwealth countries already felt a close affinity with the UK. Their education was based on the British system: they typically sat O-levels and A-levels in a UK syllabus taught in English.[5] When first encountering these 'new' nurses, patients in Glasgow and Manchester may not have appreciated the extent of the long colonial culture they held in common. A nurse who trained in Jamaica may have been just as familiar as her charges with the kings and queens of England and with the names of obscure places and traditions.

Since migrants filled vacancies in the new and popular NHS, their contribution was tolerated, if not always welcomed. The rising anti-immigration sentiment in the UK, which has been eloquently documented by Stuart Hall, a leading cultural theorist, seems also to have changed attitudes within the professions.[6] Hall argues that distinctive 'indigenous British racism' developing at that time grew out of 'a profound historical amnesia which had overtaken the British people about race and empire since the 1950s which began paradoxically with an attempt to wipe out and efface every trace of the British colonial and imperial past'.[7] This disconnection from a British colonial past would have contributed to a lack of understanding of the reasons why Black people were coming to Britain at this time. As Hall suggests, it was largely geography and distance which had enabled the long relationships to remain invisible to many in the UK.

This climate of amnesia led to a growing antipathy towards Black and minority ethnic health professionals and that, it has been argued, shaped their professional experiences.[8] Ultimately, this migration was about more than vacancy management: the expansion of the NHS meant that migrant nurses became not only permanent staff, but also permanent citizens.

INTERNATIONAL NURSE MIGRATION

Like medicine, nursing is a profession that is both well-adapted and long-accustomed to international migration. The training of nurses in developed countries has been largely viewed as similar, so nurses have moved relatively easily between the UK, USA, Australia and other wealthy countries that share equivalent systems and standards.[9] The WHO estimates that there was a global shortfall of 7.2 million healthcare workers in 2016, which is anticipated to grow to a shortage of 12.9 million care workers by 2035.[10] That need has often been met by the large-scale movement of nurses from poor economies to wealthier ones, typically between countries with historic or cultural links, such as South African nurses moving to the UK and the USA, or nurses from the Democratic Republic of Congo migrating to Belgium.[11] The numbers of nurses applying to work in the UK in the early and mid-2000s (a time of peak migration) was 147,640, an increase from 14,000 in 1978.[12] This reflects not only the increase of health worker migration globally as a phenomenon but the rising levels of largely female nurse migration.[13]

Since UK nurse training is recognised to be of a good standard, Scottish nurses are valued by other countries. Moreover, since the NHS has a reputation for quality of care, opportunities for training and good terms and conditions of employment, NHS posts are attractive to nurses from overseas. Despite a major investment in nurse training in Scotland, the nursing workforce has always needed supplementation. As both exporter and importer of nurses, Scotland therefore finds itself as an actor in a dynamic global labour market. What follows is an outline of the historical and current reasons for nurse recruitment and the changing social, political and professional context which helps to explain it. The impact this environment had on the experience of nurses who migrated is then explained through interweaving text from interviews with nurses with reference to research and policy documents which reflect the issues they raised. The conclusion reflects on nurse migration and suggests ways to engage with current migration and its impact on contemporary Scottish life.

NURSE MIGRATION IN THE UK

Nurse shortages have been an issue for the NHS since its inception. There were 54,000 nurse vacancies (around 15 per cent of the total) in the NHS when it was founded in 1948[14] within a workforce of approximately 364,000.[15] (The current nurse shortage percentage is thought to be about 9.6 per cent in England and Wales and 4 per cent in Scotland.)[16] This was also a time of significant British emigration to countries like Australia and New Zealand.[17] Although policy-makers responded by seeking to train more nurses, the advantages of recruitment from overseas then as now were also clear. The education of new nurses from the domestic population is both expensive and time-consuming, whereas fully trained overseas staff can be recruited and working in post within a few months. Nurse training over three years currently costs the NHS about £51,000.[18] A nurse recruited from overseas can be employed at £23,000 per year, with their education costs borne by the country of origin.[19]

Consequently, the UK Government sought to attract European nurses from France, Spain, Germany and Portugal.[20] They also approached Scandinavian governments in 1947 to assess potential recruitment, but these countries were likewise experiencing post-war shortages and were unable to assist.[21] The 'Balt Cygnet' scheme (part of the European Voluntary Workers programme from 1946 to 1949) did attract several thousand people who had been 'displaced' by conflict from the Baltic region and other countries to carry out basic bedside roles, but staff shortages persisted. Recruitment from the Commonwealth therefore began in 1949 and rapidly expanded, so that by 1955 there were sixteen official recruitment programmes for nurses in former British colonies, especially in the Caribbean.[22]

This approach proved successful, and the flow of qualified and student nurses continued through the 1960s and '70s. By 1977 it was estimated that over 10,500 nurses had arrived, of whom 66 per cent were from the Caribbean – about 12 per cent of the total UK nurse workforce at that time.[23] A lack of data on Scotland makes it difficult to assess actual

Figure 5.1 Awards ceremony for nurses, Royal College of Nursing, c. 1955. Royal College of Nursing Collections, P/18/1/83/4.

numbers, but photographs and documents from Scottish hospitals and health boards clearly show that some migrant nurses were working in Scotland, as well as elsewhere in the UK.

This transformation was facilitated by the Nationality Act of 1948, which granted British citizenship to people from colonies and former colonies. The legislation remained relatively unchallenged until the 1962 Commonwealth Immigrants Act, which linked citizenship to proof of employment. An amendment in 1968 further restricted access by making a distinction between those deemed 'patrials' – who had rights determined through parentage or five years' residence in Britain – and those from Australia, New Zealand and Canada, who were often not required to demonstrate this connection.[24] The legislation therefore privileged access for White Commonwealth citizens. Similar distinctions applied to professional registration with the Nursing and Midwifery Council (NMC). These were to persist for many years, and will be discussed later.

By 1971 increasingly stringent amendments to the Immigration Act of that year ended primary migration from the Commonwealth. Yet nurse migration was largely unaffected by these changes, because linkages to studentships or jobs meant that recruitment could continue. However, the political and social climate was becoming increasingly resistant to immigration. That hostility came to be encapsulated in Enoch Powell's 'Rivers of Blood' speech in 1968. Ironically, Powell was one of the government ministers who had championed overseas nurse recruitment just a decade earlier.

The 1981 British Nationality Act introduced three tiers of citizenship: British Citizens (who had the right to live in Britain), Citizens of Dependent Territories and British Overseas Citizens (both of whom had no right to remain). The Act also removed the unconditional right to family reunion. Subsequent introduction of visa requirements substantially reduced the routes, rights and numbers of migrants, and this time these changes affected nurses too.

By the 1990s the number of young people choosing to enter nursing in the UK was falling. Some analysts have attributed this to direct policy changes as the Thatcher governments reduced training places, held down wages and limited workforce growth.[25] Changing social expectations and more attractive career opportunities for young women probably played a part as well.[26] But others argued that the recruitment of migrant nurses had itself contributed to a decline in the profession's prestige. For example, the Royal College of Nursing asserted that the nursing role had been devalued because of 'the reliance on overseas nurses'.[27] Whether migrants caused perceptions of nursing to change, or whether they were responding to those changes, is a moot point. Whatever the cause, the shortage of nurses in Scotland and the rest of the UK became marked in the 1990s.[28]

New Labour investment in the NHS from 1997 led to a substantial increase in the need for nurses. One estimate suggests a 30,000 shortfall by the end of the 1990s.[29] From 1998 to 2005, therefore, there was again a determined effort to recruit directly from abroad. Large flows of nurses from hard-pressed health systems in developing countries had raised ethical issues for international recruitment.[30] An ethical code of practice for recruitment was introduced in England in 2004[31] and in Scotland in 2006.[32] Country-to-country agreements for ethical recruitment were developed, whereby countries who were part of the code determined a 'tolerable' level of nurse exports. UK public bodies ceased to recruit from developing countries with fragile healthcare systems, but formal agreements were made between the Scottish NHS healthcare bodies and their counterparts in India, China and the Philippines.[33]

Although the code setting out best practice and adherence was commended, there remained potential for private sector companies to continue to hire nursing staff from overseas without such restrictions. These 'informal' recruitment pathways outside governmental agreements could remain a route for the employment of staff, especially in the care home sector.

In 2005 the NMC, the national professional regulatory body, introduced more stringent requirements for professional registration. Immigrant nurses were required to undertake a formal adaptation programme in a university and to meet higher standards of proficiency in English language. Since few universities offered such programmes, many overseas nurses already in the UK found it difficult to gain registration.[34]

The Shortage Occupation List is a policy tool developed to help manage migration. It describes the occupations which require workers from overseas (beyond the EU), and typically five-year visas are linked to posts within those occupations. Most nursing was removed from this list in 2006 (with exceptions for specific specialist roles such as renal, paediatric or intensive-care nurses). However, it was reinstated in 2015, in part due to lobbying from the Royal College of Nursing.[35] By 2016 the demand for nurses was rising once again, with an estimated shortage of 20,000 posts UK-wide.[36]

CURRENT ISSUES

There are well-documented 'push' and 'pull' factors which underpin the decisions that individual nurses make about migration.[37] 'Push' factors include poor wages in the country of origin, economic instability, poorly funded healthcare systems, and the burdens and risks of AIDS, especially in Africa.[38] 'Pull' factors in the host country include higher wages, better living and working conditions, opportunities for professional training and a pre-existing historical relationship with the country.[39] Political factors also have a strong influence. Scotland has always had a more stable pattern of nurse employment than England, but immigration to the UK is not a devolved power, and Scottish recruitment takes place in an increasingly hostile immigration policy climate.

The policies of foreign governments are similarly influential. For example, the government of the Philippines trained nurses (and a range of other workers) as a form of human capital for export. This process began in the 1980s as a short-term solution to domestic economic difficulties, but has continued to grow. In 2013, 1.8 million temporary Filipino migrant workers emigrated to more than 190 countries, each one bearing an employment contract issued and certified by the Philippines Government.[40] Scotland recruited hundreds of Filipino nurses by this route from 2000, with health boards in Aberdeen and Glasgow being particularly active. Private-sector activity towards the recruitment of Filipinos was also occurring.

Government regulation, which has developed over the years in response to recruitment, has not necessarily improved the opportunities or risks faced by nurse migrants. In fact, they may have become increasingly vulnerable. Ethical recruitment standards provide some protection, but they were not always met, even by the NHS. In Scotland, for example, the Southern General Hospital in Glasgow was alleged in 2004 to have contributed to the exploitation of Filipino nurses by deducting wages for unsatisfactory expensive accommodation at the request of the agent.[41]

In 2013 Lothian Health Board became concerned that Black and minority ethnic (BAME) background nurses were under-represented in higher grades of the profession.[42] They surveyed their staff, and found that out of 500 nurses who identified as BAME, only twelve had progressed beyond the lowest grades, when 150 would have been expected to do so if compared to other colleagues who were not from a BAME background. The Lothian experience reflects a wider phenomenon familiar to migrant nurses: that they may be 'hyper-visible' in their physical presence, but tend to be 'invisible' in organisational structures.

NHS Lothian initiated a five-year leadership programme to support the progression of BAME nurses. The nature of the programme could give the impression that poor promotion prospects were caused by skill inadequacies of a BAME nurse. However, the policy does at least give a progressive recognition to equality requiring institutional as well as individual action.

Ethical recruitment policies were adhered to by public bodies like the NHS, but private-sector employers felt less bound by guidelines that lacked any statutory force. The consequence for migrant nurses was that they became more vulnerable to exploitation. For example, contracts specifying time commitments to an employer can be extended and nurses can be held to a specific employer through their visa and have their passports withheld. Payments also may be owed to agents or landlords, meaning that nurses may not be free to leave their posts.[43]

Some nurses who have completed their private-sector contracts, for example in a care home, can find subsequent employment as nurses in the NHS. By following this route through immigration rules, employment in private care homes can become an intermediate step in a process that results in 'international' recruitment to the NHS. For many others, the ambition to have careers in hospitals has not been fulfilled and they remain in the private care sector, typically employed in nursing homes throughout Scotland. This view of the private-care sector and the position of migrant nurses within it in 2017 mirrors to some extent the experience of migrant nurses in the 1950s NHS, who tended to be employed in the less prestigious areas of care.[44]

ASYLUM-SEEKING AND REFUGEE NURSES IN SCOTLAND, 2002–17: A NEW COHORT OF SKILLED PROFESSIONALS

In the early 2000s Scotland joined the UK-wide dispersal programme of refugees and asylum- seekers, so creating a significant new source of immigration.[45] Glasgow became part of this scheme, taking responsibility for housing approximately 12,000 people within the first three years of the scheme. Then, as now, some of those who arrived were professionals including doctors, nurses, midwives, pharmacists and physiotherapists who had trained and practised in their country of origin.[46]

They had fled war and persecution in Afghanistan, Eritrea, Ethiopia, Sudan, Nigeria, Iran and other countries. Many had completed their schooling and professional training in English.[47] The relevant professional bodies, such as the NMC, had systems in place to recognise overseas qualifications, but there was no process by which health professionals could 'adapt' their skills and experience from overseas to the needs and practices of the NHS in Britain. An ad hoc system of adaptation emerged in some universities and hospitals in England, but there was no equivalent north of the border. Since there were more than 2,000 nurse vacancies in Scotland in 2002, funding was secured from NHS Scotland to develop a system to promote professional adaptation to the needs of the NHS.

That programme became known as 'Glasgow Overseas Professionals into Practice' (GOPIP). Developed at Glasgow Caledonian University between 2002 and 2010, it supported the administrative process of professional registration, but had a holistic approach that extended far beyond approving certification. Project workers engaged closely with refugee professionals, learning in the process about the insecurities of their immigration status, and of clinical skills that could not fully be deployed because of language difficulties. A programme of academic education, practice-based adaptation and cultural integration was developed. Mentors were sought from within the NHS who had some sensitivity to the likely extra demands in the mentorship role. As a result, around 150 nurses and other health professionals were supported towards re-engagement with their former career.

Refugees who were not only seeking asylum, but also working to adapt their clinical experience to UK customs and practice, were under immense pressure. Asylum seekers in general constantly face the threat of removal, but clinicians were also having to re-establish their professional identities by undertaking practical assessments, clinical studentships and university assignments, and needed significant support. They were delighted to be in Scotland, but like the nurses who came to the UK in the 1960s and '70s, they faced not just scrutiny and discrimination in their social lives but in the workplace too.[48]

This section has outlined the broad context of global nurse recruitment in general, and of nurse migration to the UK and Scotland in particular. It has described the historical, political and policy landscape and their resulting legal and cultural influences on nurse migration to Scotland. The next section focuses on the subjective experience of some of those nurses, based on qualitative data acquired through focus groups and interviews with different groups of migrant nurses.[49]

OVERSEAS NURSES' EXPERIENCE OF MIGRATION

Documenting the experiences of migrant nurses in Scotland can provide insight into how our society engages with those who migrate and offers the potential to jointly develop ways to improve that experience. This section is based on interviews with asylum-seeking nurses and those who came to Scotland and worked there from the 1950s to 2016. Interviews were conducted with three distinct groups about their experiences of migration and professional practice and are interwoven and discussed here: (1) 6 retired nurses from the African Caribbean Women's Association (ACWA) aged between 64 and 82 years as part of the Street Level Photoworks project 'New Shoots Old Roots' (2015); (2) 12 nurses aged between 22 and 42 from the Glasgow Overseas Nurses into Practice Project (GOPIP) for refugee and asylum-seeker nurses and international nurses (2002–10); and (3) 19 nurses aged between 19 and 72 from a Witness Seminar Focus Group (WSFG), comprising retired and currently practising nurses and current student nurses (2016).

All nurse participants in these interviews – from all immigration routes and from each generation of migrants – spoke of their sense of pride in their role, and especially of working for the NHS in Scotland. The experience of practical issues generated by relocation, culture shock on arrival in Scotland and issues with colleagues and with patients and their families were also described by all participants.

An acknowledged difficulty of this kind of qualitative work with migrant health professionals is that it can be challenging to go beyond 'narratives of success, pride and ambition' since to do so would require participants to acknowledge pain, upset and disappointment.[50] That was not the case for those described here. Nearly all the nurses were able to recount personal and professional challenges and spoke openly about the covert and overt discrimination and racism that they experienced in Scotland. These experiences were not relayed as a catalogue of grievances, but with humour and some wry laughter. Nonetheless, there was considerable sadness and some dismay expressed in the witness seminar when it became clear that the adverse experiences of the first generation were still being experienced by those who came later.

ARRIVAL IN SCOTLAND, AND GETTING TO WORK AND FROM WORK SAFELY

Many nurses who migrated in the 1950s and '60s arrived with a strong sense of already 'belonging' to a Scotland and UK which were part of a shared history and culture. Those 'family ties' with the 'motherland' emerged in several interviews with retired African and Caribbean nurses, though not with nurses from other groups: 'Why go to America when they want you to pay for it – go to the motherland they will pay for

Figure 5.2 Miss Mathias, Theatre Superintendent, with West Indian nurses Sister Chinda, Sister Olube and Sister Asagie, 1962, probably taken in Nigeria. Royal College of Nursing Collections, P/18/3/62/1.

you.'[51] Another retired nurse laughed and said, 'They wanted you and you came over because it was the mother land and you do what your mother says – don't you? They had a British passport, it wasn't that they were seeking a job they had one but it was an experience.'[52]

For some it seemed it was not until arrival that nurses realised how much readjustment (and resilience) would be needed:

> In 1958 I came to Glasgow ... I came to Liverpool and it takes 14 days to get here and then I took a train to Scotland. I thought we can't stay here, I can't understand nobody and nobody can understand me. There are people when they come here they think how can you understand it when they hear the Glaswegians speak – they think phewww! They go back to London.
>
> You couldn't get a house or couldn't get a flat they wouldn't be giving you one – you would see it advertised go round there and then they say ooh it's just been taken.[53]

A Kenyan woman who arrived in the 1950s and became a Scottish nurse explains:

> You know in Kenya it was quite a high status job to be a teacher and I was a teacher there. It was high status because we were usually taught by Whites and we were the first generation of Kenyan teachers ... then I moved to the

UK and an 8 hour flight I find everything about me is obliterated I become nothing . . . you know it was such a shock to come here and realise that I am not as valued and as important as I was back home.[54]

On the other hand, readjustments were not only about how others perceived her and how that impacted her sense of self. It was also a surprised recognition of how society was structured: 'The shock coming from Kenya of seeing White people cleaning and Asians cleaning – this was completely different. In Kenya the social hierarchy positioned them at the top and Africans at the bottom.'[55]

Another spoke of her sense of relief at being in Scotland:

When I arrived from Cape Town [1980s], first of all I was so grateful because you know I could sleep the whole night without interference from the South African police . . . you know they could come into your home at any time and coming to a place where you have no disturbances was so great – I really appreciated that . . . the people of Glasgow of course were amazing – and welcoming . . . you would meet one or two who how can you say . . . were not used to seeing a Black face, but then you can find that at any point.[56]

For some it seemed that the difference in climate was their dominant impression:

I arrived in Glasgow it was very cold, very very cold – a very big house very very big house – big rooms one bathroom and one kitchen. To get hot water was very difficult. It was very cold. Snow – well I couldn't understand how the ground was so white, it was difficult for me to walk and I fell many times in the snow. Nobody explained to you what you should wear really.[57]

A feeling of safety and relief peppered some nurses' talk but it was clear this feeling was intimately linked to their ability to engage and perform in their new role in Scotland. For different reasons, which were caused by UK immigration processes rather than anxiety about engaging in their role, an asylum-seeker nurse expressed the sense of vulnerability: 'It's very scary you don't know if you will be sent back – you have the fear that you will be sent back you don't know if you will complete your life here or not its nightmarish to us, that is something I don't want to even think about.'[58] Such concerns were especially common among recent migrants who had come through asylum-seeker refugee routes, but were also noted by previous generations. Although professional identities risked being subsumed by such existential anxieties, those nurses who were able to sustain a focus on their professional role found that helpful. Not all managed to do so.

High levels of anxiety were not just expressed by those that had fled direct conflict but by others who had come from less stable political environments and had left family behind:

> I went back home and said to my father I don't want to return . . . But he said I had to. I left my children my two children and I left them with their uncle who was in the military and I went back to Glasgow. When I saw my husband back in Glasgow, I was not well and then there was a war that started – the Biafra war and I am sitting eating fish and chips and my children were running under the bed in the war. So then I said, just bring them to me and then everything was alright.[59]

Although the experience of migration was closely linked to that of working in their new country, nurses often spoke of them separately. Some nurses found the experiences of migration very difficult, while their professional adaptation was straightforward. For others, the situation was reversed. One participant found both migration and professional life very challenging:

> I went into nursing and then midwifery but it was very difficult. Very, very difficult . . . I was very homesick I used to be crying all the time – I came to Scotland in 1973. During my school days at home we had lots of teachers who were expatriates of Scotland and they had told me about the Lochs and all these things so I applied . . . I was in the nurses' home. Fortunately I met my friend. She was from the Gambia and I was from the Gambia. It was a relief to know that you had somebody.[60]

The difficulties of adaptation and integration meant that peer support remains just as crucial for recent migrants. A current student nurse described her experience as follows: 'As a Muslim student I feel like I am left out a lot because I don't socialise through drinking – everyone goes out drinking – you have to be close with someone just to be able to go and hang out – drinking is usually the first route to making friends.'[61]

PROFESSIONAL DEVELOPMENT

As discussed earlier, migrant nurses were usually directed towards less attractive specialties or to work in the private care and nursing home sector, even when there were vacancies in their preferred areas. Both recent migrants and retired nurses described the same sense of exclusion:

> I came to Scotland from Ethiopia. I worked as a general nurse and a nurse anaesthetist there for 10 years. I came to Scotland in 2003 and applied to get registration with the NMC – I was successful and could do the adaptation programme but was not allowed because I did not have a work permit. Five years later when I got refugee status and got a work permit the process of

registration with NMC had changed and I couldn't register so I applied and did a nursing course which I completed and got my degree. I took up the one year Scottish Government job guarantee and after that completed, applied for more than 30 jobs not just in Glasgow but in Edinburgh but I was never called to interview – did not get one. I applied to working in NHS Bank.

Working as a bank nurse was very stressful – tried many times to get a job [in the NHS] but I was not successful. Every day I had to go and work in different work places and work with different staff – eventually I applied to a nursing home – I have been there five years.[62]

Another nurse explained a similar difficulty:

It was a challenging experience becoming a nurse and I studied here. Actually coming to Glasgow allowed me to fulfil my ambition to be in nursing, I had many great mentors and the experience was great. I had to get my [immigration] papers – then eventually I was able to complete in 2013. I was so happy, I had my degree, I had my nursing papers then I had to get a job. I applied to more than 50 jobs and I couldn't get a job so I took up the one year Scottish Government job scheme but it was stressful and after 5 months I left and felt ill. I worked Bank nurse but I was losing my confidence and I wanted to keep up my skills so I applied for a BUPA nursing home job I have worked there for 10 months.[63]

One retired nurse spoke of the harassment she experienced trying to get to work:

Usually in the night going to duty standing in the bus stop it was when you were most insecure. We sort of used to get ourselves together so as we would not be targeted, was teenagers mostly young kids. We weren't complaining about the harassment or the insults from anybody – stones would be thrown at you. We used to be waiting for the bus to come sooner [laughs].[64]

This uncomplaining response played out in a number of ways. A nurse from Ethiopia who had fled persecution and gained refugee status explained when asked about a minor racist incident that had happened to him at work: 'From what I have fled, this sort of racism, these experiences are insignificant, nothing to me – I can manage myself fine – there is a calm in Scotland.'[65] Others were less sanguine. As one retired nurse stated concisely: 'The discrimination was awful.'[66]

Nurses were acutely aware of the potential for institutional discrimination, and sought ways to mitigate this. They spoke about the risk that a single adverse incident might harm their reputation, even if they were not at fault. Nurses would choose to work in an area where they were known and supported by their peers, rather than rely on the fairness of the organisation, or of clinicians who did not know them personally.

For some nurses, that meant working in the same ward for most of their career:

> I did two years of nursing in a nursing home and then moved to the NHS – been there a long time now. I am good with my patients very very good with my patients everybody says – but then there was somebody and she was distressed, really ill, dying of cancer. The family said she made a complaint about my care – and I was so nice to her but she [the daughter] was ambivalent and said that the mother said she was terrified of me. Then they said they had to discipline me – for what I don't know – she said she was terrified of me. I thought maybe it was about my colour I said to them 'do you think it is about my colour?' and then I thought – I cannot worry about this. I am one of those people who just does their work and then goes home – I have been working for a long time. I have been in the same ward for 11years I have been with the same Sister. Lucky for me she is nice.[67]

One student nurse, whose mother was a migrant but who had lived all her life in Scotland, shared her mother's experience in response to hearing the stories from others. It was as though she was surprised to find that her mother's account was not exceptional nor that it had not gone away: 'It's interesting how the level of discrimination has always been there. I am a student nurse and even my mum who sounds Scottish because she was brought up here but is Pakistani. But in the 70s people would say come along for an interview but when she got there they would say that the job is gone.'[68] The persistence of such direct discrimination was a source of sadness. A retired nurse at the same seminar said, 'I don't want to be negative, but it is so sad that it is still happening.'[69]

For one of the older retired nurses the seminar reinforced her thinking that her experience had actually been rather good, as they felt that things had worsened for nurses: 'In my time in nursing everyone was so grateful for what you did.'[70]

CONCLUSION

Migration is a complex undertaking – that hardly needs stating. But the complexity of the immigrant nurse experience in the UK has a number of aspects that both distinguish it from migration in general, and also illustrate some important, common features. Nurses were in the first wave of significant non-white migration to the UK from the 1950s. Unlike other migrant groups, these nurses were almost all female and had trained in what were high-status professions in their home countries. Their sense of a shared 'Commonwealth' culture did not long survive contact with their patients and new colleagues in the UK, and although their professional skills were both recognised and needed, they also found themselves exposed to systematic discrimination in favour of British and white colleagues from other Commonwealth countries.

The intimacy of their clinical role may have made this swirl of contextual factors especially intense. The first generation of migrants found themselves both highly visible, yet also overlooked; their clinical contribution to the new National Health Service was as irreplaceable as it was (sometimes) resisted. The hope of personal and professional opportunity in Britain was set against a growing social and political wariness, if not hostility, towards Black immigration. To their dismay, their professional identity – acquired with such determination, hard work and pride – seemed to offer scant protection against discrimination.

It is striking that these experiences seem not to have been unique to that first cohort of migrants from the Caribbean and Africa in the early post-war decades. They share many common features with subsequent migrant groups, including not only the experiences of refugee and asylum-seeking professionals, but also a narrative shared by a second generation – the children of those first migrants.

It is possible to detect two themes that resonate through the political and policy context, as well as the personal recollections noted in this chapter and elsewhere. First, any discussion of migration needs to take account of a sense of 'belonging' as one of its fundamental aspects. Migration necessarily involves some loss of 'home', which is offset by the promise of a new kind of belonging in the host country. For the first generation of nurse migrants, that loss seems a particularly bittersweet one, since the idea of a shared 'Commonwealth family' did not bear much relationship to the reality they experienced. The colonial promise fell short. Unfortunately, professional 'belonging', acquired through education and practice, also proved to offer less robust protection than the nurses might have hoped. The NMC and other bodies proved as defensive of professional boundaries as successive governments were of geographical borders.

This may interact with a second theme of 'intimacy'. Migration always involves movement, and therefore distance. But while it might be possible for a migrant scientist, factory worker, truck driver or agricultural labourer to keep some distance from the host population and its culture, the nature of nursing practice makes that impossible. The only comparable experience of 'intimate distance' might be domestic service or slavery. It is likely that UK clinicians, professional bodies and patients found it difficult in past decades to imagine or recognise the skills required to be an effective clinician in countries without developed health systems. But contemporary nurse migrant experience is that the systematic assessment, development and validation of those skills in the UK, for example for refugee professionals, is still not recognised by employers. That looks more like racism – just as it does when the children of migrants also face the same kind of discrimination.

These issues were until recently thought to apply mainly to non-white clinical migrants. But the emerging Home Office stance towards EU citizens working in the NHS suggests that attitudes and practices that first developed in response to BAME migration might soon be implemented for White European migrants too.

Attitudes towards migrants are slightly less negative in Scotland than in England, and concern about migration is less of an issue north of the border.[71] But immigration controls are a power retained by Westminster, and Scotland's ability to develop more inclusive policies is very limited. Tony Benn's warning that 'the way a government treats refugees is very instructive, because it shows you how they would treat the rest of us if they thought they could get away with it' seems rather prescient.[72]

One way to rebalance thinking may be to shift from the dominant narrative 'frame' of migration being based on foreigners coming to Scotland 'to get and take', to one that more accurately reflects the evidence summarised in this chapter. In other words, migrants accept major personal losses in order to offer their labour and their aspirations to the host country. Scotland has long been proud of the contribution its own emigrants made to countries all over the world. Perhaps it might also recognise the past and current contributions of Scotland's immigrants: a national story of 'giving', rather than taking.

NOTES

1. In this chapter, the term 'nurses' will be used to describe nurses and mid-wives of both genders and specialist roles, such as community, surgical, mental health, learning disability and theatre nursing.
2. E. L. Jones and S. J. Snow, *Against the Odds: Black and Minority Ethnic Clinicians and Manchester, 1948 to 2009* (Manchester: Manchester NHS Primary Care Trust, in association with the Centre for the History of Science, Technology and Medicine, University of Manchester, 2010).
3. Scottish Executive, *Code of Practice for the International Recruitment of Healthcare Professionals in Scotland* (Edinburgh: Scottish Executive, 2006).
4. I. Jackson and M. Wilson, 'Adaptation of asylum seeker and refugee nurses: Glasgow overseas professionals into practice: Unpublished Report for NHS Education Scotland', 2005; N. Jackson and Y. Carter, *Refugee Doctors:*

Support, Development and Integration in the NHS (Oxford: Radcliffe Medical, 2004); Alice Bloch, *Making it Work: Refugee Employment in the UK* (London: Institute for Public Policy Research, 2004).

5. G. Lacey and Commonwealth Secretariat, *Guidebook to Education in the Commonwealth* (London: Commonwealth Secretariat, 2012).

6. Jones and Snow, *Against the Odds*.

7. Stuart Hall, *Selected Political Writings: The Great Moving Right Show and Other Essays* (Chadwell Heath: Lawrence & Wishart Ltd, 2017).

8. Jones and Snow, *Against the Odds*.

9. An example of this is the New Zealand and Australia Trans-Tasman Agreement of 1998, which recognises qualifications of health workers, including nurses, between the two countries; the European Federation of Nurses Associations has a system for nurses from European Union countries. See Evgeniya Plotnikova, 'Recruiting foreign nurses for the UK: The role of bilateral labour agreements', PhD, University of Edinburgh, 2011.

10. Mary Edward, *Who Belongs to Glasgow? 200 Years of Migration* (Edinburgh: Luath Press).

11. Andrew F. Cooper, John J. Kirton, Franklyn Lisk and Hany Besada (eds), *Africa's Health Challenges: Sovereignty, Mobility of People and Healthcare Governance* (Oxford: Routledge, 2013).

12. A. Mejia, 'Migration of physicians and nurses: A world wide picture', *International Journal of Epidemiology*, 7:3 (1978), pp. 207–15.

13. Plotnikova, 'Recruiting foreign nurses for the UK'.

14. D. Mitchell, 'No claim to be called sick nurses at all: An historical study of learning disability nursing', PhD, London South Bank University, 2000.

15. HMSO, *Report of the Ministry of Health for the Year Ended 31 December 1952* (London: HMSO, 1953).

16. Royal College of Nursing, *RCN Labour Market Review: Unheeded Warnings. Health Care in Crisis. The UK Nursing Labour Market Review 2016* (London: Royal College of Nursing, 2016), https://www.rcn.org.uk/-/media/royal-college-of-nursing/documents/publications/2016/ocotber/005779.pdf (sic); R. Addicott, D. Maguire, M. Honeyman and J. Jabbal, *Workforce Planning in the NHS* (London: King's Fund, 2015), www.kingsfundorg.uk/sites/files/kf/field/field_publication_file/Workforce-planning-NHS-Kings-Fund-Apr-15.pdf (accessed 21 May 2017).

17. See, for instance, Megan Hutching, *Long Journey for Sevenpence: Assisted Immigration to New Zealand from the United Kingdom, 1947–1975* (Wellington: Victoria University Press, 1999); and A. James Hammerton and Alistair Thomson, *Ten Pound Poms: Australia's Invisible Migrants: A History of Postwar British Emigration to Australia* (Manchester and New York: Manchester University Press, 2005).

18. Addicott et al., *Workforce Planning in the NHS*.

19. The Migration Advisory Committee (MAC 2016) analysis shows that there is a historic pattern of peaks and troughs in the supply of migrant nurses.

This pattern offers suggestive indications that migrant nurses have been used to save costs. Nursing is an occupation in which migrants earn, on average, less than UK workers doing the same job. In most other graduate occupations, migrants earn on average more than UK workers in the same job. It is difficult not to see this as undercutting. See MAC, 'Partial Review of the Shortage Occupation List: Review of Nursing' (London: Migration Advisory Committee, 2016), https://www.gov.uk/government/publications/migration-advisory-committee-mac-partial-review-shortage-occupation-list-and-nursing (accessed 21 May 2017). See also Cooper et al., *Africa's Health Challenges*.

20. L. Doyal, G. Hunt and J. Mellor, 'Your life in their hands: Migrant workers in the National Health Service', *Critical Social Policy*, 1:2 (1981), pp. 54–71.

21. Diana Kay and Robert Miles, *Refugees or Migrant Workers? European Volunteer Workers in Britain, 1946–1951* (London: Routledge, 1992).

22. Jones and Snow, *Against the Odds*.

23. Ibid.

24. Ibid.

25. Plotnikova, 'Recruiting foreign nurses for the UK'; L. H. Aiken et al., 'Nurse staffing and education and hospital mortality in nine European countries: A retrospective observational study', *The Lancet*, 383:9931 (2014), pp. 1824–30.

26. S. Simoens, M. Villeneuve and J. Hurst, *Tackling Nurse Shortages in OECD Countries*, 19 (Paris: OECD Publication Service, 2005), https://www.oecd.org/els/health-systems/34571365.pdf (accessed 21 May 2017).

27. Jones and Snow, *Against the Odds*; Royal College of Nursing, *RCN Evidence to the Committee on Nursing* (London: Royal College of Nursing, 1971).

28. Plotnikova, 'Recruiting foreign nurses for the UK'; Aiken et al., 'Nurse staffing and education'; Simoens et al., *Tackling Nurse Shortages in OECD Countries*; J. Hallam, *Nursing the Image: Media, Culture and Professional Identity* (Oxford: Routledge, 2000).

29. Hallam, *Nursing the Image*.

30. WHO Secretariat, *Recruitment of Health Workers from the Developing World* (Geneva: WHO, 2004), http://apps.who.int/iris/handle/10665/20165.

31. Department of Health. [ARCHIVED CONTENT] UK Government Web Archive – The National Archives, *Guidance* (2004). Available at: http://webarchive.nationalarchives.gov.uk/20081027092128/dh.gov.uk/en/publicationsandstatistics/publications/publicationspolicyandguidance/dh_4097730 (accessed 26 February 2017).

32. Scottish Executive, *Code of Practice* (2006).

33. Ibid.

34. J. Buchan, 'Evidence of nursing shortages or a shortage of evidence?', *Journal of Advanced Nursing*, 56:5 (2006), pp. 457–8.

35. Royal College of Nursing, *Response by the Royal College of Nursing to Migration Advisory Committee's Call for Evidence on Partial Review of the Shortage Occupations List for Nurses* (London: Royal College of Nursing, 2015), https://www2.rcn.org.uk/__data/assets/pdf_file/0014/642101/41.15-Call-for-Evidence_Review-of-Tier-2.pdf.

36. NHS Improvement, *Evidence from NHS Improvement on clinical staff shortages* (London: NHS Improvement, 2016), https://www.gov.uk/government/uploads/system/uploads/attachment_data/file/500288/Clinical_workforce_report.pdf (retrieved 1 March 2017).

37. J. Buchan, *Here to Stay? International Nurses in the UK. Royal College of Nursing Commissioned Report* (London: Royal College of Nursing, 2002), https://www2.rcn.org.uk/__data/assets/pdf_file/0011/78563/001982.pdf (accessed 27 February 2017); J. Buchan, R. Jobanputra, P. Gough and R. Hutt, 'Internationally recruited nurses in London: Profile and implications for policy' (London: King's Fund, 2005).

38. Buchan, *Here to Stay?*; Buchan et al., 'Internationally recruited nurses in London'.

39. Buchan, *Here to Stay?*; Buchan et al., 'Internationally recruited nurses in London'.

40. F. M. E. Lorenzo, J. Galvez-Tan, K. Icamina and L. Javier, 'Nurse migration from a source country perspective: Philippine country case study', *Health Services Research*, 42:3, part 2 (2007), pp. 1406–18; K. O'Neil, 'Labor export as government policy: The case of the Philippines', *Migration Information Source* (2004). Available at: http://www.migrationpolicy.org/article/labor-export-government-policy-case-philippines (accessed 1 March 2017); B. L. Brush, 'The potent lever of toil: Nursing development and exportation in the postcolonial Philippines', *American Journal of Public Health*, 100:9 (2010), pp. 1572–81.

41. H. McGarvie, 'The NHS Slaves; Exclusive. IGangmaster leaves nurses on pounds 8 a day INHS pay him pounds 800 for every new recruit', *Scottish Daily Record & Sunday* (22 February 2004), http://www.thefreelibrary.com/THE+NHS+SLAVES%3B+EXCLUSIVE+1Gangmaster+leaves+nurses+on+pounds+8+a+day...-a0113506786 (accessed 30 May 2017).

42. J. Glover, *Nursing Career Opportunities Project* (Edinburgh: NHS Lothian, 2013), http://www.nhslothian.scot.nhs.uk/YourRights/EqualityDiversity/ImpactAssessment/Rapid Impact Assessments/Nursing Progression Project EQIA Jan 13.pdf (accessed 27 February 2017).

43. B. Anderson and B. Rogaly, 'Trades Union Congress: Forced labour and migration to the UK' (Oxford: Trades Union Congress, 2000). Available at: https://www.tuc.org.uk/international-issues/forced-labour/migration/forced-labour-and-migration-uk#_Toc95187833 (accessed 1 March 2017).

44. Jones and Snow, *Against the Odds*; C. Baxter, *The Black Nurse: An Endangered Species: A Case for Equal Opportunities in Nursing* (Cambridge: Training in Health and Race, 1988).

45. K. Wren, 'Supporting asylum seekers and refugees in Glasgow: The role of multi-agency networks', *Journal of Refugee Studies*, 20:3 (2007), pp. 391–413.

46. Jackson and Wilson, 'Adaptation of asylum seeker and refugee nurses'; Wren, 'Supporting asylum seekers and refugees in Glasgow'.

47. Jackson and Wilson, 'Adaptation of asylum seeker and refugee nurses'.

48. Jackson and Wilson, 'Adaptation of asylum seeker and refugee nurses'; Jackson and Carter, *Refugee Doctors*; Bloch, *Making it Work: Refugee Employment in the UK*; National Institute of Adult Continuing Education (NIACE), 'Refugees and asylum seekers in the UK: The challenges of accessing education and employment' (London: Institute of Public Policy Research, 2009).

49. The data is reproduced with the consent of the participants and has been anonymised at their request.

50. J. Bornat, L. Henry, P. Rajhuram and G. Wilson, 'Don't mix race with the specialty' (retired South Asian consultant geriatrician): Interviewing South Asian overseas-trained geriatricians, https://www.researchgate.net/publication/238111791_'Don't_mix_race_with_the_specialty'_retired_South_Asian_consultant_geriatrician_interviewing_South_Asian_overseas-trained_geriatricians (accessed 21 May 2017).

51. WSFG2.

52. WSFG2.

53. ACWA, HC arrived 1973.

54. ACWA, CM arrived 1965.

55. ACWA, CM arrived 1965.

56. ACWA, arrived 1980.

57. ACWA, CSS arrived 1958.

58. GOPIP, nurse arrived 2002.

59. ACWA, CSS arrived 1958.

60. ACWA, HC arrived 1973.

61. WSFG1.

62. WSFG 3.

63. WSFG 2.

64. ACWA, HC arrived 1973.

65. GOPIP, nurse arrived 2002.

66. WSFG3.

67. WSFG1.

68. WSFG1.

69. WSFG2.

70. WSFG3.

71. D. McCollum, B. Nowok and S. Tindal, 'Public attitudes towards migration in Scotland: Exceptionality and possible policy implications', *Scottish Affairs*, 23:1 (2014), pp. 79–102.

72. Benn's comment is cited in A. Paul, 'Living like a refugee: New York must do more to help its homeless', 9 October 2015, http://observer.com/2015/09/living-like-a-refugee-new-york-must-do-more-to-help-its-homeless (accessed 26 May 2017).

6

Polish Diaspora or Polish Migrant Communities? Polish Migrants in Scotland, 1945–2015[1]

Emilia Piętka-Nykaza

INTRODUCTION

Migration from Poland to Scotland is by no means a recent phenomenon. The nature and the size of immigration have been different at particular points in the history of the two countries, with the two largest inflows of Poles occurring after the Second World War and after the EU enlargement in 2004. The increase in the number of Polish migrants to Scotland has attracted considerable academic attention across a wide range of disciplines and has also generated interest from the general public and media. However, it is evident that studies on EU post-enlargement migration from Poland to the United Kingdom predominantly focus on England and Wales[2] with relatively little research exploring EU post-enlargement migration north of the border. Scotland, the focus of this chapter, provides a useful case study within a UK context because of the distinctive economic and demographic conditions of the country. Further, Scotland to date has shown a more positive public attitude towards immigration compared to the rest of the UK.

Studies on new migrant communities in Scotland tend to focus on either Accession 8 (A8) migrants[3] or eastern European nationals[4] in which Polish migrants are the dominant ethnicity.[5] Differences in definition often result in misleading generalisations about Polish migrants as representing the experiences of new migrant communities in Scotland. Indeed, Poles are the majority group among those migrants who have arrived in Scotland since 2004, but their experiences differ from migrants arriving from other central and eastern European countries.[6] Scotland-specific research on Polish migration has so far focused on either particular Polish migrant groups, including children,[7] youth,[8] and migrant workers,[9] or local case studies in Glasgow,[10] Edinburgh,[11] the Highlands and Islands,[12] Grampian[13] or Fife.[14] While these studies, when taken together, provide a vivid picture of particular Polish migrant groups at local levels, the findings are unlikely to capture fully the complexities of the experiences of Polish migrants across Scotland as a nation. The chapter therefore synthesises key academic works and local case studies of the last decade or so to provide a Scotland-wide perspective on these immigrants. It critically examines the scale of Polish migration to Scotland since 2004, the nature of the movement, diversity of social networks, and the types and variations of settlement in Scotland.

Scotland is often perceived as having a more welcoming approach towards migration than the rest of the UK, with political statements that stress Scotland's differing demographic and need for more people.[15] The synthesis therefore tries to determine how Poles have been received by the Scottish people and whether their experiences are distinctive (in relation to the rest of the UK) in terms of population structure, economic migration and the experiences of migrants regarding work, social networks and settlement.

POST-SECOND WORLD WAR POLISH MIGRATION TO SCOTLAND

The Second World War and its aftermath opened a new chapter in the history of migration from Poland to Scotland. Following the end of the Second World War, the British Government commenced the arrangements for the gradual demobilisation of the Polish Armed Forces under British command to facilitate the transition from military to civilian life of many Polish servicemen.[16] The 1947 Resettlement Act gave them and their families the right to stay and settle in the UK (including Scotland). It also provided the right to remain for ex-Displaced Persons moving to Britain via the European Voluntary Workers scheme.[17] While in 1947 there were 32,350 Poles in Scotland, by 1948 the vast majority of Polish servicemen had left for England or overseas.[18] The 1951 census of Scotland recorded 10,603 individuals living in Scotland who were designated 'born in Poland'.

By 1946 the initial positive response to Polish soldiers during the war had started to change. Now Poles were seen to have 'overstayed' and were in competition with Scots for jobs, housing and health services.[19] Many Poles in post-war Scotland were subjected to racist-sectarian hostility which was also fuelled by some elements of the popular media.[20] Yet, despite this opposition, the majority of Polish ex-servicemen and their families had no wish to return to Poland and face life there under a Communist regime.[21]

Between 1951 and 1961 the Polish military presence in Scotland was transformed into a civilian exile community. Instead of being known as a 'Polish state in exile', the Poles in Britain became '*Polonia*', a Polish community permanently settled outside their native land. Post-war migration from Poland mainly included political refugees (mostly men, ex-officers) and their family members. All of this fashioned a unity among them, which in turn encouraged the development of Polish community organisations across Scotland, with the Polish Ex-Combatants' Association (*Stowarzyszenie Polskich Kombatantów* – SPK) being the most successful. The establishment in 1948 of the Polish Catholic Mission in Scotland (*Polska Misja Katolicka w Szkocji*) played an important role in maintaining religious beliefs and church connections among Poles in Scotland.[22] The firm attachment to Catholicism, together with legitimate pride and patriotism expressed in the rejection of the Soviet-imposed regime in Poland, helped to construct a successful post-war Polish community in Scotland. Even though the impact of these institutions in later years proved to be transitory due to the death of their founders, some of the members of the 'second generation' continued their traditions and maintained the ethos of the ethnic community.[23]

Between 1961 and 1991 the number of 'Polish-born' persons in Scotland continued to fall. According to the 1991 census, there were 73,700 Polish-born people living in the United Kingdom in that year, which fell to 58,000 in 2001, mainly due to the ageing of the older generation (57 per cent of Poles in the census were aged over 64),[24] but also because of return migration to Poland during the 1990s as the Soviet empire disintegrated.[25] Despite an increase in the number of Polish migrants moving to the UK throughout the 1990s and early 2000s, the contemporary migration of Poles to Scotland only gained momentum after the accession of Poland to the European Union in 2004. The next section focuses on that period.

SCALE OF EU POST-ENLARGEMENT MIGRATION FROM POLAND TO SCOTLAND

Historically, Scotland has been a country of net out-migration. Until the 1990s there were more people leaving than moving into the country. In comparison to other countries of the UK, Scotland experienced population decline from a peak of 5,227,000 in the mid-1970s to 5,055,000 in 2002. The relative increase in population since the early 2000s has been largely driven by immigration, with migrants from the EU Accession 8 countries and Poland being the most significant in number. Overall,

369,000 people in Scotland in 2011 were born outside the UK. Of these, 55,231 were born in Poland (15 per cent of all those born outside the UK). This figure makes Poland the third most common country of birth after Scotland and England and, interestingly, even ahead of Northern Ireland and Wales. The level of migration from Poland has played an important role in resolving some of the population issues in Scotland.[26]

Quantifying the exact number of Polish migrants living in Scotland (and the UK) is difficult due to the limitations of existing data.[27] The available sources, including the Worker Registration Scheme (WRS) and the registrations of National Insurance numbers, indicate that Polish migrants who have moved to Scotland since 2004 are predominantly young (81 per cent of those who registered with the WRS between May 2004 and 2009 were aged between 18 and 34).[28] Yet, although the evidence confirms that these migrants are overwhelmingly young, three-quarters of Poles are not university graduates[29] and many of them have limited competence in English.[30]

Another characteristic of the recent EU post-Accession migration from Poland to Scotland is that people are travelling from all regions of Poland and tend to be widely dispersed across Scotland (and the UK), living in both urban and rural areas rather than 'clustering' in a few locations. Distinct patterns of Polish settlement in the UK are generally influenced either by pre-existing migration networks, the demands of recruitment agencies (see the discussion on migration networks) or employment opportunities.[31]

The areas of Scotland that have attracted the highest absolute inflows of A8 migrants (including Poles) are a mix of large cities (Edinburgh and Glasgow) and mainly rural local authorities (Perth and Kinross, the Highlands and Aberdeenshire). A8 migrants (including Poles) form the most relatively significant proportions of the workforce in some rural areas of Angus, Perth and Kinross and Aberdeenshire (see Table 6.1).

Analysis of the Scottish population census for 2011 illustrates a difference in population change due to migration in Scotland. For example, it indicates that the majority (63 per cent) of migrants to Scotland arrived between 2001 and 2011. In comparison to other parts of the UK, Scotland has the largest proportion of recent migrants. The increase of Polish migration to Scotland has been proportionately much greater than to England. Polish migrants now form 15 per cent of all non-UK foreign-born residents living in Scotland and 8 per cent in England.[32]

Table 6.1 Total WRS registrations, May 2004–April 2011, and WRS registrations as a proportion of workforce jobs, 2011

Local Authority	WRS registrations, May 2004–April 2011	WRS registrations, May 2004–April 2011/ workforce jobs 2011
Angus	4,945	24.7
Perth and Kinross	10,300	23.4
Aberdeenshire	7,450	14.1
Highland	7980	12.7
Argyll and Bute	1,865	9.8
Scottish Borders	2355	9.4
West Lothian	3,755	7.4
Fife	6,180	7
City of Edinburgh	12,585	6.3
Moray	1,325	6.3
Shetland Islands	480	6
Aberdeen City	5,935	5.5
Stirling	1,645	5.5
East Lothian	975	5.1
Midlothian	935	4.5
Dumfries and Galloway	1,410	4.1
Glasgow City	10,905	3.9
Dundee City	2,120	3.7

Source: D. McCollum, L. Cook, C. Chiroro, A. Platts, F. MacLeod and A. Findlay, 'Spatial, sectoral and temporal trends in A8 migration to the UK 2004–2011: Evidence from the worker registration scheme', CPC *Working Paper Number 17* (Southampton: ESRC Centre for Population Change, 2012), p. 17.

ECONOMIC MIGRATION OF POLISH MIGRANT WORKERS TO SCOTLAND SINCE 2004

EU post-enlargement migration is often described as the temporary, circular and fluid mobility of young migrants, governed by short-term economic need rather than aspirations for long-term settlement.[33] These fluid migration patterns are fashioned by open borders and labour markets between the EU member states.[34] Many Poles, for instance, have experienced a high level of unemployment at home (20 per cent in 2003), which makes emigration a rational response to domestic economic difficulties.[35] Therefore, finding work is a key motivation for migrants before and after they leave Poland.[36] Considerable attention has therefore been paid to the economic context of Polish migration, including to the UK, of their experience of work. These studies show their concentration in particular sectors of the Scottish economy (see Table 6.2).

Table 6.2 Percentage of A8 migrants in sectors of the economy in Scotland

Sector	WRS registrations, May 2004–April 2011, as percentage of employee jobs, April 2011	
	United Kingdom	Scotland
Agriculture	25.00%	29.60%
Hospitality and catering	10.10%	11.40%
Manufacturing	2.90%	3.30%
Construction	1.80%	3.20%
Transport	1.70%	1.90%
Retail	1.00%	0.80%
Health and medicine	1.10%	0.70%
Total (all sectors in economy)	3.60%	3.60%

Source: McCollum et al., 'Spatial, sectoral and temporal trends in A8 migration to the UK 2004–2011: Evidence from the worker registration scheme', p. 12.

It is evident that high proportions of A8 migrants (including Poles) are found in the agriculture (more than a quarter of all employees) and hospitality sectors. These patterns are linked to specific segments of the labour market in Scotland and the UK which have come to depend on migrant labour.[37] These sectors, however, mainly offer low- or semi-skilled jobs. The concentration of Polish migrants in them is not only a Scottish phenomenon, but also a feature across the UK. Similarly, there is evidence of a mismatch between the educational attainment of Polish migrants and their current occupations.[38] The high concentration of Poles in these sectors is likely to be a consequence of their entry level, which often provides the easiest route into work for newly arrived migrants. Employment in low- and semi-skilled occupations is often perceived as a potential 'cost' of migration for Polish migrant workers during their stay in Scotland.[39] It is also related to limited recognition of Polish qualifications and previous work experience in Poland. Poor English language competence has also been identified as a key factor restricting occupational mobility, so improving language skills is a particularly salient issue for many Poles, especially those who have found employment below the level of their qualifications.[40] Indeed, one study confirmed that a sample of migrants who improved their English language skills subsequently managed to gain jobs with better pay and improved working conditions.[41]

Yet gaining increased competence in English can be difficult for many Polish migrants due to their work patterns (such as shift work). Many Eastern Europeans (including Poles) have been trapped in low-skilled jobs and experience difficulty in finding the time and the energy to improve their English while working long hours, doing multiple jobs and trying to balance family and work life.[42] These experiences mainly relate to older and less-skilled migrants who are restricted to low-paid occupations due to their poor language skills, but who at the same time have little desire to return to Poland where their prospects in the labour market are worse.[43] Although Poles in Scotland work below their level of qualifications, they tend to report improvement in their material position compared to previous experiences in Poland. As a result, some of them have compromised and accepted employment below their qualifications due to the greater economic and material benefits arising from their migration to Scotland.[44]

ATTITUDES TOWARDS POLISH MIGRANTS IN SCOTLAND

Examination of the impact of Polish migration to the UK has focused on changes to the labour market and provision of public services. This has taken centre stage in government and media debates about immigration from the EU, where it is perceived as a 'problem' due to it causing pressures on public services including housing, education and health.[45] This concern, however, is not shared by the Scottish Government. It sees Scotland as having 'a different need for immigration than other parts of the UK', especially in securing demographic stability and sustainable economic growth in Scotland.[46] As a result, there is broad political consensus that Scotland 'needs' and 'welcomes' migrants.[47] More welcoming attitudes towards migration are also evident among the general public in Scotland, according to opinion polls.[48] In contrast, according to the British Social Attitudes Survey,[49] three-quarters (75 per cent) of the UK public favour a reduction in immigration and almost half (45 per cent) agreed that it undermined 'British cultural life'. The most recent Scottish Social Attitudes Survey,[50] however, suggests that 40 per cent of Scots (an increase from 33 per cent in 2010) consider immigration a factor in making the country 'a better place'. Several case studies have also shown the relatively positive attitude towards migration and migrants in Scotland.[51] Nevertheless, public attitudes to migration in general and to Polish immigration in particular can be considered to be much more complex than this positive picture suggests and the issues merit further analysis.

While the Scottish Government seeks to encourage immigration into Scotland, public attitudes towards an increase in the number of migrants arriving in Scotland are less enthusiastic. The recent Scottish Social Attitudes Survey[52] found that in comparison to 2010, fewer Scots (from

46 per cent in 2010 to 38 per cent in 2015) worry about losing their identity if more people from Eastern Europe come to Scotland. Yet, despite this, public concern about the impact of greater ethnic diversity due to migration from Eastern Europe remains at a high level. Further, in 2015, one in three people (32 per cent) expressed the view that 'people who come here from Eastern Europe take jobs away from other people in Scotland' (a decline from 37 per cent in 2010).[53] Negative perceptions about eastern European migration on the Scottish labour market were particularly high among those aged 18 to 24 (46 per cent in 2010), in working-class occupations and on lower income bands (50 per cent in 2010).[54] The reported levels of higher concern among these groups could be partly explained by the recent growth in employment of Polish migrant workers in sectors that traditionally employ young people (the hospitality sector) as well as working-class people (the food-processing sector). These hostile attitudes can create barriers to ensuring a receptive environment for Polish migrants who are mainly working in these low-skilled occupations. Studies in Glasgow[55] have found that a substantial minority of new migrants have experienced hostility in the form of verbal threats (17 per cent of respondents) and to a lesser extent verbal abuse (8 per cent of respondents). Similar findings were reported in a study in Fife, with 5 per cent of respondents reporting physical abuse due to their perceived ethnicity or nationality.[56]

Public opinion and attitudes towards migration in Scotland are both reflected in and shaped by the media. The media tends to describe 'migration' issues in terms of expressing its support or critical reaction towards government policies.[57] The differences in migration policy between the Scottish Government in Holyrood and the UK Government in Westminster are also reflected in both tabloid and broadsheet press coverage. Following the accession of Poland to the EU in 2004, there has been some agreement among certain sections of both the British and the Scottish press that Polish migrants have helped to reduce labour shortages and so have brought economic benefits to the UK. Polish migrants were described as 'young', 'educated', skilled' and 'eager to work' long and flexible hours.[58]

However, the tone of British press coverage has changed significantly since 2007, when the focus shifted towards the fear of a 'flood' of cheap labour from Poland taking jobs from 'native workers' and putting financial pressure on public services.[59] This change in attitude could be explained by the economic downturn from 2007 onwards, as well as by the imposition of austerity measures by successive UK governments. It might also be influenced by fears of new waves of migration from

Bulgaria and Romania after they joined the EU in 2007.[60] Nevertheless, it is argued that Polish migrants in Scotland in particular have helped address two significant demographic problems: an ageing population and labour shortages. Polish migrants, therefore, are presented in the Scottish press as *complementary* to the economy, keen to integrate and to make Scotland their new home. This distinctive perception of Polish migrants has also been used by the Scottish press to justify the need for greater devolved powers for the Scottish Government over immigration.[61] In contrast to the negative attitudes often to be found in English tabloids, media coverage in Scotland has consistently depicted Polish migration as one of a series of 'solutions' for population stability, skills shortages and economic growth in Scotland.

Although political assertion and public attitudes at the national level towards migration remain important, much of the debate about the reception of new migrants occurs at the local level. The limitations of data on migration from Poland provide a challenge for local authorities in meeting the demands of new migrant communities. This is especially problematic as the dispersal of Polish migrants across Scotland brought them to localities (such as the Highlands and Islands and Fife) which were inexperienced in receiving international migrants. Increased migration of Polish families into areas with little history of receiving migrant families placed pressure on schools and local authorities for places for English language support.[62] To respond to the increasing needs of interpreting services, many schools tend to use Polish pupils who have better English language skills, but this obviously places a considerable responsibility on them.[63]

As part of the process of integrating new migrants, several local authorities across Scotland have prepared special 'welcome packs' (also available in the Polish language) to provide them with information on how to access public services. Some other public bodies, such as the police[64] and the NHS,[65] have done the same. Despite their availability, however, official sources of information are less likely to be used by migrants. Instead, Polish migrants tend to seek information about health services from members of their extended families or from doctors in their country of birth.[66] Accessing information about services in Scotland is often difficult due to language barriers, so having a member of staff who speaks the Polish language has been identified as a helpful way to respond to migrant needs.[67] Polish migrants tend to have a reasonably good knowledge of public services and how to access them, but understanding how things work comes mainly from other Poles rather than from information provided by public bodies. This emphasises the important role of social networks among Polish migrants in providing important information, and perhaps also questions the accessibility of information to migrant communities provided by public bodies in Scotland.

SOCIAL NETWORKS AND POLISH MIGRANT COMMUNITIES IN SCOTLAND

Polish migrant social networks are increasingly seen as crucial to understanding decisions about migration, migration patterns and settlement.[68] Polish migrants are involved in complex ethnic and family relations in Scotland that play an important role in shaping their migration experiences. For many of them, the family is central to their decisions about settlement in the UK.[69] The pattern of Polish migrant families migrating to Scotland in most cases involves men first moving to find a job, with partners and children joining them later.[70] Concerns about the future of their children in Scotland play an important role in the decision to settle there. For example, one study shows that many Polish parents think that their children would have more opportunities in education and employment in Scotland than in Poland.[71] Indeed, since 2004, Polish migrant children have become one of the fastest-growing groups in the school-age population in Scotland. In 2012 the number of pupils speaking Polish as a main home language was 8,255, which made Polish pupils the largest population after students who speak English at home.[72]

Family migration to Scotland introduces many changes in the power dynamics of parent–child relationships.[73] As Polish children learn English more quickly through their schooling, they often become 'cultural brokers' to their parents by helping them familiarise with the host community and mediating their access to a diverse range of public services.[74] Their children's function as 'cultural experts' often challenges traditional family roles, gendered hierarchies and relationships.[75] Furthermore, many Polish migrant parents learn the English language through their children due to the issues mentioned earlier regarding access to English language classes.

Family networks with a wide range of relatives, including siblings, cousins, parents and grandchildren, play important roles in facilitating the settlement of Poles in Scotland. These include emotional, informational and practical support, such as arranging accommodation and employment or helping with access to public services. Family relations and having children abroad also plays a key role in making decisions about settlement in Scotland.[76] Once children enter the education system, many Polish parents are unwilling to disturb their learning and take them away from a system with which they have become familiar.[77] Having children of school age further helps many Polish women to integrate into their local communities by taking part in playgroups or school activities. Once the family as a whole becomes settled in Scotland, the likelihood of returning to the country of origin often permanently recedes.

Many Polish migrant households continue to function across borders, because movement to Scotland usually involves leaving some family members behind. They therefore become part of a complex set of trans-national relationships both in Scotland and Poland. Open borders within the EU enable Polish migrants to travel on low-cost airlines and commu-nicate by new forms of technology such as the Internet (e-mails, Skype) on a regular basis. As a result, Poles move between places and maintain connections between 'home' in Poland and Scotland before deciding whether to settle on a permanent basis or not. However, the result of the European Union membership referendum in June 2016 may introduce changes to free movement between the EU and the UK, and could therefore have a profound impact on these transnational relationships. The retention of complex social and family relations across borders also provides important ongoing sources of practical and emotional support. For example, many families have their Polish relatives move to Scotland on a temporary basis to help with childcare responsibilities. Others exercise caring at a distance or undertake 'transnational mothering', with migrating adults doing the caring and supporting of children over the phone.[78] These transnational family relations, however, can also represent 'competing obligations', with significant emotional strain for both migrants and the families left behind.[79]

POLISH MIGRANTS' SOCIAL NETWORKS AND FORMS OF COMMUNITY ORGANISATIONS: POLISH DIASPORA OR ETHNIC COMMUNITIES?

EU post-enlargement Polish migrants in Scotland experience a complex range of relations within their community, including kinship, friendship and ethnic community ties that involve different levels of trust and reci-procity. Their daily lives are, however, linked to specific, trusted groups of networks between family members and close friends.[80] These relation-ships are the main source of information and support, and more often than not are carried from Poland itself rather than being constructed after arrival. EU post-enlargement Polish migrants in Scotland tend to distinguish two types of ethnic relations: those organised around small kinship groups or/and friendship, and more generalised connections often seen as less trustworthy.[81] Indeed, in comparison with their counterparts who settled in Scotland after the Second World War, the more recent arrivals tend to report a lack of trust and reciprocal relations with other Polish migrants. This finding directly challenges the assumption that Polish migrants can access information and support from broader networks within their ethnic community. Poles themselves acknowledge that the immigrant community is split along class boundaries, divisions between different migrant cohorts and lack of contact beyond small kin and friendship clusters.[82] This fragmentation within the various Polish communities is not only typical for Scotland. Similar studies in London,[83] Lancashire[84] and Southampton[85] likewise indicate that Poles tend to be 'bonded' among small, close-knit networks or family groups and not within larger homogeneous 'ethnic communities'. Despite this, there is a feeling among the migrants that some form of community should and could exist.[86]

While the post-war migration constituted one 'Polonia' living in exile, the EU post-enlargement Polish migrants often perceive members of their ethnic community as competitive and even threatening. This low level of trust is related to a widely recognised stereotype of 'immoral Poles' but also to internal fissures among the Polish migrant communities along social divisions of class, gender and age. The post-war migration mainly consisted of ex-officers and servicemen who settled in Scotland for political reasons. But the socio-demographic composition of recent arrivals and their migration strategies and patterns are substantially different. Those who settled after the Second World War wished to maintain their national identity in 'exile' but that does not necessarily apply to those who arrived at the beginning of the new millennium. Since they remain internally divided, the concept of a coherent and collective diaspora does not fit their experiences of ethnic relations following their migration to Scotland.

In response to increasing numbers migrating from Poland to Scotland with special consumer needs, several voluntary and profit-driven outlets have been established since 2004.[87] They have become important in responding to the complex social, economic and cultural needs of Polish migrants by providing them with informational support, initiating institutional networks and assisting them with access to public services in Scotland. These include, for example, travel and recruitment agencies, interpreting services, tax and benefit advisors, lawyers, money-sending agencies, Polish delis and restaurants, and a wide range of services offered by and to Polish migrants, including health services (dentists),

Figure 6.1 A Polish shop on Gallowgate, Glasgow, August 2017.
© Angela McCarthy.

car repair, construction services, hairdressers and beauticians, babysitters, transport services, interpreters and photographic services. The establishment of new Polish community organisations has changed the landscape of many streets in Scottish towns and made the presence of Polish migrants in Scotland more visible.

Since 2004 a wide range of online social networks dedicated to new Polish migrants has developed. These online communities (for example, emito.net and glasgow24.pl) provide migrants with guidance on how to access public services in Scotland, starting with English language classes to advice on how to apply for welfare benefits. They allow Poles to share via online forums their migration experiences, acquire support and advice, arrange meetings or share information about the quality of services offered by other Poles. As such, these online forums create a form of social assistance and play an important role in developing migrants' social networks across Scotland. In addition to online communities, Polish migrants in Scotland have set up their own media channels, including the newspapers *Szkocjapl* and *Emigrant*, and radio stations such as Szkocjafm and Sunny Govan Radio in Glasgow. It could be argued that all of these developments may have helped to bring the community closer together despite the tensions within it already described.

The increase in the number of diverse Polish migrant organisations might in part be explained by the fact that already established post-war Polish organisations did not reflect the diverse needs of the new waves of post-accession Polish migrants in Scotland. The purpose of the post-war Polish community organisations was mainly political, placing a large emphasis on maintaining a Polish identity. The needs of new EU post-enlargement migrants were more instrumental and related to their initial settling needs, such as finding a job, renting a flat and starting a bank account. The post-war community ventures were mainly managed by second-generation Poles who had different experiences and attitudes to Poland than the new Poles coming to Scotland in 2004. These differences between old and new Polish migrants have resulted in an increase in the number of new Polish community organisations being established to provide social, cultural and educational services across Scotland.[88]

In addition to the long-established Scottish Polish Cultural Association in Edinburgh and the Sikorski Polish Club in Glasgow, a number of new Polish community organisations, including the Polish Cultural Festival Association, the Polish Association Aberdeen and the Fife Polish Association, have established new structures to meet the needs of new migrants across Scotland. The purpose of these bodies is mainly to promote Polish culture and heritage through organising national celebrations, art exhibitions, performances and festivals, and to promote the integration of Poles into Scottish life.

While most of the 'for profit' and voluntary Polish organisations offer their services to adults, since 2004 several Polish Saturday Schools have been established in towns and cities across Scotland. These schools, however, have a different structure to the first one established after the Second World War for Polish children of Polish servicemen in Scotland. Current Polish Saturday Schools run their classes mostly on Saturday mornings and offer instruction in Polish language, history and geography. The Polish Catholic Mission in Scotland provides spiritual guidance and religious services such as masses, the sacraments and religious lessons in Polish for Polish children in Aberdeen, Edinburgh, Glasgow, Dundee, Perth and Inverness.[89]

FORMS OF SETTLEMENT AMONG EU POST-ENLARGEMENT POLES IN SCOTLAND

While members of the post-war Polish community could not return to their home country and therefore had to settle in Scotland, EU post-enlargement Polish migrants can travel and move between places, maintaining active connections between both Poland and Scotland. Whereas the drivers of Polish migration to Scotland are fairly well evidenced, their fluid migration patterns make their longer-term intentions or actual settling practices difficult to assess and thus remain open-ended. Polish migrants have been described as 'regional free movers' who are seeking 'intentional unpredictability'[90] and therefore are more likely to engage in temporary, circular or transnational mobility than in long-term, permanent migration. Consequently, EU post-enlargement migration is often described as a 'liquid migration', where migrants do not settle permanently but move back and forth between their home and receiving countries.[91]

These fluid migration patterns among Polish migrants can also be explained by open borders among the enlarged EU member states and the ease of access to information about destination countries through the web and social media and reduced telecommunication or travel costs.[92] Not surprisingly, therefore, Polish migrants do not have fixed ideas regarding the duration of their stay in Scotland. Instead, they tend to focus on a range of economic (for example, having a job, house and car) and social (having a family and friends) connections that anchor them in Scotland in describing their settling practices.[93] However, the result of the European referendum in June 2016 will introduce changes to the status of EU citizens living in the UK and therefore may have an impact on migration patterns from Poland. Consequently, Polish migrants may no longer be able to benefit from free movement between the EU and the UK, which will have an impact on the fluidity of their migration patterns and open-ended character of their settlement.

Migrants' decisions about settling often include a combination of individual and structural factors that have an impact on migrants' perceptions of settling or returning.[94] This, however, means that remaining in Scotland is not a uniform process for all new Poles. One study identified four main settling practices among Polish migrants living in Scotland. They include settlers, over-stayers, and circular and economic migrants.[95] The difference between Polish migrants' settling practices depends on several factors including: attitudes to home and the country of residence; feelings of constancy, security and familiarity with the social and material environment; and social (family and children) and economic forms of attachment to home and the country of residence.[96] Settled Polish migrants tend to develop various forms of attachments, including economic and psycho-social links, and therefore want to stay in Scotland and have no plans to move abroad. Over-stayers tend to postpone decisions to migrate from Scotland, as they have achieved a degree of economic stability and live a comfortable life in Scotland but experience little emotional attachment to the new place of residence. Another practice, that of circular migration, involves those Poles who maintain multiple relationships with their country of origin and residence through regular trips to Poland or other locations for short periods of time. The final settling practice is that of economic migrants whose stay in Scotland is characterised by the fulfilment of their economic goals.[97]

Decisions about settlement or return are not linear processes, and considerations about settlement and return can always take new turns. Until 2016, EU post-accession Polish migrants in Scotland were not an entirely predictable population with different strategies of migration and return. However, the result of the European referendum may change that.[98] When the UK leaves the EU, Poles may no longer be able to benefit from free movement and maintain transnational relations across borders. This could force some migrants to make a final decision about 'staying' or 'going'.[99]

CONCLUSION

The context and nature of different migrations from Poland to Scotland have changed over time. The political character of post-war migration, with strong connections to the Catholic faith, and an expressed pride and patriotism among post-war Polish migrants, created a baseline for the successful structure and organisation of '*Polonia*', the Polish community permanently settled outside Poland. The experiences and the organisation of Polish EU post-enlargement migrants, however, differed, and that diversity needs to be acknowledged. Recent Polish migrants have tended to form various community organisations with a range of profiles in response to the complex needs and interests of this migrant group. Despite these forms of community organising, there is consensus among studies of Polish migrant experiences that Poles are not a cohesive ethnic group and that notions of 'diaspora' or 'community' are misplaced.[100] Internal divisions within the new Polish migration are founded on social class, migration strategies and settling practices. 'New' Poles in the UK (including Scotland) tend to be structured along the lines of 'personal' communities formed by close personal relations within family members and friends. These relations are not spatially bounded, as most Poles still continue to have equally close and dense transnational networks with their family and friends back in Poland.

By examining the experiences of the largest non-UK migrant group in Scotland, this chapter has sought to examine whether the experiences of

Poles in Scotland are distinctive (in relation to the rest of the UK). The synthesis has shown that Polish experiences in Scotland are complex and nuanced. Analysis of the 2011 census demonstrates that the impact of Polish migration has been different for Scotland by helping the country to achieve demographic growth and fill gaps in the labour market. Despite the absolute number of migrants who came to Scotland since 2004 being less than those to England, Polish migrants form the largest foreign-born population in Scotland. The analysis in the chapter also shows that political and media debates on EU migration in Scotland are distinctive. English newspapers often describe Poles as cheap labour, which places pressure on the employment market and public services. In Scotland, however, the debate is more balanced and overall coverage more positive. Yet, while the Scottish Government wishes to encourage immigration, the public is less enthusiastic. Analysis of the Scottish Social Attitudes Surveys of 2010 and 2015 indicates that despite general public attitudes towards migration in Scotland being more welcoming than in the rest of the UK, any increase in the number of eastern European migrants (including Poles) would cause concern among disadvantaged groups. These more negative attitudes are especially to be found among some younger people and lower working-class sections of the population. Nevertheless, local case studies have found only limited evidence that migrants have experienced hostility in the form of verbal threats or physical abuse.

While this chapter shows differences between Scotland and the rest of the UK in terms of public, media and political debates concerning Polish migration, it remains difficult to be certain whether the Polish migrant experiences north of the border are substantively different from elsewhere. This is because there are very few comparative studies providing sound empirical data on various regions across the UK. Even so, some similarities in Polish migrant experiences can be identified. Polish migrants throughout the UK tend to be found in low-skilled occupations, such as agriculture, food processing and the hospitality sectors. The evidence suggests, as well, a general mismatch between the educational qualifications of Polish migrants and their most common occupations in the UK.[101] In addition to work, settlement practices across the UK are quite similar. Migrants from Poland have been described as 'regional free movers' who are more likely to engage in temporary, circular or transnational mobility and do not have a fixed idea regarding duration of stay.[102] We can conclude by suggesting that Polish settlement in Scotland,[103] as in England,[104] tends to be open-ended, with the decision whether to remain depending on a range of economic and social factors.[105] There can be little doubt, however, that the result of the EU referendum in June 2016 will introduce uncertainties about the status of EU citizens living in the UK which will affect future Polish attitudes to settlement, belonging and mobility.

NOTES

1. I am grateful to Professor Colin Clark for his edits on a draft of this chapter and to Professor Sir Tom Devine for his extensive editing of the final version.
2. A. White, 'Polish migration to the UK compared with migration elsewhere in Europe: A review of the literature', *Social Identities*, 22:1 (2016), pp. 10–25.
3. Accession 8 (A8) migrants are the citizens of the eight countries that joined the European Union in 2004, including Czech Republic, Estonia, Hungary, Latvia, Lithuania, Poland, Slovakia and Slovenia.
4. Eastern European nationals are citizens coming from the post-Communist block, including Bulgaria, Czech Republic, Estonia, Hungary, Latvia, Lithuania, Poland, Romania and Slovakia.
5. See, for example, D. Sime, R. Fox and E. Piętka, 'At home abroad: The life experiences of Eastern European migrant children in Scotland' (Glasgow: University of Strathclyde, 2011); D. McGhee, S. Heath and P. Trevena, 'Post-accession migrants: Their experiences of living in "low demand" social housing areas in Glasgow', *Environment and Planning*, 45 (2013), pp. 329–43; S. Shubin and H. Dickey, 'Integration and mobility of Eastern European migrants in Scotland', *Environment and Planning*, 45 (2013), pp. 2959–79; R. Kay, M. Flynn, P. Trevena, S. Shubin, H. Porteous and C. Needler, 'Social support and migration in Scotland: Interim report' (Glasgow: University of Glasgow and Swansea University, 2016).
6. P. Trevena, 'How comparable are the experiences of Poles to those of other EE migrants in the UK?' (Presentation at the Polish Migrants' Experience of Life in the UK since 2004 conference, University College London, School of Slavonic and East European Studies, London, 17–18 April 2015).
7. D. Sime and R. Fox, 'Migrant children, social capital and access to services post migration: Transitions, negotiations and complex agencies', *Children and Society*, 29:6 (2015), pp. 524–34.
8. M. Moskal, 'Polish migrant youth in Scottish schools: Conflicted identity and family capital', *Journal of Youth Studies*, 17:2 (2014), pp. 279–91.
9. E. Piętka, N. Canton and C. Clark, '"I know that I have a university diploma and I'm working as a driver": Defining the EU post-enlargement movement of highly skilled Polish migrant workers to Glasgow, Scotland', in B. Glorius, I. Grabowska-Lusinska and A. Kuvik (eds), *Mobility in*

Transition: Migration Patterns after EU Enlargement (Amsterdam: Amsterdam University Press, 2013), pp. 133–54.

10. Blake Stevenson, 'A8 nationals in Glasgow' (Glasgow: Glasgow City Council, 2007).

11. P. Orchard, A. Szymanski and N. Vlahova, 'A community profile of EU8 migrants in Edinburgh and an evaluation of their access to key services' (Edinburgh: Scottish Government, 2007).

12. P. de Lima, B. Jentsch and R. Whelton, 'Migrant workers in the Highlands and Islands' (Inverness: Highlands and Islands Enterprise, 2005).

13. P. de Lima, M. Chaudhry, R. Whelton and R. Arshad, 'A study of migrant workers in Grampian' (Edinburgh: UHI Policy Web, 2007).

14. Fife Research Co-ordination Group, 'Migrant workers in Fife – survey 2007' (Fife: Fife Council, 2007).

15. Scottish Government, 'Scotland's future' (Edinburgh: Scottish Government, 2013) p. 16.

16. P. D. Stachura, '"God, honour and fatherland": The Poles in Scotland, 1940–1950, and the legacy of the second republic', in T. M. Devine and D. Hesse (eds), *Scotland and Poland Historical Encounters, 1500–2010* (Edinburgh: John Donald, 2011) pp. 159–72.

17. J. Zubrzycki, *Polish Immigrants in Britain: A Study of Adjustment (Studies of Social Life)* (Hague: Springer, 1956).

18. T. Kernberg, 'The Polish community in Scotland', PhD thesis, University of Glasgow, 1990, p. 203.

19. Stachura, '"God, honour and fatherland"', p. 161.

20. R. Clements, 'Press reception of Polish migrants in Scotland, 1940–2010', in Devine and Hesse (eds), *Scotland and Poland*, p. 178.

21. Zubrzycki, *Polish Immigrants in Britain*, p. 85.

22. T. Kernberg, 'The Polish community in Scotland', p. 261.

23. Stachura, '"God, honour and fatherland"', p. 168.

24. S. Drinkwater, J. Eade and M. Garapich, 'Poles apart? EU enlargement and the labour market outcomes of immigrants in the UK', *IZA Discussion Paper No. 2410* (Bonn: Institute for Study of Labour, 2006), p. 5.

25. A. Fihel and E. Pie tka, 'Funkcjonowanie polskich migrantow na brytyjskim rynku pracy', *CMR Working Papers* (Warsaw: Centre for Migration Studies, University of Warsaw, 2007), p. 9.

26. H. Packwood and A. Findlay, 'Immigration to Scotland and the constitutional change debate: Geography, difference and the question of scale', *CPC Working Paper Number 42* (Southampton: ESRC Centre for Population Change, 2014), p. 2.

27. House of Lords, 'The economic impact of immigration, volume I: Report, Select Committee on Economic Affairs, 1st Report of Session 2007–08' (London: The Stationery Office Limited, 2008), p. 20.

28. Home Office, 'Accession monitoring report, May 2004–March 2009' (London: Home Office, 2009), p. 10.

29. A. Fihel and P. Kaczmarczyk, 'Migration: A threat or a chance? Recent migration of Poles and its impact on the Polish labour market', in K. Burrell (ed.), *Polish Migration to the UK in the 'New' European Union: After 2004* (Farnham: Ashgate, 2009), p. 35.

30. A. White, 'Young people and migration from contemporary Poland', *Journal of Youth Studies*, 13:5 (2010), p. 566.

31. P. Trevena, D. McGhee and S. Heath, 'Location, location? A critical examination of patterns and determinants of internal mobility among post-accession Polish migrants in the UK', *Population, Space and Place*, 19:6 (2013), pp. 671–87.

32. Packwood and Findlay, 'Immigration to Scotland and the constitutional change debate', p. 2.

33. A. Favell, 'The new face of east–west migration in Europe', *Journal of Ethnic and Migration Studies*, 34:5 (2008), pp. 701–16.

34. R. Black, G. Engbersen, M. Okólski and C. Pantiru (eds), *A Continent Moving West? EU Enlargement and Labour Migration from Central and Eastern Europe* (Amsterdam: Amsterdam University Press, 2010).

35. Drinkwater et al., 'Poles apart?', p. 2.

36. K. Burrell, 'Staying, returning, working and living: Key themes in current academic research undertaken in the UK on migration movements from Eastern Europe', *Social Identities,* 16:3 (2010), p. 300.

37. D. McCollum and A. Findlay, 'Employer and labour provider perspectives on Eastern European migration to the UK', *CPC Working Paper Number 14* (Southampton: ESRC Centre for Population Change, 2011).

38. P. Trevena, 'Why do highly educated migrants go for low-skilled jobs? A case study of Polish graduates working in London', in B. Glorius et al. (eds), *Mobility in Transition: Migration Patterns after EU Enlargement*, pp. 169–89; A. White, *Polish Families and Migration since EU Accession* (Bristol: Policy Press, 2011).

39. Piętka et al., '"I know that I have a university diploma and I'm working as a driver"', p. 148.

40. C. Clark, N. Canton and E. Piętka, '"The thing is that we haven't come here for holidays": The experiences of new migrant communities from central and eastern Europe who are living and working in Glasgow' (Edinburgh/London: British Council and the Institute for Public Policy Research, 2008).

41. McCollum and Findlay, 'Employer and labour provider perspectives on Eastern European migration to the UK', p. 18.

42. Kay et al., 'Social support and migration in Scotland: Interim Report', p. 3.

43. McCollum and Findlay, 'Employer and labour provider perspectives on Eastern European migration to the UK', p. 23.

44. Piętka et al., '"I know that I have a university diploma and I'm working as a driver"', p. 148.

45. A. Rudd, 'Speech to Conservative Party', Birmingham, 4 October 2016, htttp://press.conservatives.com/post/151334637685/rudd-speech-to-con servative-party-conference-2016 (accessed 1 June 2017).
46. Scottish Government, 'Scotland's future', p. 267.
47. R. Pillai, 'The reception and integration of new migrant communities' (London: Institute for Public Policy Research, 2007), p. 35.
48. D. McCollum, B. Nowak and S. Tindal, 'Public attitudes towards migration in Scotland: Exceptionality and possible policy implications', *Scottish Affairs*, 23:1 (2014), pp. 79–102.
49. A. Park, E. Clery, J. Curtice, M. Phillips and D. Utting, 'British social attitudes: The 29th report' (London: NatCen Social Research, 2012), p. 30.
50. A. Stout, 'Scottish social attitudes 2015: Attitudes to discrimination and positive action' (Edinburgh: Scottish Government, 2015), p. 4.
51. See, for example, M. Lewis, 'Warm welcome? Understanding public attitudes towards asylum seekers in Scotland' (London: Institute for Public Policy Research, 2006); A. Hussain and M. Miller, *Multicultural Nationalism: Islamophobia, Anglophobia and Devolution* (Oxford: Oxford University Press, 2006).
52. Stout, 'Scottish social attitudes 2015', p. 4.
53. Ibid., p. 4.
54. R. Ormston, J. Curtice, S. McConville and S. Reid, 'Scottish social attitudes Survey 2010: Attitudes to discrimination and positive action' (Edinburgh: Scottish Centre for Social Research, 2010), p. 93.
55. Stevenson, 'A8 nationals in Glasgow', p. 33.
56. Fife Research Co-ordination Group, 'Migrant workers in Fife: Survey 2007', p. 1.
57. R. King and N. Wood (eds), *Media and Migration: Construction of Mobility and Difference* (London and New York: Routledge Research in Cultural and Media Studies, 2001).
58. Clements, 'Press reception of Polish migrants in Scotland', p. 179.
59. J. Semontan, 'Public perception of A8 migrants: The discourse of the media and its impact' (Glasgow: University of Glasgow and BEMIS Empowering Scotland's Cultural Minority Communities, 2011), p. 6.
60. Clements, 'Press reception of Polish migrants in Scotland', p. 180.
61. Ibid., p. 184.
62. M. Moskal, 'Polish migrant children's experiences of schooling and home-school relations in Scotland', *CES Briefing No. 54* (Edinburgh: Centre for Educational Sociology, University of Edinburgh, 2010).
63. Ibid.
64. Scottish Police set up the dedicated website https://www.facebook.com/ SzkockaPolicja for Polish migrants to provide information about their services in the Polish language and to offer Poles an opportunity to contact the police in the Polish language.

65. NHS Scotland provides a number of health guides in the Polish language.

66. D. Sime, '"I think that Polish doctors are better": Newly arrived migrant children and their parents' experiences and views of health services in Scotland', *Health and Place*, 30 (2014), pp. 86–93.

67. Kay et al., 'Social support and migration in Scotland: Interim report'.

68. See, for example, L. Ryan, 'Transnational relations: Family migration among recent Polish migrants in London', *International Migration*, 49:2 (2011), pp. 80–103; L. Ryan, R. Sales, M. Tilki and B. Siara, 'Family strategies and transnational migration: Recent Polish migrants in London', *Journal of Ethnic and Migration Studies*, 35:1 (2009), pp. 61–77, and White, *Polish Families and Migration since EU Accession.*

69. Ryan et al., 'Family strategies and transnational migration'.

70. Sime et al., 'At home abroad'.

71. Ibid.

72. The Scottish Government, 'Pupil census supplementary data: Pupil census 2012 supplementary data' (Edinburgh: Scottish Government, 2012).

73. Moskal, 'Polish migrant youth in Scottish schools', pp. 279–91.

74. D. Sime and R. Fox, 'Home abroad: Eastern European children's family and peer relationships after migration', *Childhood*, 22:3 (2014), p. 378.

75. D. Sime and E. Piętka-Nykaza, 'Transnational intergenerationalities: Cultural learning in Polish migrant families and its implications for pedagogy', *Language and Intercultural Communication*, 15:2 (2015), p. 219.

76. E. Piętka-Nykaza and D. McGhee, 'EU post-accession Polish migrants' trajectories and their settling practices in Scotland', *Journal of Ethnic and Migration Studies* (2016), pp. 1–17.

77. D. McGhee, S. Heath and P. Trevena, 'Competing obligations and the maintenance of physical co-presence: The impact of migration and structural constraints on post accession Polish families in the UK', *Families, Relationships and Society*, 2:2 (2012), pp. 229–45.

78. Sime and Fox, 'Home abroad', p. 378.

79. McGhee et al., 'Competing obligations and the maintenance of physical co-presence'.

80. E. Piętka, 'Encountering forms of co-ethnic relations among Polish community in Glasgow', *Studia Migracyjne – Przegl d Polonijny*, 37:1 (2009), pp. 129–51.

81. Ibid.

82. Ibid., p. 137.

83. L. Ryan, R. Sales, M.Tilki and B. Siara, 'Social networks, social support and social capital: The experiences of recent Polish migrants in London', *Sociology*, 42:4 (2008), pp. 672–90.

84. N. Gill and P. Bialski, 'New friends in new places: Network formation during the migration process among Poles in the UK', *Geoforum*, 42:2 (2011), pp. 241–9.

85. D. McGhee, P. Trevena and S. Heath, 'Social relationships and relationships

in context: Post-Accession Poles in Southampton', *Population, Space and Place*, 21:5 (2015), pp. 433–45.

86. White, 'Polish migration to the UK compared with migration elsewhere in Europe: A review of the literature'.
87. M. Garapich, 'The migration industry and civil society: Polish immigrants in the United Kingdom before and after EU enlargement', *Journal of Ethnic and Migration Studies*, 34:5 (2008), pp. 735–52.
88. Piętka, 'Encountering forms of co-ethnic relations among Polish community in Glasgow'.
89. See Polish Catholic Mission in Scotland website, available at http://www.kosciol.org (accessed 31 May 2017).
90. Favell, 'The new face of east–west migration in Europe'.
91. Engbersen et al., '"A van full of Poles": Liquid migration from Central and Eastern Europe', in Black et al. (eds), *A Continent Moving West*, pp. 7–22.
92. M. Metykova, 'Only a mouse click away from home: Transnational practices of Eastern European migrants in the United Kingdom', *Social Identities: Journal for the Study of Race, Nation and Culture*, 16:3 (2010), pp. 325–38.
93. Piętka-Nykaza and McGhee, 'EU post-accession Polish migrants' trajectories and their settling practices in Scotland'.
94. S. Drinkwater and M. Garapich, 'Migration strategies of Polish migrants: Do they have any at all?', *Journal of Ethnic and Migration Studies*, 41:12 (2015), pp. 1909–31.
95. Piętka-Nykaza and McGhee, 'EU post-accession Polish migrants' trajectories and their settling practices in Scotland', p. 1.
96. Ibid., p. 6.
97. Ibid., p. 14.
98. Electoral Commission, 'EU referendum results', 2017, available at: http://www.electoralcommission.org.uk/find-information-by-subject/elections-and-referendums/past-elections-and-referendums/eu-referendum/electorate-and-count-information (accessed on 1 May 2017).
99. C. Moreh, D. McGhee and A. Vlachantoni, 'Should I stay or should I go? Strategies of EU citizens living in the UK in the context of the EU referendum', *Briefing Paper 35* (Southampton: ESRC Centre for Population Change, 2013).
100. See discussion in Piętka, 'Encountering forms of co-ethnic relations among Polish community in Glasgow'; Ryan et al., 'Social networks, social support and social capital'; Gill and Bialski, 'New friends in new places'; McGhee et al., 'Social relationships and relationships in context'.
101. Clark et al., '"The thing is that we haven't come here for holidays"'; Piętka et al., '"I have a university diploma and I'm working as a driver"'; Trevena, 'Why do highly educated migrants go for low-skilled jobs?'; White, *Polish Families and Migration since EU Accession*.

102. See discussion in Favell, 'The new face of east–west migration in Europe'; Engbersen et al., '"A van full of Poles"'; and Piętka-Nykaza and McGhee, 'EU post-accession Polish migrants' trajectories and their settling practices in Scotland'.
103. Piętka-Nykaza and McGhee, 'EU post-accession Polish migrants' trajectories and their settling practices in Scotland'.
104. Drinkwater and Garapich, 'Migration strategies of Polish migrants'.
105. Piętka-Nykaza and McGhee, 'EU post-accession Polish migrants' trajectories and their settling practices in Scotland'.

7

Education and the Social Mobility of Chinese Families in Scotland

Eona Bell

> In Chinese culture it's all about doing better. They expected you to work really hard when you were little, but it was all about building up, and going to uni, making a better life for yourself. They would never stand in your way.
> 'James',[1] Scottish-born Chinese, aged 26, 2005

Representations of Chinese communities in the West are polarised. Chinese immigrants are seen to be highly successful in education and business yet, compared with other minority ethnic groups, their stories are often overlooked and their participation in public life is low. As representatives of a 'model minority', Chinese immigrants have been lauded for achieving prosperity through self-motivation and plain hard work, and for doing so without provoking the social and political tensions which have arisen in relation to other ethnic groups – a positive perspective on what can otherwise be read as marginalisation. In her influential critique of previous studies of globalisation, Aihwa Ong[2] describes Chinese migrants as exemplary cosmopolitans, 'flexible citizens' who readily move both their families and capital around the globe, unencumbered by political ties to the nations in which they reside. On the other hand, tales of illegal migration and the drug trade have led to the reproduction of racist images of the Chinese as a 'yellow peril' threatening Western communities and moral order – a stereotype which has endured over many decades across various locations.[3] This chapter places Scotland's Chinese population within this complex and disparate global diaspora. The particular focus will be on differences in access to education between the generations, and between successive waves of migrants to Scotland from Hong Kong and China. The idea of meritocracy, and the belief that anyone can rise out of poverty through schooling, has attained the status of a 'national myth' – that is, a story which people tell about themselves[4] – in both Scottish and Chinese cultures. Nevertheless, as this chapter argues, belief in the possibility of social mobility through education may be insufficient to overcome barriers of language, social inequality in access to schooling, gender ideology and other factors which can frustrate individual attainment.

PRE-1945 CHINESE MIGRATION TO SCOTLAND

A small but steady flow of people has travelled from Scotland to China since at least the eighteenth century, not least because of British commercial and diplomatic interests in Asia.[5] But few Chinese made the opposite journey before the 1900s. The earlier history of a Chinese presence in Scotland merits further research, but it was small and consisted mainly of temporary visitors, including students such as Huang Kuan, who studied in Edinburgh from 1850 to 1855, becoming the first Chinese graduate from a Western school of medicine. In England and Wales, by contrast, settled Chinese communities were recorded in the dockland areas of London in 1851[6] and those of Liverpool and Cardiff by 1911.[7] Chinese seamen were present in Glasgow at the time of the 1919 harbour riot, one of a series of disturbances in British cities, when labour leaders including the 'Red Clydesider' Emanuel Shinwell enforced a 'colour bar' on black and Chinese sailors on British merchant ships, and white working-class people, frustrated by the shortage of post-war jobs, abused and attacked foreign workers.[8] Few of these sailors, however, appear to have settled permanently in Scotland.

In the interwar period, a handful of Chinese made their homes in Scotland through personal ties, often formed in the context of Britain's colonial history. For example, one Chinese domestic servant accompanied her Scottish employers when they returned from service in the Far East in the 1930s. On leaving their employment she remained in Edinburgh and opened one of the first Chinese restaurants in the city. Another pre-Second World War Chinese restaurant is recorded in Chambers Street in Edinburgh, close to the university.[9] Meanwhile, the son of a Chinese seaman opened a restaurant, Wah Yen on Govan Road in Glasgow, during the 1940s.[10] The location of this restaurant, near the Glasgow docks, suggests that a large part of the clientele may have been Chinese sailors.

POST-WAR GROWTH OF THE SCOTTISH CHINESE POPULATION

Researchers working on Chinese communities in Britain have frequently lamented the inadequacy of population estimates, which are generally assumed to under-report the true figures. Dorothy Neoh MBE, a founding member of the former San Jai Project for Chinese children and families in Glasgow, puts this down partly to the 'Chinese dislike of bureaucracy' but the language barrier and insecurity over immigration status may also have deterred registration.[11] With that caveat, the growth of Scotland's Chinese population, in relation to that of the UK as a whole, is evident from census figures from the past sixty years, as shown in Table 7.1.

The roots of the present-day Chinese community in Scotland lie in the wave of migration from Hong Kong and the rural New Territories to Britain after the Second World War. Under British colonial government, Hong Kong people had rights to settle in the UK, particularly after the passing of the 1948 British Nationality Act. Most of these post-war migrants came from farming and fishing communities which were undergoing massive change and disruption following the establishment in 1949 of the People's Republic of China (PRC). Hong Kong and the New Territories received thousands of refugees from the PRC, at the same time as agricultural markets were closed off by the political upheaval. In response to growing unemployment and housing shortages, the British colonial government encouraged large-scale emigration, which at first involved young men from the poorest rural communities

Table 7.1 Ethnic Chinese population in Scotland and the UK, 1951–2011

	Scotland	UK total
1951	837	2,600
1961	1,316	10,310
1971	6,300	96,000
1985	10,000*	150,000
2001	16,310	247,403
2011**	33,706	393,141

Sources: Census reports England and Wales 1951–2011; Scotland 1951–2011
* Rough estimates by community groups cited by Chan[12]
** The doubling of the Chinese population between 2001 and 2011 may be partly attributable to new migration by students and other mainland Chinese, and partly to the relatively young age of the ethnic Chinese population. However, there are difficulties in comparing the two census figures since the ethnic category 'Chinese' was moved from the 'Other' group in the 2001 UK census to a new category of 'Asian/Asian British' in 2011.

but later attracted those from richer villages.[13] Many of them went first to London, finding work with their kinsmen in Chinese restaurants catering to a new British taste for 'exotic' food. Although at first these men saw themselves as temporary sojourners, the prospect of the 1962 Commonwealth Immigrants Act, which would limit immigration, prompted many of them to bring their wives and children to settle permanently in Britain. At this point, during the 1960s, Chinese families moved north to Scotland, and also to the Netherlands and Nordic countries, in search of fresh business opportunities.[14]

During the 1970s, the Chinese community in Scotland started to become more cohesive, with restaurant owners – almost exclusively male – forming business associations, and women coming together informally to organise mother-tongue language classes for their children, who they realised were at risk of losing their Chinese language skills as they entered the Scottish education system. The Edinburgh Chinese School was opened in 1971 and the Glasgow Chinese School in 1972. However, the geographic dispersal of the Chinese population meant that many families, especially in rural Scotland, had only infrequent contact with other Chinese people. In the late 1970s, some 1,500 Vietnamese Chinese people arrived in Scotland as refugees after the end of the Vietnam War. After the initial emergency resettlement, some stayed in Scotland and became integrated with the Hong Kong Chinese community, though the majority left to join a larger Vietnamese population in the southeast of England.[15]

In the 1980s, local authority funding became available for minority ethnic organisations: welfare providers were established for the Chinese in Scotland, such as the Edinburgh Chinese Elderly Support Association, and the San Jai Project for Chinese women and children in Glasgow. The Chinese community schools also benefited from national policies which encouraged the learning of minority languages in Britain, and the curriculum became more organised, with students able to gain national qualifications in Cantonese. Textbooks and other support were provided by the Hong Kong Government Office in London, which served as a point of contact for Chinese in Britain until 1997.[16]

In percentage terms (at 411 per cent), the growth of Scotland's ethnic Chinese population since the 1990s was much greater than that of England. In this period, the composition of the Chinese population of Scotland has changed considerably as a result of migration from places other than Hong Kong. Taiwanese electronics companies opened manufacturing plants in Lanarkshire during the 1990s, bringing with them several hundred Taiwanese staff and their families. However, the largest change has been from the new wave of migration from the PRC, which relaxed its rules on travel and migration in the post-Mao era, allowing millions to go abroad. In 1991 the number of people arriving in Scotland from mainland China was negligible, although there were 5,910 immigrants from Hong Kong. A decade later, in 2001, there were over 7,000 migrants from Hong Kong and 3,329 recorded from the PRC. The 2011 census recorded a total 15,338 migrants from China to Scotland.[17]

Recent changes in the political environments of both Scotland and Hong Kong have had important implications for the Scottish Chinese population. The year 1997 saw both the handover of Hong Kong from Britain to China and the devolution of certain political powers from the UK Parliament to Scotland. Scotland's devolved government since 1997 has positively encouraged inward migration, for example through the Fresh Talent: Working in Scotland Scheme of 2004–8.[18] The decade or so preceding the handover of Hong Kong to China saw a rise in international migration of professional people from Hong Kong to the West; a small number of these came to Scotland and elsewhere in the UK, although many more emigrated to Canada and Australia.[19] After 1997, Hong Kong began a process of political, cultural and linguistic reintegration with mainland China. The Mandarin language, for example, has been promoted as an official language alongside the local Cantonese and English. Recent protests and public demonstrations under the banner of the Umbrella Movement give some indication that this process is not welcomed by all Hong Kongers, and the post-1997 changes have led to a reassertion by many of Hong Kong's distinctive culture, expressed through the Cantonese language and reflecting an entrepreneurial, cosmopolitan outlook which does not sit easily with the policies of the PRC.[20] Thus, it seemed significant that in my research, many Chinese Scots chose to self-identify as 'Hong Kong people' rather than 'Chinese'.

The Scottish Chinese population has grown particularly since 2000 in student areas, such as Anderston and Hillhead in Glasgow and Southside in Edinburgh.[21] It is likely that the Chinese in these areas are largely university students, since the total number of students from China studying at Scottish universities has increased continuously year on year from 4,220 in 2007/8 to 8,545 in 2013/14, falling slightly to 8,450 in 2014/15. Chinese students now make up around 40 per cent of the total Chinese population in both England and Scotland.[22]

Apart from students, new arrivals have included professional people, undocumented economic migrants, particularly from the poor Fujian and Zhejiang provinces in southern China, and a few hundred asylum seekers from the PRC who have been housed in Glasgow as part of the UK government's dispersal scheme.[23]

There is some interaction between the old and new Chinese migrants in Scotland, as new migrants often work in restaurants, doing jobs which Scottish-born Chinese youth no longer want to do. Mainland Chinese students often teach in the Chinese language schools. As with the Chinese community in Liverpool,[24] the Hong Kong Chinese in Scotland are generally settled, with established social networks, while more recent migrants from mainland China tend to be more mobile and may have difficulty integrating with the Cantonese-speaking community because of occupational, linguistic and cultural differences. On the other hand, some new migrants arrive as students or professional people possessing social capital which earlier generations of Chinese migrants lacked. Existing associations and support services have been set up to meet the needs of the Hong Kong Chinese, and are now having either to adapt or make way for new organisations for the Mandarin speakers. Meanwhile, new migrants are forming associations of their own, including Young Chinese Professionals Scotland, and the Alba Cathay Chinese School in Edinburgh.

As for settlement patterns, Garnethill in Glasgow has long been an economic and residential hub of the Chinese community in the West of Scotland, and Chinese businesses found a new and highly visible home in Chinatown in Cowcaddens in 1992. However, geographical concentration of that kind is not typical of the Scottish Chinese population, which is very widely dispersed across the country. Census data show that Chinese people have settled in every part of Scotland, probably to avoid competition between ethnic businesses such as restaurants and Chinese medicine shops. Unlike some other minority ethnic groups, then, many Chinese Scots have only infrequent contact with other Chinese, apart from their immediate family members.

EXPERIENCES OF SCHOOLING AMONG CHINESE PEOPLE IN SCOTLAND

When I was beginning my research as a social anthropologist among Chinese families in Scotland, a wise friend, with long experience of professional engagement with Scotland's immigrant communities, told me, 'If you want to know the Chinese, go to their schools. The others have their temples, but the Chinese have their schools.' He was referring to the community-led Saturday schools which exist in many Scottish towns and cities, teaching Chinese languages and culture primarily, but not exclusively, to Scottish-born Chinese children. Chinese immigrants are far from unique in running community language schools, as in 2006 more than one hundred schools in Scotland provided classes in at least twenty-one community languages.[25] Even so, community schools play a special part in the history of the Chinese population. A survey of school students in the East of Scotland found that students of Chinese heritage, compared with other minority groups, were the most likely to attend them.[26] These community language schools are significant for Chinese parents in Scotland, who are keen for their children to know the Chinese written characters widely regarded as crucial to the identity of a 'Chinese' person. They also value the schools as safe places where both children and adults are able to explore and negotiate new and complex social and cultural identities,[27] and community schools are an important focus for charitable giving and volunteering within the Scottish Chinese community.[28]

The high value placed on education by Chinese families has been noted by researchers in China itself, as well as in Western countries where ethnic Chinese have settled.[29] Education has long been a cherished route to prosperity in Chinese societies. In imperial China, a poor boy could achieve material advancement and social prestige by passing national examinations to enter the civil service, and in the very different political environment of the contemporary PRC, parents invest heavily in their children's schooling, which they believe will improve the fortunes of the whole family. Many scholars argue that Chinese migrants overseas carry with them these cultural beliefs in the importance of education as a route to success.[30]

'Valuing education' has been identified as a stereotypical attribute of British Chinese pupils, expressed both by British Chinese people themselves and by their teachers.[31] If hard work forms part of a person's ethnic identity and self-worth, then this could be a strong motivating factor in education. Experiments have shown the effects of socio-cultural stereotypes on individual performance: black students underperformed on an academic test when attention was drawn to their ethnicity.[32] This so-called 'stereotype threat' can also have positive effects, motivating students from stereotypically high-achieving groups.[33]

This argument appears to be borne out by Scottish Government statistics for 2014/15 which show that Asian-Chinese school leavers had the highest levels of attainment of any ethnic group, with 88 per cent of school leavers achieving at least one qualification at SCQF level 6 or better, far higher than the 59.8 per cent of White-Scottish leavers achieving this level.[34] These figures do not, however, distinguish between the Scottish-born children and grandchildren of Chinese immigrants, and those who have arrived directly from Hong Kong or China specifically to pursue an education in Scotland, and it is highly problematic to assume that all ethnic Chinese people share the same cultural values and attitudes.

It is also useful to consider how members of subordinate groups adjust their personal aspirations downwards because of constraints external to themselves. British Chinese children might do well at school but take the safe option of work in the catering trade because, rightly or not, they anticipate failure in other fields of employment.[35]

The classic sociological works on education and social mobility in Western societies – setting aside the factor of ethnic identity – suggest that education is a means of reproducing class values, and that urban, middle-class parents are more likely to encourage their children to succeed at school, thereby demonstrating their social distinction.[36] In the past, children of Hong Kong Chinese immigrants struggled in British schools because their working-class families lacked the 'cultural capital' necessary for success in Western education, and British teachers despaired of the Chinese children's ability to settle and integrate with their classmates.[37] However, British Chinese children showed a remarkable ability to adapt to their new surroundings, quickly learning English and helping their parents to adjust to the new social setting.[38] In the space of just a few decades the British Chinese overall seemed to have overcome many of the barriers of race, language and class, and were achieving considerable upward social mobility.[39]

The key research question, then, was to explore ethnographically the everyday parenting practices by which Scottish Chinese parents may support their children's learning. A related question was whether the experience of migration affected Chinese parents' attitudes to schooling. The Chinese in Britain have attracted relatively little scholarly attention, and a third question concerned changes in British Chinese family life since the 1970s, when research suggested that family relationships were severely strained by the process of migration and the nature of work in the catering trade. Finally, in the contemporary context of diversity within the Scottish Chinese population, how did differences of class and subethnic origin affect the degree to which Chinese migrants conform to the stereotype of being diligent students?

The discussion that follows draws upon long-term ethnographic fieldwork conducted in Edinburgh, Glasgow and Fife between 2005 and 2007. As a volunteer teacher of English as an Additional Language and as a tutor, I made regular visits to Scottish Chinese family homes, and I attended two Chinese community schools as a student of Cantonese language, calligraphy and Chinese knotting. In addition, over eighteen months I participated in a wide range of social activities at community centres, museums, festival celebrations, church services and private gatherings. In addition to observations from everyday life, I recorded data on at least forty ethnic Chinese individuals, including people born and brought up in Hong Kong, China and Scotland. Twenty were women aged 18–75, ten were men aged 18–90 and ten were children aged 8–17.[40] Evidence from these life-story narratives of Chinese Scots of different generations suggests that attaining upward mobility is highly contingent on external factors, including differences of class and gender, migration status, and political and colonial histories, which may support or frustrate individual attainment and mobility.

Despite the long tradition of respect for learning in Chinese society, until relatively recently the opportunities to progress by this route were restricted to a small elite, in which boys were always favoured over girls and most schools were in private hands.[41] In the PRC since 1949, great strides have been made towards universal education provided by the state, but inequalities of opportunity persist to the present day, with far better educational facilities for students in urban areas than in the countryside.[42] Likewise, in Hong Kong, rural children were less likely to attend school than their urban peers until 1971, when free primary education was offered for all. Only in 1978 did the government guarantee three years of compulsory secondary education.[43] The political turmoil of the early years of the PRC and especially the years of the Cultural Revolution had caused enormous social upheaval and destroyed existing institutions, including schools in both mainland China and Hong Kong. The effects were particularly severe in the rural areas from which many migrants came.[44] Hence, the majority of Chinese Scots born before 1965, and especially older women, received only a basic education, if any, while Chinese people born in either Scotland or Hong Kong after that date may be assumed to have received at least nine years of schooling and be far better equipped to take up opportunities for higher education and employment.

One of the wealthiest Chinese restaurant owners in the East of Scotland, a man I call Cheng, was born in 1926 in a Cantonese-speaking fishing village in the northern New Territories. In common with many single-surname villages in the region, it had a small school, funded by the lineage organisation, where boys were given an elementary education by a classically trained scholar. These schools were colloquially known in

Cantonese as *bobojai*, referring onomatopoeically to the beatings which were regularly handed out to the students. Cheng attended this school for just three months, when he was ten years old, but then the teacher died and was not replaced. The Japanese invaded Hong Kong in 1941. Daily survival became the family's priority, and Cheng's brief schooling ended when he joined his parents at work on the fishing boat.

His village had a long history of outward migration, mainly to Malaya and South East Asia, but in the 1950s people started to migrate to England from all over the New Territories. It was becoming increasingly difficult to make a living, as the small fishing boats faced competition from larger vessels. Cheng was by now in his late twenties and married with three sons. His parents asked a relative to organise a work permit for him to emigrate to Britain. Following the tradition of the mutually reliant Chinese family, Cheng's duty was to earn sufficient money to support his ageing parents, unmarried siblings, wife and children.

Like many of his contemporaries, Cheng found work in a restaurant in London, remitting money home while saving sufficient capital to bring the family to Britain, which he achieved in 1972. They moved to Leicester, where they ran their own fish-and-chip shop and the children completed secondary school, before relocating to a small Scottish town in 1979. None of the four children attended university because, according to Cheng, the family could not afford to support them. Instead, they all helped in the family business.

Cheng's story demonstrates that education was unavailable as a route to upward social mobility for many of the first generation of Chinese Scots who, living through times of dramatic social and political upheaval in Hong Kong and China, used migration as a means to survive and to fulfil their family obligations. Men and women of Cheng's generation, who are now in their eighties and nineties, had very little schooling before they migrated, and the isolated and arduous nature of catering work made it extremely difficult for them to learn English as adults. Previous research has pointed to the emotional and practical hardships they have faced because of the language barrier.[45]

Over the three decades of his working life in Britain, through long hours of hard work, and at the cost of prolonged separation from his family, Cheng achieved financial independence and the respect of others in the local Chinese community, who recognise the work he has done latterly as a volunteer in various charitable projects. In contrast to the restaurateurs of the London-based Man lineage described by James L. Watson, who have become property millionaires across several countries,[46] or the transnational elite Chinese businessmen whom Ong defines as the quintessential 'flexible citizens',[47] Cheng's success is small in scale. His pride is in the stability and prosperity of his family, who live close to him in Scotland, and he sums up his own achievements as a self-made man, telling me in Cantonese: 'I came here with only £10 in my pocket and now I have my own restaurant and three children in business.'

Gender has also restricted the educational attainment of Chinese girls and women in Scotland, at least for the first generation of immigrants in the 1960s and '70s. This reflects the traditional preference for sons in Chinese culture, which historically has led to families investing in the education of boys rather than girls, especially when resources were scarce. The logic was that on marriage a girl would be 'lost' to her husband's family, whereas a boy would continue the family line and provide care to his parents in old age. As the following case study illustrates, in some families these attitudes persisted after migration to Scotland.

Lily was born in Glasgow in 1974, to Hakka parents who were still in their early twenties and had emigrated with Lily's paternal grandparents, her aunts and uncles from a farming community on the Hong Kong–China border. The relatives worked together in a restaurant which they co-owned. Lily attended school in Glasgow from the age of five, but in retrospect feels she was badly let down both by her parents and by school staff. The family, numbering eight or nine people, lived in a two-bedroom flat until the overcrowding caused such tension that the grandparents moved out to a separate house with their six young grandchildren. They cared for the children while the parents worked full-time in the restaurant, some miles away. Lily, as the oldest granddaughter, was required to bathe and supervise the babies, under the fierce eye of her grandmother. She describes a childhood isolated from her peers as the grandmother, who spoke no English, forbade her to play outside the house. Once a week, on the day the restaurant was closed, Lily and her siblings spent a few hours with their mother and father. Their parents expressed their love for their children through gifts of toys and clothes, but could offer little emotional support.

Lily was unhappy at primary school, mainly because she struggled with English, having no one at home who spoke it, and no television in the house. Although she received some remedial English language teaching, she feels it was inadequate. Other children teased her because of her poor English and physical appearance. Until she was in her late teens, all her friends were Chinese. Overall, Lily feels let down by the Scottish school system of the 1980s and sees her education as a missed opportunity.

From the age of thirteen, she and her brother helped their parents in the takeaway at weekends, hiding in the kitchen washing dishes because they were under the legal working age. She enjoyed this work and is now proud to have acquired good practical skills at an early age, learning to cook, shop, and launder clothes. This gave her the confidence to leave home at sixteen, when she moved in with the Scottish-born Chinese boyfriend who became her husband. The couple continue to earn a living from the catering trade, although once their children were born Lily became a full-time mother. Neither she nor her husband wanted their children to experience the separation from parents which they believe tarnished their own childhoods, and the family restaurant business is now sufficiently profitable for them to pay employees, and no longer rely on unpaid family labour.

Just as data from Hong Kong and China point to a rise in girls' educational attainment following the introduction of free universal education, attitudes and behaviour have also changed among Chinese families in Scotland, to the extent that no research participants younger than Lily reported any discrimination against daughters with regard to schooling.

Next, it may be that class and regional differences in the backgrounds of Chinese Scots affect their attitudes to education. Although the Chinese population of the US has a somewhat different history of migration, settlement and exclusion from that in Britain, some useful comparisons may be made with regard to their approach to education. Both class and race are said to affect the educational paths of Chinese Americans. A study of middle- and working-class Chinese American university students found that all felt pressure from their parents to succeed academically, but only middle-class parents really expected their children to reach the most prestigious professions after graduating from elite universities.[48] The 'downtown Chinese' parents, who worked in the ethnic enclave economy, aspired to a secondary tier of professions, including pharmacy and accounting, for their children; these were more likely to enrol at the regional college. Historically, the majority of Chinese in Britain came from similarly poor backgrounds in Hong Kong, and have worked in the ethnic catering trade after migration. However, there have been instances of 'downward' social mobility for graduates who have moved from professional positions in Hong Kong or China to more lucrative work in British restaurants,[49] and in recent years, ethnic Chinese migrants have come from and entered a wider range of occupations. This suggests that Western academic definitions of 'class' may fail to capture some of the meanings of education and work for non-Western immigrants.[50]

While Lily's family came from a poor village, another research participant, whose family came from urban Hong Kong, took a different approach to her children's education. Mrs Shek graduated from a Hong Kong university before emigrating to Scotland and opening a restaurant with her husband in the 1970s. Their young children remained in the care of Mrs Shek's parents in Hong Kong until they reached school age, when she brought them to Scotland. She and her husband were too busy to help their children with their schoolwork and so decided to send them to private schools, assuming that the teachers would give the direction they required. An Edinburgh-born Chinese man described this ironically as a 'typically Cantonese approach: if you have a problem, just throw money at it.' The cost represented a significant financial sacrifice, as Mrs Shek told me: 'For years we lived in a tiny flat, and I drove a very old and ordinary car. All our money went on my son's school fees.' She also boasts that although she was working in a takeaway and had very little time to spend with her son, she used their time together for the maximum benefit: driving to school every morning, she would question him about his lessons and ask whether he had any problems or difficulties understanding the teacher.

Finally, it has been argued that variability in school achievement by minority ethnic groups in the West may be due less to intrinsic 'cultural' differences than to differences in the group's history in relation to the majority culture. In US schools, for instance, immigrant children whose families have migrated voluntarily tend to flourish, while those who were incorporated unwillingly into an alien culture, such as refugees, former slaves or indigenous peoples, do not.[51] This model may work well in the context of US race relations, but does not account so well for the situation in Britain. Research in the late 1970s and '80s indicates that the first generation of Chinese pupils to enter British schools, like Lily, did not flourish, despite their 'voluntary immigrant' status. The barriers of language and geographic isolation, along with the pressures of family work in catering, formed structural impediments to their learning.[52]

A counter-argument runs that structural factors, independent of the minority group, affect minority pupil attainment. These may include the promotion of race equality in schools, and efforts to improve teachers' ability to respond to specific pupil needs, including support for speakers of English as an Additional Language.[53] The proportion of non-white pupils in a local authority area can also influence the commitment to and investment in targeted educational resources.[54] This would support Lily's belief that Scottish schools in the 1970s were at fault for failing to meet the specific needs of immigrant children.

In relation to migration histories, I found that children born and brought up entirely in Scotland tended to have a more positive experience of school than those who were born or spent their early years in Hong Kong. Many of the children born in Scotland to Chinese parents in the 1980s had a different childhood experience from that of Lily and Mrs Shek's children, perhaps because their parents were more secure financially, and after several years in Britain, more confident about their children's integration into wider society. Lisa, who was born in Dundee in 1980, saw herself as no different to her white Scottish peers:

I don't actually have many BBC [British-Born Chinese] friends – just a few close friends and relatives – but they don't see themselves as Chinese, they think of themselves as Scottish. I see myself as Scottish Chinese, I suppose, but then I think – does it really matter? The people I know see themselves as Scottish, they just don't relate to issues like BME, racism and so on. They might get the odd racist comment now and then, maybe when you're at the pub, but it's not a big deal. We are quite integrated socially and have Scottish friends.

Lisa's parents were employed by other Chinese immigrants in the catering trade, so did not rely on the help of their children to keep a family business afloat; on the contrary, having experienced the social exclusion and long working hours demanded in the restaurant trade, they urged their children to study and qualify for a different career. Lisa considers herself 'lucky' that her parents did not push her towards a particularly prestigious profession, such as medicine or law, but encouraged her to 'live outside the box', by which they meant she should not be constrained by stereotypes, but make a life for herself in Scotland by working hard at school, integrating into local society and finding a 'Western' job. Lisa chose to go to art college, and has found employment in the voluntary sector. Other research participants of Lisa's generation worked in graphic design, architecture, public sector management, retail, IT and finance. They have attained the parents' dream for them of white-collar jobs, enabling a degree of security and comfort in their lives which was beyond the reach of the first generation of Hong Kong immigrants. Some of their peers, however, including Lisa's two brothers, opted to stay in the ethnic catering trade, as a positive choice, perhaps motivated by high earnings, or by a personal disinclination to higher education. As Lisa described it: 'I wouldn't say it's an easy option, in the sense that the work is very difficult, very demanding, but for someone who isn't focused, who doesn't know what their options are, hasn't heard of apprenticeships and that kind of thing, it can be a fall-back option.'

New Chinese migrants in Scotland since the 1990s have been much more likely than the early migrants to cite education as a primary motive for leaving Hong Kong or China. However, there are once again class differences in how this shapes their migration, and in the prospects which are opened up for their children.

The Wongs were the only example I encountered of the 'astronaut family', a term coined for middle-class Hong Kong Chinese who moved abroad – typically to Australia, Canada or the US – because of uncertainty around the 1997 handover to China, but maintained a home in Hong Kong in the hope that their fears were unwarranted.[55] The husband would continue to live and do business in Hong Kong while his 'astronaut' wife and children were overseas. Rachel Wong and her husband had been thinking of sending their son to school in Scotland because of the good reputation of its private schools, but decided to do so earlier than they had planned when the SARS virus hit Hong Kong in 2003. Rachel and her son left immediately and came directly to Scotland, where she bought a flat and enrolled the boy at one of the most prestigious boys' schools. At the time of my fieldwork, Rachel was running a small boutique, selling goods imported from Hong Kong through her husband's extensive business connections. She was active in one of the Chinese Christian churches and also attended meetings of the Chinese Women's Group, but saw her husband only infrequently.

Mrs Li arrived in Edinburgh with her husband and two teenage sons in autumn 2007, but did not expect to return to Hong Kong as most of their relatives had migrated to Scotland decades before. When I asked why they had come, Mrs Li told me, with some surprise at my question, that it was 'for a better life for the children'. They had lived in urban Hong Kong where Mr Li worked as a painter and decorator and she was a housewife. With the boys now aged eleven and sixteen, they decided to join their extended family in Edinburgh, where both parents would be given work in one or other of the family restaurants. The children were enrolled in the local state secondary, where their cousins were already pupils. Located in one of the most deprived parts of Edinburgh, the school had a record of low academic achievement. However, there was no question of the children going anywhere but the local school, to which they could walk alone while their parents were at work.

As I got to know the family, I often wondered how exactly the parents thought their sons would benefit from the move. Kevin, who was sixteen, spoke poor English and was desperately homesick. His Hong Kong school report suggested he had never been a high achiever academically, but was more interested in sports. Painfully shy and depressed, he struggled to make any friends at the Edinburgh school, let alone adjust to the new, English-medium curriculum. His younger brother, Johnny, had a more extravert personality and the added advantage of being in the same class as his Scottish-born cousin, who despite warnings from teachers could whisper to Johnny in Cantonese if he needed help in lessons. Johnny was enrolled in the Chinese Saturday School with his cousins, attending basketball club as well as Cantonese classes, and soon made new friends. Kevin, meanwhile, refused to come to Chinese school. He never left the flat, except to go to school or family events, spending most of the time on the Internet or playing computer games alone.

Lacking financial and cultural capital prior to migration, working-class Chinese like the Li family faced far greater obstacles to social mobility than other new migrants coming from middle-class and professional backgrounds.

SCOTLAND'S CHINESE POPULATION IN INTERNATIONAL PERSPECTIVE

The preceding section has drawn out some of the continuities and differences between Chinese immigrants of different generations and social backgrounds in Scotland. I have also related the Scottish data to similar research on other overseas Chinese communities. At this point it may also be helpful to highlight some broader points of contrast and comparison between the experiences of Chinese in Scotland and elsewhere. This is possible as, with a few exceptions,[56] most previous research on the 'British' Chinese population has focused exclusively on people living in England, which of course has its own distinctive history of 'race' and class relations.

Recent studies of the Chinese population in the island of Ireland have also shown how the specific local dynamic of community relations shapes the experience of minority ethnic people. Ironically, despite the sectarian tensions within Northern Irish society, Chinese immigrants perceived it as a safer place for newcomers than some English inner cities.[57] Similarly, Asian (Chinese, Indian and Pakistani) migrants to Scotland experienced significant racial discrimination in both housing and job markets but overall thought Scotland was a more tolerant and friendly place to live than England. This may be because the total black and ethnic minority population of Scotland is smaller than in the rest of the UK, and therefore is not perceived as a threat. It has often been pointed out that Chinese and other Asian immigrants are tolerated because they set up their own businesses rather than competing with local people for jobs; and in their work in catering or corner shops, they establish good relationships with local residents.[58] It has further been argued that Scots use 'territorial' markers such as birthplace, accent, upbringing and commitment to the country as criteria for national 'belonging', whereas in England, people are more likely to be defined by their family origin and cultural background.[59] On this basis, a Scottish-born Chinese person, fluent in English and educated in Scotland, or a first-generation immigrant who invested in a business in Scotland, would be more readily accepted as 'Scottish' than their counterpart in England, where more attention is paid to ethnic or racial difference. This optimistic view was, however, negated by those of my research participants who had experienced racial abuse in Scotland, and by other evidence that racist attacks are often under-reported by Chinese in Britain.[60]

Another aspect of Scottish culture which might contribute to a distinctive experience for migrants, compared with those in other places, is the theme of the liberating power of education which has entered the Scottish national mythology, along with the figure of the 'lad o' pairts', the child from humble origins who works his way up through learning to success.[61] David McCrone has shown that the educational opportunities for children of the skilled working class and petit bourgeoisie are better in Scotland than in England. He points out that while the study of contemporary Scottish social structure may not conclusively prove that Scotland is overall a more meritocratic, egalitarian society than the rest of the UK, the hegemonic belief that it is so weighs on individual hopes and aspirations.[62]

Based on his experience as a community worker in the 1980s, Alfred Chan reported that Chinese people in Edinburgh were more 'middle class' than in London. They were, for example, more likely to hire help in their restaurants in order to spend time with their families, and worked only six days a week compared with seven days in London. Chinese people were also attracted to Edinburgh because they believed the schools to be better than in English cities, and they viewed it as a quiet and safe environment where their offspring would be protected from the temptations of a larger city.[63] My own research confirmed that many Scottish Chinese parents were prepared to sacrifice income for the sake of a better quality of life, defined as having leisure time and opportunities to spend time together as a family.[64] While none of my informants could make explicit comparisons between Scotland and England as places to bring up a family – very few of them had actually lived in England, and those who had were men of the older generation who left childcare to their wives – they did prefer the calmer lifestyle, milder climate and more spacious homes available in Scotland, in contrast with hot and densely populated Hong Kong. I also found they were unlikely to travel to England, unless they had relatives there. They were more likely to spend holidays in Hong Kong, or with relatives in the US or Canada, than to visit London or explore other parts of the UK. Even so, Chinese in Scotland remain aware of issues throughout the UK as most Scottish Chinese family homes subscribe to a British Chinese TV channel broadcasting from the South East of England, and most pick up free copies of Chinese-language newspapers, published in or near London but distributed through Chinese supermarkets throughout the UK.

Community organisations of various kinds have been established to counteract the isolation of Chinese migrants. These include Chinese business associations, Christian churches, women's groups, information and advice centres, lunch clubs, and sheltered housing for the elderly. These tend to cater to the needs of Chinese in specific cities or regions of Scotland, as opposed to having national reach. This points to a process of group-making on the grounds of locality. As with Chinese people in Vancouver, who formed associations based on a variety of shared characteristics,[65] Chinese in Scotland use their place of work or residence as the basis for new group formation, as much as other possible criteria for common interest such as surname, country of origin, occupation or language.

Although most Chinese Scots have no religion, there are Chinese Christian churches in several towns and cities, including congregations of the Chinese True Jesus Church, made up almost exclusively of people with family ties to the tiny Ap Chau Island to the west of the New Territories. The Ap Chau people, who had eked a living by fishing, emigrated in large numbers to Elgin and surrounding towns in Aberdeenshire in the late 1960s and early 1970s to work in restaurants owned by their relatives and fellow islanders.[66] Congregations also exist in Edinburgh and Newcastle, as well as the South of England. Members of the True Jesus Church in Britain have a tradition of marrying within the church, and because of their religious teaching abstain from smoking and gambling, which marks them out from other Chinese migrants. Another subgroup with shared family origins are the Hakka Chinese – members of a minority ethnic group with distinctive cultural practices and a separate language from the majority Cantonese in Hong Kong.

Hong Kong Chinese emigrant communities in English cities were often organised according to centuries-old social networks, based on shared surnames and descent from a single ancestor. These 'lineage' or 'ancestral associations' were central to the ritual, social and economic life of South China (including Hong Kong), and played a key role in emigration to Britain.[67] I found no evidence, however, of any kin-based association among the Chinese population of Edinburgh, although the Kut-O Association links Hakka immigrants in the West of Scotland. A study of Chinese immigrants to Edinburgh in the late 1960s uncovered no fewer than thirty different surnames among the cohort. This suggests that the nuclear family was a more important influence than the wider kin group in Chinese migration to Scotland, as families attempted upward social mobility to improve their social position through the restaurant trade.[68] As one scholar notes, 'the notion of "family" was what supported the Chinese immigrant in the chosen place of settlement'.[69]

Since 2000 British Chinese community websites such as Dimsum[70] and the British Chinese Online Discussion Board have played an important part in ethnic community-building among the widely dispersed Chinese population of the UK,[71] but they were little used by the Chinese Scots in my sample. Any who were active on social media chose to use 'mainstream' channels, the most popular at the time of my research being MySpace and later Facebook. Again, it appeared that people established relationships with other Chinese whom they met in everyday life, whether as work colleagues, at community groups or at Chinese schools, but did not seek out connections with a larger 'British Chinese community'.

CONCLUSION

In this chapter I set out to explore how Chinese families in Scotland have used education as a strategy to secure upward social mobility for themselves and their children. The ethnographic research was designed to understand better the differences of class and subethnic origin which might affect the degree to which Chinese migrants conform to the stereotype of being hard workers and diligent students. The case studies in the preceding sections illustrate that this has not been a uniform pattern, but one shaped by particular individual circumstances, including gender, social class, place of origin, reasons for migration, and the availability of schooling for migrants of different generations.

It is evident that significant changes have occurred in the Scottish Chinese population since the 1950s, and particularly since the arrival of wives and children from Hong Kong in the 1970s, when family relationships were severely strained by the process of migration and the nature of work in the catering trade. First-generation migrants were unable to benefit from the new opportunities offered by migration, because they lacked the basic literacy needed to advance in education and professional careers. On the other hand, for subsequent generations there is no longer the same pressure to excel in education since, once settled in Scotland, many Chinese families are content to enjoy a settled, stable life. The education of children is now valued intrinsically, an integral part of a model of childhood which includes play, leisure and self-realisation. It is important to parents that children should be released from the obligation to contribute to the family income. This is a sharp contrast to the experience of older Chinese Scots, before and after migration, who were required to earn money for the household as soon as they were able.

Almost all Scottish Chinese parents in the research wanted their children to work hard at school, and defined themselves as good and responsible parents if they enabled this. But they also wanted their sons and daughters to be happy. This can be seen as part of a general shift towards a form of family life unlike that of the previous generation. I have argued elsewhere[72] that there has been a move within Scottish Chinese families towards a more child-centred approach to parenting and family life. Many parents who experienced deprivation in their own childhoods value the opportunities which contemporary Scottish schools offer, and encourage their children to take up extra-curricular activities, including sport and music, for the sake of a richer and more rounded life. Most resist the idea of their children going to work while they are still at school.

To a large extent, these values are no different to those of non-Chinese, middle-class parents in contemporary Scotland, and I found no cases of the 'pushy' parenting which has been documented in studies of Chinese families in England[73] and, controversially, in Chinese-American Amy Chua's 2011 memoir, *Battle Hymn of the Tiger Mother*.[74] My Scottish-Chinese informants recognised the stereotypes but generally did not consider that they themselves – or indeed anyone they knew personally – were 'tiger mothers'. One Edinburgh Chinese mother wrote to me in an email (2011):

> The UK version of Amy Chua would be Vanessa Mae's mother, the famous violinist. She was on a TV programme, telling about her tyrant mother and her childhood. I suppose it all depends on [the] individual mother – how much does she want their child to be successful and famous. For me, the

most important is: the children will be able to get a decent job and that they are happy with it.

Going beyond the stereotypical association of ethnic Chinese with educational achievement, it is important also to consider other values that act as drivers to individual and collective ambition. In contemporary Chinese societies these have included the value of family and, perhaps increasingly in the younger generation, materialism and what Yan has described as 'selfish individualism'.[75] Hong Kong, in particular, has been noted for a strongly materialistic culture. Education is treated very pragmatically as a means to achieve the main measures of success, which are economic security and the possibility of self-realisation through freedom of career choice. The evidence from Chinese families in Scotland appears to support Vivian Louie's argument concerning the New York Chinese: that success in education depends on class, both prior to immigration and in the host country.[76] But further, in Scotland today there is a growing realisation among Chinese immigrants and their descendants that education may not be the only or best route to achieving the goal of a materially successful and fulfilling life.

NOTES

1. All names of research participants in this chapter are pseudonyms.
2. Aihwa Ong, *Flexible Citizenship: The Cultural Logics of Transnationality* (Durham, NC: Duke University Press, 1999).
3. For a detailed discussion, see Christopher Frayling, *The Yellow Peril: Dr Fu Manchu and The Rise of Chinaphobia* (London: Thames & Hudson, 2014).
4. David McCrone, *Understanding Scotland: the Sociology of a Nation* (London: Routledge, 2001).
5. See Ian Wotherspoon, *The Scots and China, 1750–2000: Issues, Ideas and Identities* (Edinburgh: CreateSpace, 2013).
6. Anthony Shang, *The Chinese in Britain* (London: Batsford Academic and Educational, 1984).
7. Gregor Benton and Edmund Terence Gomez, *The Chinese in Britain, 1800–Present: Economy, Transnationalism, Identity* (Basingstoke: Palgrave Macmillan, 2008).
8. Jacqueline Jenkinson, 'Black sailors on Red Clydeside: Rioting, reactionary trade unionism and conflicting notions of "Britishness" following the First World War', *Twentieth Century British History*, 19:1 (2008), pp. 29–60.
9. J. A. G. Roberts, *China to Chinatown: Chinese Food in the West* (London: Reaktion Books, 2002), p. 172.

10. British Chinese Heritage Centre, 'Glasgow', http://www.britishchineseher itagecentre.org.uk/34-project/the-evolution-and-history-of-british-chinese-workforce (last accessed 2 January 2017).

11. Dorothy Neoh, 'The Chinese community in Scotland', in J. Beech (ed.), *Scottish Life and Society: The Individual and Community Life*, vol. 9 (Edinburgh: John Donald, 2005), pp. 604–17.

12. Alfred Chan, *Chinese in Scotland: Their Education, Employment and Social Needs in Britain in the Past Twenty Years* (Glasgow: University of Glasgow Press, 1987).

13. James L. Watson. 'The Chinese: Hong Kong villagers in the British catering trade', in James L. Watson (ed.), *Between Two Cultures: Migrants and Minorities in Britain* (Oxford: Oxford University Press, 1977), pp. 181–213.

14. Nick Bailey, Alison Bowes and Duncan Sim, 'The Chinese community in Scotland', *Scottish Geographical Magazine*, 110:2 (1994), pp. 66–75.

15. Vaughan Roberts and Samantha Hale (1989), 'The geography of Vietnamese secondary migration in the UK', Research Paper in Ethnic Relations No.10, Centre for Research in Ethnic Relations, University of Warwick. Available from www2.warwick.ac.uk/fac/soc/crer/research/publications/research_pa pers/rp_no.10.pdf (last accessed 3 March 2017).

16. Benton and Gomez, *The Chinese in Britain*, p. 254.

17. Scottish Government, *Scotland's Diaspora and Overseas-Born Population*, http://www.gov.scot/Resource/Doc/285746/0087034.pdf (last accessed 14 March 2017).

18. Mika Danson, 'Fresh or refreshed talent: Exploring population change in Europe and some policy initiatives', *Diversities*, 9:1 (2007), pp. 13–34; Luke Cavanagh, Franca Eirich and John-Glyn McLaren, 'Fresh Talent: Working in Scotland Scheme: An evidence review' (Edinburgh: Scottish Government, 2008). Available from http://www.gov.scot/Publications/2008 /08/15155422/0 (last accessed 14 March 2017).

19. Janet W. Salaff, Siu-lun Wong and Arent Greve, *Hong Kong Movers and Stayers: Narratives of Family Migration* (Urbana: University of Illinois Press, 2010).

20. Carol Jones, *Lost in China? Law, Culture and Identity in Post-1997 Hong Kong* (Cambridge: Cambridge University Press, 2015).

21. CODE/Joseph Rowntree Foundation, *How has Ethnic Diversity Changed in Scotland?* (Manchester: ESRC Centre on Dynamics of Ethnicity, 2014).

22. Scottish Government. International Student Statistics, http://www.gov. scot/Publications/2016/03/9265/3 (last accessed 6 February 2017).

23. The 2011 census showed that 74 per cent of Scotland's ethnic Chinese population was born outside the UK. Scottish Refugee Council, *Where are Refugees Coming From?*, http://www.scottishrefugeecouncil.org.uk/ assets/0410/WhereRefugeesAreComingFrom.pdf (last accessed 14 March 2017).

24. Sean Beck, 'Meeting on the margins: Cantonese "old-timers" and Fujianese "newcomers"', *Population, Space and Place*, 13:2 (2007), pp. 141–52.

25. Joanna McPake, *Provision for Community Language Learning in Scotland* (Stirling: Scottish CILT, 2006), http://www.gov.scot/resource/doc/920/0039475.pdf (last accessed 1 January 2017).

26. Joanna McPake, *Mapping the Languages of Edinburgh* (Stirling: Scottish CILT, 2004).

27. Andy Hancock, 'Unpacking mundane practices: Children's experiences of learning literacy at a Chinese complementary school in Scotland', *Language and Education*, 26:1 (2012), pp. 1–17.

28. Eona Bell, 'Challenges to ethnic cooperation among Hong Kong Chinese in Scotland', in Ellen Judd, Charles Stafford and Eona Bell (eds), *Cooperation in Chinese Communities* (London: Bloomsbury, forthcoming 2018).

29. Jin Chi and Nirmala Rao, 'Parental beliefs about school learning and children's educational attainment: Evidence from rural China', *Ethos*, 31:3 (2003), pp. 330–56; Andy Hancock, 'Attitudes and approaches to literacy in Scottish Chinese families', *Language and Education*, 20 (2006), pp. 355–73; Andrew B. Kipnis, *Governing Educational Desire: Culture, Politics, and Schooling in China* (Chicago: University of Chicago Press, 2003); Vivian S. Louie, *Compelled to Excel: Immigration, Education, and Opportunity among Chinese Americans* (Stanford, CA: Stanford University Press, 2004).

30. Frank N. Pieke, 'Chinese educational achievement and "folk theories of success"', *Anthropology and Education Quarterly*, 22:2 (1991), pp. 162–80.

31. Louise Archer and Becky Francis, *Understanding Minority Ethnic Achievement: Race, Gender, Class and 'Success'* (Abingdon: Routledge, 2007).

32. Claude M. Steele and Joshua Aronson, 'Stereotype threat and the intellectual test performance of African Americans', *Journal of Personality and Social Psychology*, 69 (1995), pp. 797–811.

33. Margaret Shih, Todd L. Pittinsky and Nalini Ambady, 'Stereotype susceptibility: Identity salience and shifts in quantitative performance', *Psychological Science*, 10 (1999), pp. 80–3.

34. Scottish Government, *Summary Statistics for Attainment, Leaver Destinations and Healthy Living*, No. 6: 2016 Edition, http://www.gov.scot/Publications/2016/06/4523 (last accessed 1 January 2017).

35. Chan, *Chinese in Scotland*.

36. Pierre Bourdieu and Jean-Claude Passeron, *Reproduction in Education, Society and Culture* (London: Sage, 1990, 2nd edn); Paul E. Willis, *Learning to Labour: How Working-Class Kids Get Working-Class Jobs* (Farnborough: Saxon House, 1977).

37. Anne Garvey and Brian Jackson, *Chinese Children* (Cambridge: National Educational Research and Development Trust, 1975).

38. Watson, 'The Chinese: Hong Kong villagers', p. 202.
39. Yuan Cheng, 'The Chinese: Upwardly mobile', in Ceri Peach (ed.), *Ethnicity in the 1991 Census*, vol. 2: *The Ethnic Minority Populations of Great Britain* (London: HMSO, 1996), pp. 161–80.
40. This data is still in possession of the author. The case studies that follow, unless referenced otherwise, are drawn from the author's research.
41. John Cleverley, *The Schooling of China: Tradition and Modernity in Chinese Education* (Sydney: Allen & Unwin, 1991, 2nd edn).
42. Lijun Chen, Dali Yang and Qiang Ren, 'Report on the state of children in China' (Chicago: Chapin Hall at the University of Chicago, 2015). Available from http://www.chapinhall.org/research/report/report-state-children-china (last accessed 14 March 2017).
43. Mark Bray and Ramsey Koo, *Education and Society in Hong Kong and Macao: Comparative Perspectives on Continuity and Change* (Hong Kong: Springer Press, 2005).
44. Steve Tsang, *A Modern History of Hong Kong* (London: I. B. Tauris, 2007).
45. Ruby C. M. Chau and Sam W. K. Yu, 'Social exclusion of Chinese people in Britain', *Critical Social Policy*, 21:1 (2001), pp. 103–25.
46. James L. Watson, 'Virtual kinship, real estate, and diaspora formation: The Man lineage revisited', *Journal of Asian Studies*, 63 (2004), pp. 893–910.
47. Ong, *Flexible Citizenship*, pp. 112–13.
48. Louie, *Compelled to Excel*.
49. Shang, *The Chinese in Britain*.
50. Archer and Francis, *Understanding Minority Ethnic Achievement*.
51. John Ogbu, *Minority Education and Caste: The American System in Cross-Cultural Perspective* (New York: Academic Press, 1978).
52. Garvey and Jackson, *Chinese Children*; Great Britain Commission for Racial Equality, *The Needs of the Chinese Community in Scotland and the North East of England* (London: Commission for Racial Equality, 1988).
53. Gina Netto, Filip Sosenko and Glen Bramley, *Poverty and Ethnicity in Scotland: Review of the Literature and Datasets* (Joseph Rowntree Foundation, 2011), http://www.jrf.org.uk/publications/review-poverty-and-ethnicity-scotland (last accessed 14 December 2016).
54. Glen Bramley and Noah K. Karley, 'Home ownership and educational achievement: School effects as neighbourhood effects', *Housing Studies*, 22:5 (2007), pp. 693–722.
55. Yuying Tsong and Yuyi Liu, 'Parachute kids and astronaut families', *Asian American Psychology: Current Perspectives* (New York: Psychology Press, 2009), pp. 365–80.
56. W. C. A. A. Bradley, 'The Chinese in Ei [Edinburgh]: Study of adjustment of the restaurant group' (Masters thesis, University of Edinburgh, 1973); Chan, *Chinese in Scotland*; Andy Hancock, 'Attitudes and approaches to literacy in Scottish Chinese families', *Language and Education*, 20 (2006),

pp. 355–73; C.-M. Liu Garland, 'The role of the True Jesus Church in the communal development of the Chinese people in Elgin, Scotland', in Elizabeth Sinn (ed.), *The Last Half-Century of Chinese Overseas* (Hong Kong: Hong Kong University Press, 1998), pp. 425–46; Neoh, 'The Chinese community in Scotland'.

57. Mary Delargy, 'Language, culture and identity: The Chinese community in Northern Ireland', in Máiréad Nic Craith (ed.), *Language, Power and Identity Politics* (Basingstoke: Palgrave Macmillan, 2007), pp. 123–45; Nicola Yau, 'Celtic tiger, hidden dragon: Exploring identity among second generation Chinese in Ireland', *Translocations*, 2 (2007), pp. 48–59.

58. Bashir Maan, *The New Scots: The Story of Asians in Scotland* (Edinburgh: John Donald, 1992).

59. Peter E. Hopkins, 'Young Muslim men in Scotland: Inclusions and exclusions', *Children's Geographies*, 2:2 (2004), pp. 57–72; Richard Kiely, Frank Bechhofer and David McCrone, 'Birth, blood and belonging: Identity claims in post-devolution Scotland', *Sociological Review*, 53 (2005), pp. 150–71.

60. Sue Adamson et al., *Hidden from Public View? Racism Against the UK Chinese Population* (London: The Monitoring Group, 2009). Available from http://www.sociology.leeds.ac.uk/assets/files/research/cers/Min%20 Quan%20Finished%20Report.pdf (last accessed 14 March 2017).

61. Keith Hope, *As Others See Us: Schooling and Social Mobility in Scotland and the United States* (Cambridge: Cambridge University Press, 2009).

62. McCrone, *Understanding Scotland*.

63. Alfred Chan, *Employment Prospects of Chinese Youth in Britain: A Research Report* (London: Commission for Racial Equality, 1986).

64. Eona Bell, 'Ethical dilemmas for Hong Kong Chinese parents bringing up children in Scotland', in Charles Stafford (ed.), *Ordinary Ethics in China* (London: Berg, 2013), pp. 80–99.

65. Edgar Wickberg, 'Global Chinese migrants and performing Chineseness', *Journal of Chinese Overseas*, 3 (2007), pp. 177–93.

66. Garland, 'The role of the True Jesus Church', pp. 425–46.

67. James L. Watson, *Emigration and the Chinese Lineage: The Mans in Hong Kong and London* (Berkeley, CA: University of California Press, 1975).

68. Bradley, 'The Chinese in Ei [Edinburgh]'.

69. Neoh, 'The Chinese Community in Scotland', pp. 604–17.

70. Now archived at http://www.webarchive.org.uk/ukwa/target/7176209/ source/subject (last accessed 14 March 2017).

71. David Parker and Miri Song, 'Inclusion, participation and the emergence of British Chinese websites', *Journal of Ethnic and Migration Studies*, 33:7 (2007), pp. 1043–61.

72. Bell, 'Ethical dilemmas for Hong Kong Chinese', pp. 80–99.

73. Archer and Francis, *Understanding Minority Ethnic Achievement*.

74. Amy Chua, *Battle Hymn of the Tiger Mother* (London: Bloomsbury, 2011).

75. Yunxiang Yan, *The Individualization of Chinese Society* (Oxford: Berg, 2009).
76. Louie, *Compelled to Excel*.

8

African Migrants, Asylum Seekers and Refugees: Tales of Settling in Scotland, 2000–15

Teresa Piacentini

Ehm . . . personally I hate the bus just now . . . I really hate the bus. Because you just get on the bus and the way people look at you and things like that. I think one thing, when I came to Glasgow I didn't know anybody here, but I knew Rexon . . . I called him up and he told me he lived in Pinkston Drive so I lived with him for maybe a week or so and I got a flat in Pinkston Drive. Then . . . I don't know, maybe after a couple of months of living in Glasgow I knew that Pinkston Drive was . . . a very bad place to live. It has a kind of stigma, asylum seekers and things like that. So one thing I've experienced is when you are going to tell people you live in Pinkston Drive and, you know, you are African, you are just associated with asylum . . . They think you are asylum seeker and people look at you like you are being a drain on the resources of Glasgow

Adegoke, Cameroonian student

In Edinburgh, the problem doesn't appear in this negative way, not like it has been since 2000. When you saw an African in Edinburgh, you knew that he was either a student or worked in the hospital or in an old folks home . . . you see a different side to things. But in Glasgow, Africans were asylum seekers

Guy, Cameroonian, migrant worker

These words bring together place, space, migration route and 'race' in a complex and nuanced way and capture a moment in Scotland's very recent immigration history since 2000. They offer a useful starting point for this chapter on the settlement experiences of African people seeking asylum in Central Scotland. They reveal something fascinating about the way in which migration trajectory intersects with place to produce particular experiences of settlement. As Adegoke and Guy so perceptively observe above, the spaces and places certain immigrants occupy shape the experiences they have and how certain identities ('asylum seeker', 'refugee') come to supersede others.

The focus of this chapter is the experiences of some of the Congolese, Ivoirians and Cameroonians living in Glasgow since 2000, many of whom came to be relocated to the city through compulsory dispersal as asylum seekers needing accommodation, and the associations that they developed as part of their story of 'settling in'. In describing how these associations emerged and their many roles and functions, the chapter explores how practices of community building are shaped by two different migration routes in two different geographical places: through dispersal policy as enshrined in the 1999 Immigration and Asylum Act (in the city of Glasgow); and resettlement via the Gateway Protection Programme (in the town of Motherwell). In order to explore the similarities and differences that emerge when thinking through these routes, 'settling in' and how these intersect with place, I draw on extensive ethnographic fieldwork with five Glasgow-based African community associations over a thirty-month period (between 2007 and early 2011) and forty-eight in-depth interviews with members, as well as conversations with members, from one Motherwell-based Congolese association.

The associations in this research were selected based on a number of criteria. First, I identified them from my previous experience of working as a French interpreter in and around Glasgow from 2000 to 2010. This role gave me a broad base of knowledge from which the research could be developed, as well as a unique insight into the way policies affecting many asylum seekers and refugees were implemented in practice and experienced. Second, at the beginning of the work in 2007, these were the only established 'non-political' groups from Central and Western Africa in Glasgow. Third, they had each been in formal existence as constituted associations for roughly the same length of time (since 2003/4). This meant that they had each emerged from a broadly similar (UK) political context, which, though evolving throughout the duration of the project, provided a useful framework for studying how the associations developed in a comparative sense and the constraints and opportunities they have experienced. Fourth, the political geography of members' nationalities added another interesting comparative layer: the colonial histories of their home countries were predominantly French/Belgian and so they did not necessarily share a linguistic, historical, political or cultural connection to the UK.

In drawing from their experiences, this chapter seeks to do three things. It tries first to analyse how community building is carried out by dispersed African asylum seekers and refugees in Glasgow. Rather than adopting a discourse of 'integration', which is present in much of the scholarly and policy literature in relation to refugees, this chapter stresses grassroots mobilisation as a way for newly establishing asylum seeker and refugee communities to 'settle in' on their own terms. Second, the chapter offers an examination of how experiences of settlement, feelings of belonging and 'rooting in' come to be shaped by place, by different migration routes and by differences in immigration status. Third, by looking backwards and forwards, it concludes with observations about future dispersal programmes and what lessons may be learned, particularly with reference to the most recent incarnation of Gateway Protection Programme, the Syrian Vulnerable Persons Resettlement Programme.

NEW PLACES, NEW BELONGINGS: DISPERSAL TO GLASGOW

People of African origin and descent have had a long historical contact with Scotland and the Scottish people. From the eighteenth century, this presence has been perceived as dominated by slavery and colonialism, and as such, contemporary African experiences for the most part have remained framed by the rubric 'Scotland, Slavery and Empire'. This is despite the reality that African/Caribbean peoples have been coming to Scotland for a variety of reasons, including employment and study. Since 2000, however, Scotland's African population has grown significantly and the first point of departure in this story of increased African immigration is a consideration of dispersal. This is the process by which the UK Home Office moves asylum seekers, on a no-choice basis, to one of a number of UK cities in order to effectively 'spread the burden' of asylum away from the South East of England.[1] In itself, dispersal as a policy response is not new, but has formed an occasional part of Britain's immigration strategy since the 1970s with Ugandan Asians and Vietnamese 'boat people' and in the 1990s with refugees from Bosnia and Kosovo. Overall, these groups were accepted within the UK, albeit with some wariness.[2] In due course, dispersal policy was to radically change the ethnic geography of the city of Glasgow.

In these instances of refugee immigration, the UK Government has typically relied heavily upon the voluntary sector and already established communities for much of the resettlement work of dispersed programme refugees.[3] Until the 1990s, the UK had no domestic asylum legislation. Prior to 1999, therefore, the ethnic geographies of the UK largely reflected the agency of the minority groups themselves, with the majority of newly arrived refugees settling in areas where they had family or friends, or where there were pre-existing communities, most commonly London or the South East of England.[4] Precursors to the 1999 dispersal system of asylum seekers were the 1994 Bosnia Project and the 1999 Kosovan Programme, both of which were viewed as relatively successful in integrating refugees in UK society as individuals settled in the long-term in dispersal areas.[5] The dominant model in Scotland since 1995 has been one of multi-agency working, recognising the value of close collaboration in matters of settlement and support. Moreover, the absence of any pre-existing Bosnian (and Kosovar) communities in any part of the UK prior to these programmes may have constrained the onward migration decisions of refugees. Therefore, it was this, rather than a desire to stay in areas of original dispersal, that led to their continued settlement.[6]

The 1999 Immigration and Asylum Act was to dramatically alter some of these patterns of settlement. Alongside compulsory relocation on a no-choice basis, this legislation was part of a wider set of measures aimed at people claiming asylum. New forms of social and economic segregation, including the removal of the right to work and access to education and mainstream welfare in the UK were introduced. In addition, a nationally coordinated resettlement and support system, the National Asylum Support System (NASS), was established.[7] Moreover, as it had done historically, the UK Government at the time (and since) has made explicit its aim of expanding the role and expectations of voluntary sector agencies and community groups in the provision of services in new dispersal areas.[8]

Support and accommodation were provided to asylum seekers via contracts with housing providers, to populate housing that was in 'low demand' and was unpopular with both tenants and applicants. There was also a strong association between dispersal locations and social deprivation, a pattern which has been well documented.[9] Glasgow City Council (GCC) was the first, and remains the only, local authority in Scotland accommodating dispersed asylum seekers in high-rise accommodation across a number of neighbourhoods in Glasgow. Most asylum seekers in the city were housed in Glasgow Housing Association property until a contract change in 2012.[10] Current estimates are that there are around 20,000 refugees and asylum seekers resident in Scotland, mainly in Glasgow, a development that has significantly altered the ethnic geography of the city. But behind this demographic change due to asylum migration is a much bigger story about Scotland's increased ethnic minorities which is worth highlighting. In the ten years between the 2001 and 2011 censuses, Scotland's ethnic minority population grew. Ethnic minorities are people who have described themselves as other than 'white Scottish' and so includes 'white other British' who are

Scotland's first minority, followed by Poles, Scotland's second minority group. Moreover, Scotland's diversity has increased both overall and in every local authority across the country.[11]

LA VIE ASSOCIATIVE: NEWLY SETTLING AFRICANS AND THEIR ASSOCIATIONS IN GLASGOW

Many asylum seekers come from non-Commonwealth countries which have a relatively limited historical relationship with the UK and subsequently there are few existing 'communities' there. It is important to note that not all asylum seekers are non-white, although the majority are. Across the UK, the ten leading countries of origin in 2011 were Iran, Pakistan, Sri Lanka, Afghanistan, Eritrea, China, Nigeria, Libya, Sudan and Bangladesh.[12] It is difficult to know how this maps onto the Scottish context, as data relating to the nationalities of asylum applicants in Scotland are not provided by the Home Office, but the languages most commonly spoken by applicants in 2012 can give us an indication of the leading countries of origin. The first is Farsi (22 per cent), the second Arabic (21 per cent) and the third English (16 per cent).[13] African immigration to Scotland is a special case, and comparing census data between 2001 and 2011 gives some indications of the growth in people identifying as 'black African' (African and Caribbean). In 2001, Springburn in North Glasgow, a key dispersal site in the city, had 322 African residents and the highest proportion in Scotland. By 2011 Springburn's African population had increased rapidly to 2,360, and is now followed by other wards in Glasgow and in Aberdeen, all of which had fewer than 100 African residents in 2001 but between 690 and 1,100 residents by 2011.[14] Significant numbers of these African people are asylum seekers from countries that previously did not have significant immigrant representation in Glasgow. According to the 2011 census, the African population in Scotland has grown from 5,000 in 2001 to 30,000 in 2011. This six-fold increase between 2001 and 2011 has been put down to dispersal, immigration and family building, and has created new areas of settlement larger than the ones that had been its main clusters in 2001.[15]

Dispersal across the UK was challenging both for the majority of people arriving and for the host communities. For the many hundreds of people coming to Glasgow, with its overwhelmingly white population and distinctive urban culture, the experience of settling in was daunting. The absence of already established minorities and communities to provide social and cultural connections meant extremely limited access to social networks of co-nationals, which posed problems of social and emotional isolation. It was against this background that a number of African associations began to emerge through a process of collective self-help. As Joelle, an Ivoirian asylum seeker, remarked:

I met a Congolese woman at the hotel ... we had been sent to Glasgow together ... I didn't really know Glasgow and she took me to the African shop Solly's. So one day I was on the bus going to Solly's and there were two women on the bus talking, they were talking French, Africans you know ... and before getting off I said to one of them, you are from the Ivory Coast, the other I knew wasn't because of her accent, and she said yes. And that's how I met Annie ... and she said to me we are putting together a small group, because we are on our own here. I gave her my number, and that's how I joined the group. When I went along to the first meeting, it was in Layla's flat in my own block, and I could see that these were all people who were feeling very isolated ... And the president at the time, she had said she wanted to create this group because she had also felt too isolated at the beginning, she knew others would feel the same and she didn't want people to go through that ... and that we were all asylum seekers too.

The 'ghettoisation' of asylum seekers in areas with high levels of migrant concentration produced social and spatial segregation of the kind that Joelle describes above and that Adegoke referred to at the beginning of this chapter.[16] Unsurprisingly perhaps, given their limited resources which might have enabled them to move more freely about the city, asylum seekers tended to restrict their movements to the same neighbourhoods of their daily encounters, such as bus stops, post offices, local shops, schools and churches, at community drop-ins and English language classes (English for Speakers of Other Languages, ESOL). These all became central to the creation of social connections, sharing of knowledge and 'rooting in'.

Given the restrictions on work and education, people claiming asylum quickly found each other in these spaces of encounter, forming informal friendship groups, which then became formally constituted associations. Each of these associations had what can be described as a broad and a core membership. The broad membership included members who attended drop-ins or monthly meetings as interested members, or association-organised events, with a less direct responsibility for the running of association business. This was instead the role of core members who were responsible for keeping the association going, often holding office-bearing roles such as President (or Chair), Vice-President, Secretary, Vice-Secretary, Treasurer, Vice-Treasurer, and other roles as decided from time to time, for example, Public Relations Officer, Advisor, Social

Affairs Secretary, Membership Officer. Core members would also represent the association at meetings with external partners such as the Scottish Refugee Council or integration networks.

Association des Femmes Ivoiriennes de Glasgow (AFIG) was set up in 2004 by a small number of asylum-seeking women from the Ivory Coast. AFIG had a broad membership of around 25 and a core group of 10 active members. Africa Umoja Scotland is a generalist African charity, established in 2002, by a group of Congolese asylum-seeker men and women. It has approximately 100 listed members, with a core membership of around 10, although numbers have fluctuated since 2007. Cameroonian Association and Sympathisers in Scotland (CAMASS) started to meet as a solidarity group in January 2003, formalising activities in 2004. It has a mixed membership of around 60, with a core group of around 30 members meeting regularly. Association of English Speaking Cameroonians in Scotland (ASSECS) formed in 2004 as a small social group of English-speaking Cameroonians. Founding male and female members were in fact members also involved in CAMASS but, as Anglophone Cameroonians, they felt under-represented within a Francophone group. It has a core membership of about 25 members, and a broader grouping of around 50. Karibu's beginnings date to 2001, when a small group of Swahili- and French-speaking African women asylum seekers came together in the north of Glasgow. A registered charity since 2007, it runs two social enterprises, ESOL classes and a monthly drop-in. It has an estimated membership of 100 female members from Sub-Saharan Africa. Motherwell African Refugee Community Association (MARCA) established itself in 2009, with a small membership of around 15, and supports Congolese refugees dispersed to Motherwell. These associations share a number of characteristics and Figure 8.1 captures their multifaceted nature.

In each case, founding members met each other through chance encounters on buses, in shops, in high-rise flats, in service-provider offices and at Home Office reporting centres. The combination of the novelty of their surroundings, of social isolation and boredom, and poverty and dependence, all of which characterised the experience of compulsory dispersal, brought people together. In each case, with the exception of ASSECS, most members were asylum seekers. ASSECS members were mainly migrants who had come to Glasgow for work or study. Each association would meet in members' homes, with the exception of Karibu, which also runs a monthly drop-in at a local church hall. The associations each offer members a place to socialise and meet people from a similar ethnic background as well as provide behind-the-scenes

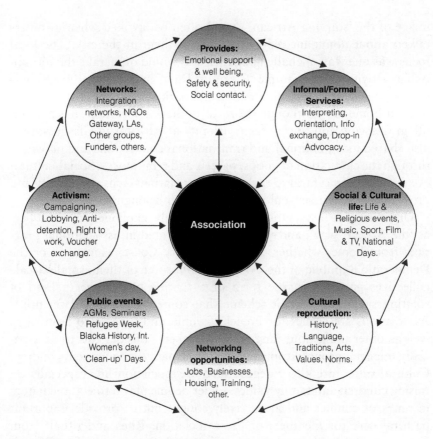

Figure 8.1 Association roles and functions.

support, advice and information. Much association time is taken up with issues around the asylum process, the translation of Home Office letters into meaningful language, signposting to support service and advocacy and campaigning work to basic information on getting by, where to shop for African food and how to use the public transport system. As the Ivoirienne asylum seeker Joelle reported:

> Meetings were a way to come together, to try to enjoy ourselves together, eat our food, talk about home, listen to music . . . and to forget. But also to say, you know, I got this letter what does it mean, or, you know, if you needed to speak to your lawyer, or to know if your lawyer has a good reputation, or for advice or information, if someone has had the same experience, what they did, that kind of thing[.]

An important objective is the attempt to improve Scottish attitudes to asylum seekers and raise more awareness of Africans in Glasgow. The image of the 'starving African' would often be invoked when members talked about dominant representations of them in the city. The local focus was one way of challenging this, and would often take the form of public activities, for example 'Clean up Days' in their local neighbourhoods (which were also dispersal neighbourhoods), the rationale being 'it's our home too'. Although the focus of these associations has been on life in Glasgow and raising their visibility as Africans in Glasgow, they also shared local, national and transnational connections and networks through the circulation of goods, parcels and remittances. Social-cultural events have been central to each of the associations' sense of identity and provide a way to assert cultural identity and belonging.

Organising as associations was commonly explained by members as 'the African way', and was directly replicated in associational practices from home, whether that be the Ivory Coast, Cameroon or the Democratic Republic of the Congo. Within some of them, smaller-scale collectives grew up in the form of a *tontine* or *Ndanje* (a kind of rotating saving and credit scheme that some members had set up).[17] Associations are spaces for French, Swahili and Lingala to flourish as well as other indigenous languages. Members consider this to be especially important for the transmission of the native languages to children. Cultural values are also foregrounded in association life: especially on raising children and family values. Older people play a role as mediators in times of conflict and are actively sought out to provide important pastoral care for members of the association. Rites and rituals from home are respected, reproduced and sometimes reinvented to fit with life in Glasgow. Finally, each association sometimes organises high-profile public events such as national days, International Women's Day events, Commonwealth Day celebrations, community clean-up days and Refugee Week community events that are widely attended by their members, as well as other African groups and the broader Scottish community.

From this broad overview, three conclusions can be drawn. First, these associations provide both a set of specific functions of support for their members, enabling the strengthening of cultural and ethnic identities *and* a critical space to mobilise and challenge structural factors affecting them. Second, members' routes to the UK, in these cases mainly through asylum, directly shape what these associations do and the types of services they provide to members. Third, place, in terms of dispersal neighbourhoods, offered important opportunities to mobilise and challenge the relative invisibility of the migrant groups.

'DOWNTOWN YAOUNDÉ': RECONNECTING TO HOME AND AFRICAN-NESS THROUGH THE ASSOCIATION

As explained above, African associations meet monthly in members' homes. This act of opening one's private home space to others is beneficial in a number of ways. First, it offers a degree of certainty in an unpredictable environment when awaiting a decision from the Home Office. This became an important element of the process for developing belonging for individuals and groups in a safe space, providing some familiarity in a place of newness. Second, it creates opportunities to collectively and individually preserve cultural heritage, enact ethnic identity and adapt these to the new environment. As Sandrine, a Cameroonian woman, put it:

> ASSECS during these years has played a very crucial role by creating a platform where new English Speaking Cameroonians coming to Scotland can meet in our homes and speak pigin, and eat eru [wild leaf vegetable], achu [pounded cocoyam] and fufu-corn [cassava] giving them that sense of home. ASSECS also has played some very important role to supporting members both emotionally, physically and psychologically.

This leads to the re-creation of 'home' practices, of homeliness, and the renewal of African identities through food and music and sociability. Third, the reshaping of the private home space as the community space provides ways to familiarise immigrants with the new (the city) while practising the old (social practices from the homeland). Femi, a male Cameroonian asylum seeker, reflected with a sense of nostalgia:

> Now that I have the group, when we are together it feels like downtown Yaoundé [laughs]. Really it does, because when you are together, it's like . . . it's like you are transported through time, you are back there . . . You visit your friends like you do back home, you talk like back home, you eat the food, you laugh at the same things, you listen to music, you feel so at home . . . [smiles broadly]. Yes! I can say this; it makes you feel at home . . . And you know because you meet every month, you look forward to it. It's like you know you are going home every month, it sounds crazy but that is how it feels. You know in Cameroon, you don't live alone like here, your door closed, and no contact with people outside. No. You live with other people. And even, you know, after . . . when I go home, I am alone, I feel sad, but then I feel happy 'cos I know they are there so it makes me feel at home too.

This homely familiarity is not to be underestimated or undervalued: it recreates important moments of ethnic and cultural identity and belonging in a social and political context of restrictions, poverty, social isolation, boredom and waiting. The associations work very hard to keep their members culturally, emotionally, socially and practically connected to both their past and their new present. This is done through an intensive sharing and circulation of cultural practices and rituals – through dance, song, music, food, ideas, storytelling, life celebrations, wakes, *tontine* and *ndanje* – and of material goods, including music, DVDs, beauty products, clothes and material for making clothes, magazines, books and so on. All of this suggests the significant ways in which the ordinary event of the meeting held in the new home space can do something quite extraordinary, connecting people up across time, place and space. These are effectively leisure moments, and such leisure moments for refugees should be recognised as forms of belonging and freedom. Music, food and dancing are known for their importance in cultural reproduction, but also have liberating effects, to exist not only as refugees at these times but also as Cameroonians, Ivoirians and Congolese, and as Africans.[18] Familiar practices, expressed in clothing, are used to reproduce national identities in exile, and this is often the case for community events – national days, AGMs or as part of Refugee Week – as well as ritual events, such as births, christenings and weddings.

Figure 8.2 AFIG National Day celebration. © Teresa Piacentini.

Figure 8.3 CAMASS AGM, Sighthill, Glasgow, 2010. © Teresa Piacentini.

Figure 8.4 AFIG church christening, St Roch's church, Royston, Glasgow, 2010. © Teresa Piacentini.

These events again represent safe spaces for the expression of cultural and sometimes a political identity; they are moments of visible and proud assertions of cultural origins and African-ness in Scotland. Interestingly, they are also spaces for asserting forms of hybridity,

Figure 8.5 Traditional christening celebration, St Roch's church hall, Royston, Glasgow, 2010. © Teresa Piacentini.

Figure 8.6 Karibu tartan textile initiative, 2010. © Teresa Piacentini.

with cultural symbols from Scotland appropriated, merged and adapted to communicate a message of new forms of belonging, suggesting in material and symbolic terms a hybrid of African-ness and Scottish-ness.

ACHETER AFRICAIN: MEETING THE NEEDS OF GLASGOW'S AFRICAN POPULATION

'Settling in' is also about creating those opportunities to build foundations beyond the social and cultural. The emergence of hybrid shops tells another part of this story of African migration to Scotland. They have been slowly appearing across Glasgow and most obviously in the Southside, where there are neighbourhoods with long-established minority ethnic communities. The Southside area covers Govanhill and Pollokshields, both with the highest black and minority ethnic populations in Glasgow, according to the 2011 census: Pollokshields East (53 per cent), Pollokshields West (37 per cent), Govanhill (33 per cent).[19] Over the course of generations, these localities have become popular destinations because of the number and range of their 'ethnic' shops. Karibu members explained that after they had visited the drop-in (which took place in Govanhill), they would do their food shopping from the local shops in the heart of East Pollokshields neighbourhood (Albert Drive) or Govanhill (Allison Street). Both streets combine tenement flats with grocery stores, halal butchers, banks, lawyers' offices, travel agents, telecommunications businesses and shops selling textiles and cloth, all services tailored to the specific needs of the majority South Asian population. When I asked Malika, a Congolese member of Karibu, whether Congolese cooking used the same ingredients as South Asian cooking, she told me that people initially shopped there for spices and herbs, but then they could also buy manioc flour, cassava root, plantains and yams, as well as large bags of rice and maize meal, all staples in much African cooking. The local shops had good deals on international phone cards and for sending money home via one of the many Western Union services on offer. Also, slowly and steadily since 2000, many South Asian grocers have been stocking manioc flour alongside gram flour, and cassava root and plantains alongside okra and gourds. The main thoroughfares of these neighbourhoods are also changing as their numerous stores either advertise African foods or combine them with those of other ethnicities in order to appeal to an increasingly varied customer base.

These developments, however, are not unique to the Southside, as in other dispersal areas in Glasgow and across the city similar types of shops and services have opened for business. Both they and established food markets have become landmarks in their own right, often used to help people navigate unfamiliar neighbourhoods. Many people talk about localities in terms of these shops or which bus to take to get from A to B in relation to those situated on a particular route:

Figure 8.7 Govanhill greengrocer, Glasgow, 2016. © Teresa Piacentini.

Figure 8.8 African café, Pollokshaws, Glasgow, 2015. © Teresa Piacentini.

At the AGM of the Congo Brazzaville Association, Heloise a member and also then president of Karibu was invited to make a speech. The President wanted to honour one member in particular for her hard work and commitment to the community. She began to speak very passionately. She reminded members that they had to be proactive, they had to take action, and they could not wait for things to happen but had to make it happen for themselves. She compared the African community to the Pakistani community and the Chinese community, saying that they had worked hard and built their community and their place in Glasgow, but that they too had begun with very little. They had become political players, they were economically independent, and they looked after their own. But, she said, the African community still had much work to do, to make its mark, to make its contribution. She made reference to the need in Glasgow for shops selling specialist goods, clothes, music and so on. The spirit of this speech was very much in keeping with the earlier JFK quote: what can you do for your country, your 'community'.[20]

Heloise's remarks highlight the self-representations of Africans in Glasgow in seeing themselves not only in terms of 'African-ness', but as a Black, Asian or Minority Ethnic (BAME) population, aligning with other minorities. At community events speakers would often make reference to what was unique about them – their African-ness – alongside their national identity, while at the same time emphasising what they perceived as shared values and symbols that they identified with other 'racialised minorities', interchangeably signified as 'Asian Muslims', 'Pakistanis' or 'Asians' rather than with the wider (and 'whiter') Scottish community. They based this knowledge on the development of what they saw as an ethnicised economy that also serviced their needs, the Asian supermarkets and shops they frequented, but also in the presence of BAME people in politics and employment. They looked for visible cues to then draw comparisons with 'what could be' for them in the future. Their understanding was that the local Indian, Pakistani, Bangladeshi and Chinese populations in Glasgow had been new like them when they arrived and were now settled and integrated. This was a story also retold to them by others.

One CAMASS National Day event brought together around fifty Cameroonians and friends for an evening of music, traditional dance, fashion and food. A Glasgow SNP Councillor, Jahangir Hanif, had also been invited as a guest of honour. After the entertainment, Councillor Hanif made a speech making direct references to comparisons with the 'African' and 'Asian' community. He drew parallels between the two communities, about a shared work ethic, belief in family values, and about how their respective 'ethnicities' can be mobilised as a political, economic and cultural resource. He addressed this group as the next generation of immigrants settling who could bring their expertise and make their mark on Glasgow and Scottish society. Statements such as these, to be retold by members to each other and others (as Heloise did in the earlier field note), reflect a desire for settlement and a projection of themselves as part of the Scottish minority landscape, not as temporary residents.

The notion of a community life-cycle, moving at different paces for different settled and settling groups, and of a changing social and cultural landscape, visibly materialises in these neighbourhoods and on these routes. Victoria Road, the main road passing through the heart of Govanhill, is also changing. Since fieldwork began in 2007, a number of new 'African' stores have become established selling foodstuffs, beauty products, music and DVDs. In addition, there is an 'international barbers' and an 'African' beautician/hairdresser, all within walking distance of each other in Govanhill. They display posters and photos in their windows to promote the ethnic products used and styles favoured by their 'Asian' and 'African' clientele.

These examples highlight a new and interesting development in Glasgow, which is a marker not only of 'settlement', but of how African migrants adapt to their changing physical and material landscape, and how this landscape adapts to them. By this I mean the ways in which the newly settling African population attempts to build institutional completeness in the sense of a drive to establish institutions that will increase a population or ethnic minority's relative autonomy vis-à-vis the wider society.[21] There is also evidence of others adapting, with already well-established ethnic stores 'rebranding' in offering 'Asian, African and European food'. This, I would suggest, is not just about settlement but finding a cultural home within the established 'South Asian communities' and how these established populations also adapt to changes in the cultural landscape. People cross the city of Glasgow to go to these shops. Again, as with the associations meetings in the high-rise flats, in these cultural spaces there is a sense of sanctuary and safety through the familiarity they offer. That shops are adapting sends a message that this extended clientele is also welcome through their doors. They provide a place to feel safe in a 'new place', experiences of which were otherwise marked by the sense of hostility and racism towards asylum seekers and refugees. Indeed, they are a long way from the bleak rubbish-strewn welcome to Glasgow many faced when they first arrived in the high-rise flats.

Dispersal of course takes different forms, and in 2007 a separate group of Congolese refugees were settled outside of Glasgow. The remainder of this chapter explores some of their experiences.

GATEWAY PROTECTION PROGRAMME AND CONGOLESE REFUGEES TO MOTHERWELL: A DIFFERENT TALE OF SETTLING IN

In 2005 North Lanarkshire Council (NLC) agreed to take part in the Gateway Protection Programme (GPP), the UK's official refugee resettlement programme to which it became a signatory in 2004. As with asylum, the participating local authorities tend to be those in areas with low-demand housing. Of the eighteen authorities involved in 2012, twelve were in the North of England and one in Scotland (North Lanarkshire).[22] NLC was the only council to do so (until the introduction of the Syrian Vulnerable Person Resettlement Scheme in 2015). Under GPP, highly vulnerable refugees and their families, identified by the UN's refugee agency UNHCR, are resettled under arrangements between councils and the Home Office. GPP offers a legal route for a quota of UNHCR-identified refugees to move to the United Kingdom and enjoys cross-party support. The programme is distinct from and in addition to ordinary provisions for claiming asylum in the United Kingdom.

In 2007 seventy-seven refugees from the Democratic Republic of Congo were resettled in Motherwell, a large town and former burgh in North Lanarkshire, Scotland, located 17 miles south east of Glasgow. Motherwell has a population of 32,120, with a much smaller population of BAME (0.2 per cent) compared to Glasgow (11.6 per cent) according to the 2011 census.[23]

GPP refugees have permission to work, and to access mainstream benefits and further education, and in Motherwell were housed across the town in low-level social housing. A number of the Congolese resettled there were involved in the Glasgow-based associations, taking part in meetings and community events. Part of this came about through bridging work between Africa Umoja Scotland and NLC. Through its informal work and networks, Africa Umoja Scotland has emerged as a prominent African community group and played a key role in supporting the settlement of Gateway resettled refugees in Motherwell. When the Congolese families arrived in Motherwell, it liaised between the families and NLC in the early months, providing essential interpreting and translation services as well as acting as general cultural advisors to the Council. Karibu was also involved in supporting Congolese women, and both associations contributed to ensuring the flow of information between Congolese people in Glasgow and Motherwell, building links to their culture, heritage and social networks in Scotland and beyond.

Given they had immediate access to work, education and mainstream benefits, as might have been expected, the experiences of Gateway resettled Congolese were different to dispersed Africans in Glasgow. Families were allocated social rented accommodation in different parts of Motherwell, to ensure that no 'refugee ghetto' would be created. The main support role was provided by a team of existing Tenancy Support Workers, three of whom were seconded to work with the refugees.[24] But perhaps the most striking difference with their dispersed counterparts in Glasgow was the absence of associations in the experience of settling in and the performance of cultural identity and belonging. The latter was central to asylum seekers in Glasgow but apparently of little relevance in Motherwell. There, some refugees spoke about a reluctance to form a community association or indeed identify as a community, a pattern evidenced in other research conducted with Motherwell Congolese refugees, which found a resistance to the establishment of a refugee association, which refugees believed would impede integration.[25]

In contrast to the dispersed Congolese, Ivoirians and Cameroonians in Glasgow, the Motherwell Congolese refugees had strong connections with other Congolese refugees with whom they had bonded in the refugee camps and who were settled elsewhere in the UK and in other European cities. Therefore, a different kind of diasporic community emerged in Motherwell, but one that was much more transnational in nature, in contrast to the largely localised diaspora in Glasgow. It could be argued that the dispersal programme produced quite different effects: paradoxically the African communities in Glasgow had to find much more sustained and creative ways to settle in because of their more precarious position. This is not to suggest that the more precarious the position the better the settlement outcome. Far from it. But it does highlight that the interplay of migration route and place produces really quite different settlement responses and effects.

It is instructive to compare and contrast some of the settlement experiences and outcomes. Both Glasgow and Motherwell have a long history of inward migration involving white minorities (Irish, East Europeans and other migrant workers) and this shared memory of immigration might have contributed to local people welcoming new migrants.[26] However, in both sites there have been experiences of racism, a feeling that 'local people' were in fact a little reserved and distant. Yet most refugees in both locations believed that this simply reflected the wide range of human nature, with 'good and bad everywhere'. In Glasgow and Motherwell, some spoke of experiencing racism, but this time from new neighbours and local people in predominantly 'white' neighbourhoods. Many talked about dispersal sites as places of threat and fear, of being racially abused in their housing estates, at bus stops, in supermarkets and on the streets, including Virginie, a female Ivoirian asylum seeker:

> Ehm at the beginning it was a bit difficult because when I went out, I was often alone and it was a bit hard because I would often come across young people who are a bit ... who don't really like to see black people out and about ... so I often had quite a few problems with them. But after, you know, I got used to it and I would say to myself well it's normal you know ... when I got to know them and they got to see me more and more I saw they were decent people, we just didn't know each other you know, and also, we don't have the same skin, we don't have the same ways of seeing things ... I think it was because we didn't know each other, I think that over time ... well they are going to get used to seeing us.

Virginie went on to explain she was reluctant to report racialised crime or victimisation because she did not want to be seen as 'a trouble maker'. That people did not want to raise this as a problem demonstrates one of the ways in which society operates within a racialised order and how social relations are indeed racialised.[27] It is important not to use assumptions about the apparent absence of racism to consolidate the myth that it does not exist in Scotland, a rose-tinted refugee-ified retelling of the story that 'We're a' Jock Tamson's bairns'. Racism is part of Scotland's past and present. The present focus on post-Brexit racism as a new phenomenon risks erasing people's long-endured experiences of, and resistance to, everyday and institutionalised racism and anti-immigrant sentiment.[28] However, how Africans talked about racism reveals having to find ways of negotiating their difference to help them cope with the experiences of heightened visibility as 'black' Africans, and their invisibility as marginalised and stigmatised asylum seekers with limited rights.[29]

Virginie's assessment of the situation featured in the narratives of other asylum seekers in Glasgow and refugees in Motherwell. Members would speak about being told to 'go home' and being racially abused at bus stops and at the concierge stations of the high-rise flats by 'locals', either young people or others described as being drunk or on drugs. Experiences would be recounted in equally pragmatic terms: they 'didn't want to cause trouble'; they felt it more important to 'keep their head down'; that 'white' Scottish people were simply 'not used to seeing black faces' and over time this would improve as 'more "black" people settled in Glasgow'.[30]

The following field note illustrates the kind of racism encountered. During a CAMASS meeting in a church hall in the north of Glasgow, a group of young people we had seen hanging around outside the hall began to enter, asking if they could use the toilet. The hall was in the heart of a housing scheme of high-rise flats and most likely the local neighbourhood of these young people. The members allowed them to come in but they continually interrupted and became disruptive. After about 20 minutes, two CAMASS members said to them they could not stay anymore as it was a private meeting. The young people, who looked to be in their mid-teens, started swearing at the members, shouting racial abuse and that it was 'their' church hall and 'they had every right' to enter as they wished. Although we didn't feel necessarily in danger, things were taking an ugly turn. A CAMASS member then called the police to report the abuse. Two police officers arrived 30 minutes later, by which point the young people had gone. When I talked through what had happened with other members, they simply shrugged and said it happens a lot and that it was best just to keep their heads down and avoid drawing attention. From their experience, also, the police always arrive too late for anything to be done.

Racism was indeed an everyday occurrence, either as anti-immigrant and racist abuse shouted in the street or in the form of more nuanced micro-aggressions, such as unsolicited touching of children's hair on buses or people asking whether as French-speaking Africans they spoke 'real French'. For the Congolese, Ivoirian and Cameroonian asylum seekers in Glasgow, the racism they experienced had less of an impact on their daily lives than the effects of trying to cope with the uncertainty as they awaited a decision on their asylum claims. However, it did shape their experience of settling in. Of note is that these racist acts occurred in localities and contexts that simply cannot always be avoided, such as bus stops, shops, post offices and at entrances to high-rise blocks. One of the most frequently deployed risk-avoidance strategies in Glasgow was to avoid being outside the relative safety of the home space in the evening.[31] Similar experiences were reported in Motherwell. Despite instances of racist behaviour, people were reported as being generally friendly,[32] but undoubtedly the housing strategies in both sites have contributed to the racialisation of asylum seekers. Their settlement in Glasgow in high-rise flats became identified with those seeking asylum and led to a kind of racialised ghettoisation.[33] Adegoke already explained some of this at the beginning of the chapter. Being African in a high-rise neighbourhood came to be equated with immigrant status – both in Glasgow and indeed elsewhere, as Adegoke and Guy reminded us earlier. In contrast, the 'whiteness' of Motherwell and their dispersal across the town to avoid this ghettoisation meant the Congolese as black Africans would equally stand out as different because of their immigration status as refugees. Racism and racialisation could not be avoided, was difficult to challenge and revealed its pervasive nature in Scotland.

As with Glasgow, the Motherwell Congolese frequently visited each other's homes, and this has been central to developing a sense of community and sustaining relationships. In Glasgow these were more formalised through the organisation of associations, but they occurred in less formal and less structured ways as well. What became clear from association practices and from conversations with Motherwell Congolese was that, regardless of location, the rituals of life celebrations were transported from home and adapted to the new setting in Scotland. It was also clear that people gained mutual support by being able to discuss issues to help and understand their new lives. These social relationships and sense of both shared national identities and an African identity made it possible to continue to function on an everyday basis both at an individual and family level, which would not otherwise be the case. In both places people talked of their friends as 'family' and it was clear that they meant this in a close and deeply felt sense. For many, local church communities – Catholic, Pentecostal, Baptist, Jehovah Witness and non-denominational Christian – were also extremely important. As well as providing a sense of meaning, belonging and consistency, practising a faith provided opportunities to meet 'local Scottish' people, build social networks and fulfil important roles, for example as pastor, member of the choir or working in the church café. In Glasgow there has been far greater opportunity with more churches across a number of faiths. There is now a Congolese French-speaking church established in the north of the city that has attracted a growing congregation.

Although these parallels do exist, there remain several differences. Motherwell's smaller BAME population meant that the Congolese refugees were going to be much more visible compared to ethnically diverse parts of Glasgow. In this respect, we can see place and race intersecting in a very explicit way. GPP provides access to services, a broader range of rights and entitlements and hence greater 'stability' and security from the outset. Dispersed asylum seekers are subject to a much more punitive asylum process underpinned by uncertainty and liminality. It was precisely this context that was a key driver in encouraging the Congolese, Cameroonians and Ivoirians in Glasgow to organise into associations. The greater unpredictability of their lives led to a pressing need for emotional and cultural support, information sharing and practical support, all of which engendered a different kind of response. In Glasgow the concentrated housing of asylum seekers in high-rise neighbourhoods produced a kind of 'thrown togetherness' that in turn facilitated the development of kinship networks and sociability, creating spaces and opportunities for reproducing and adapting cultures.[34]

Despite regular contact among themselves, Motherwell Congolese did not necessarily see themselves as a 'group' and were resistant to the formation of a locally based refugee community organisation specifically for Congolese families (despite varying levels of contact with Congolese and other African families in Glasgow). By contrast, for the Glasgow associations a central aim was to create a space for asserting their presence in the city, to become visible and make their voices heard, to set down roots in what was a highly precarious set of circumstances for many. In Glasgow the extremely difficult conditions of dispersal led to the development of a much wider formal and informal network of advocacy and support, of integration networks, dedicated services, information, ESOL, drop-ins and gender-based services than exist in Motherwell. The Gateway programme there did not provide these types of supports perhaps because the built-in twelve-month support programme accompanying its implementation did not recognise the same immediate and long-term needs and responses. Finally, there has not been the emergence of significant levels of ethnic commercial enterprise in Motherwell, in contrast to Glasgow where businesses are developing to meet gaps in consumption and services. This is not a result of a lack of demand, as many Congolese travel to Glasgow to shop, but rather because there were simply not the numbers of either Congolese or wider BME communities to make commercial enterprise a sustainable endeavour.

Place is relevant. While Glasgow and Motherwell have both experienced large-scale Irish immigration in the past and both are post-industrial landscapes, the differences between the city of Glasgow and the town of Motherwell are marked. The more multicultural Glasgow has a much greater capacity to absorb diversity and to provide the infrastructure that supports the development of commercial activities servicing different communities. Motherwell, on the other hand, is less equipped to cope with this absorption of diversity and the creation of spaces of ethnic conviviality, and its much smaller BAME population remains a significant feature of the obstacles individuals face in enacting and practising cultural identities. But beyond that there is the question of the (in)visibility of BAME people – and particularly Congolese/African nationals – across the wider range of public services, in housing, in social services, education, employment, advice services and so forth. Motherwell's limited experience of supporting asylum seekers may also imply the continued 'refugeeness' of its Gateway residents present and future.

SOME CONCLUDING THOUGHTS LOOKING FORWARD . . .

This chapter has explored how different configurations of routes and places interplay to produce quite different settlement outcomes, ways of practising community and of living and reproducing culture and rooting in. It has unpacked ways in which some of Glasgow's African associations have grown and developed, the circumstances of their emergence and how this is shaped by migration route and place. In so doing it has offered an analysis of how 'settling in' comes to be experienced and cultural identity is embodied and performed, and how both are shaped by the contingencies of one's immigration status, with all of the limitations and opportunities those contingencies may bring. As sociologists, the ways in which we imagine and conceptualise stories of settlement, belonging and identity are deeply rooted in the distinctive social, spatial, cultural and political patternings of different urban environments. What I hope to have shown is that spaces of encounter are about much more than the interpersonal, that there are material, political, structural and spatial dimensions that interplay and that migration route and place are two of them.

Even in the short time since my fieldwork was carried out, the city landscape and skylines have changed. Fast forward to 2017 and many of the high-rise flats that dominated the dispersal neighbourhoods where the Congolese, Ivoirians and Cameroonians developed their new communities, built up their associations and set down markers of settlement have been demolished. The high-rise flats, the community flats they housed and shopping centres sprawling beneath them, the post offices, many of those spaces of encounters that were so critical for the development of social bonds and networks have gone. With the demolition programmes has come decanting and relocation, mostly to areas of tenement living and low-level social housing across the city. What this might mean for spaces of encounter for the development of practices of community is uncertain at this point. The refugees described in my research tell new stories of settling in, shaped by this decanting process – tales once more of newness, of not fitting in, of visibility, and in some cases a longing for those high-rise flats 'where it all began'. For the Motherwell Congolese there is an overall sense of settling in, but different kinds of uncertainty exist relating to job and financial security. Despite this, the Congolese community continue to view their lives positively, making it possible to continue to function on an everyday basis, and this, it would seem, is the key similarity between both sites.[35]

Revisiting my research sites has also taken place in a changing political context in which migration has become a dominant story. We have watched as hundreds of thousands of refugees risk their lives on the 'migrant trail' on foot across the Balkan route and over water on the Mediterranean crossings. While our gaze was averted, the UK Government passed the new Immigration Act 2016, arguably its most restrictive and punitive set of immigration laws and policies to date. Brexit has happened, won arguably on a ticket of emboldened xenophobia and anti-immigrant rhetoric. Donald Trump's presidential win has ushered in ill-thought-through extreme vetting orders for certain refugees entering the US alongside promises of building walls. All of this directly shapes the reception and settlement of asylum seekers and refugees in ways that affect the possibilities and opportunities for development of community.

Since 2015, Scotland has been proactively welcoming Syrians through the rather more high-profile Syrian Vulnerable Persons Relocation Scheme, which is modelled on the Gateway programme. To date there have been two thousand arrivals in Scotland and they are being settled in every local authority in the country. For many local authorities it has been a very new experience, as they have never undertaken this kind of settlement before. According to work done by the Community Development Alliance Scotland,[36] there is evidence that the process has been rushed, with four weeks' preparation too short a lead-in time for the necessary structures and support to be put in place. Moreover, because all of Scotland's local authorities are accepting refugees under the Syrian programme, many are being dispersed across Scotland, often to rural areas with very little ethnic diversity and low BAME populations. They have limited infrastructures in place to support them, such as interpreting services, ESOL support in schools and appropriate religious institutions. Issues around employment are also important, particularly in rural areas, where language barriers will be particularly pronounced and where there may be limited opportunity to match skills and expertise. There is, however, some good evidence of multi-partnership working, and this follows the historical patterns of collaboration and multi-agency working in Scotland, as seen with dispersal, the Motherwell Gateway programme, and historically with the reception of Chilean exiles in the 1970s in the West of Scotland. Most studies exploring refugees' experiences in Scotland focus on the experiences of 'refugees', but Diana Kay's study, with its specific focus on the experiences of Chilean exiles in Scotland, is one exception. Interestingly, her analysis of material deprivation, of the effects of the social space of relocation in Scotland in council estates, of feeling betwixt and between, of marginalisation, and of social isolation as experienced by women in particular in the absence of family, directly echoes the experiences of African asylum seekers and refugees that have informed this chapter.[37] But responses to these experiences have been markedly different, from the setting up of associations to address isolation and collectively reimagine and reproduce the experience of home, to the creation of opportunities to establish social, cultural and economic foundations for 'settling in'.

The African asylum seekers and refugees whose experiences are recounted in this chapter felt compelled to respond to their marginalisation in the way they have because of their route into the UK and the places they were sent to. UK immigration policy has changed dramatically since the 1970s. In the present incarnation of dispersal and the current political context, if the experiences of Gateway Congolese in Motherwell and dispersed Congolese, Ivoirians and Cameroonians in Glasgow tell us anything, it is quite clear that more than ever we need to be aware of the intersections of migration trajectory and place, and how these impact upon settlement experiences. Comparing and contrasting the experiences of Africans in Glasgow and Motherwell shows that these combine to produce quite particular outcomes for communities of new populations seeking to settle.

NOTES

1. R. Sales, 'The deserving and the undeserving? Refugees, asylum seekers and welfare in Britain', *Critical Social Policy*, 22:3 (2002), pp. 456–78; P. Hynes, *The Dispersal and Social Exclusion of Asylum Seekers: Between Liminality and Belonging* (Bristol: Polity Press, 2011).
2. E. Kelly, 'Asylum seekers in Scotland: Challenging racism at the heart of government', *Scottish Affairs*, 33 (2000), pp. 23–44; L. Kelly, 'Bosnian refugees in Britain: Questioning community', *Sociology*, 37:1 (2003), pp. 51–68.
3. D. Joly, *Haven or Hell? Asylum Policies and Refugees in Europe* (Basingstoke: Macmillan, 1996).
4. A. Bloch, *The Migration and Settlement of Refugees in Britain* (Basingstoke: Palgrave, 2002).
5. Kelly, 'Bosnian refugees in Britain'.
6. V. Robinson and C. Coleman, 'Lessons learned? A critical review of the government programme to resettle Bosnian quota refugees in the United Kingdom', *International Migration Review*, 34:4 (2000), pp. 1217–44.
7. Hynes, *The Dispersal and Social Exclusion of Asylum Seekers*.
8. R. Zetter and M. Pearl, 'The minority within the minority: Refugee community based organisations in the UK and the impact of restrictionism', *Journal of Ethnic and Migration Studies*, 26:4 (2000), pp. 675–98.
9. K. Wren, 'Supporting asylum seekers and refugees in Glasgow: The role of multi-agency networks', *Journal of Refugee Studies*, 20:3 (2007), pp. 391–413; Hynes, *The Dispersal and Exclusion of Asylum Seekers*; J. Darling, *Producing Urban Asylum Initial Findings*. Research Report (2015), online at https://www.research.manchester.ac.uk/portal/files/31440035/FULL_TEXT.PDF
10. D. Sim, 'Refugee onward migration and the changing ethnic geography of Scotland', *Scottish Geographical Journal*, 131:1 (2015), pp. 1–16.
11. CoDE Briefing, *How has ethnic diversity changed in Scotland?* (2014), online at: http://www.ethnicity.ac.uk/medialibrary/briefings/dynamicsof diversity/code-census-briefing-scotland_v2.pdf (last accessed 20 December 2016).
12. S. Blinder, *Migration to the UK: Asylum*, Briefing Paper (Oxford: University of Oxford Migration Observatory, 2013).
13. Scottish Refugee Council, http://www.scottishrefugeecouncil.org.uk/media/facts_and_figures/asylum_applications_uk_figures
14. CoDE, *How has ethnic diversity changed in Scotland?*
15. Ibid.
16. Bloch, *The Migration and Settlement of Refugees*.

17. T. Piacentini, 'Missing from the picture? Migrant and refugee community organizations' responses to poverty and destitution in Glasgow', *Community Development Journal*, 50:3 (2015), pp. 433–47.

18. G. Hage, 'At home in the entrails of the west: Multiculturalism, ethnic food and migrant home-building', in H. Grace, G. Hage, L. Johnson, J. Langsworth and M. Symonds (eds), *Home/World: Space, Community and Marginality in Sydney's West* (Annandale, NSW: Pluto, 1997), pp. 99–153; H. Lewis, 'Music, dancing and clothing as belonging and freedom among people seeking asylum in the UK', *Leisure Studies*, 34:1 (2014), pp. 42–58.

19. Glasgow City Council, *Briefing paper: Population by Ethnicity in Glasgow* (2013), online at http://www.glasgow.gov.uk/CHttpHandler.ashx?id=17783&p=0 (last accessed 2 December 2016).

20. Field note, GCBA AGM.

21. R. Breton, 'Institutional completeness of ethnic communities and the personal relationships of immigrants', *American Journal of Sociology*, 70 (1964), pp. 193–205.

22. Sim, *Refugee Onward Migration*.

23. Glasgow City Council, *2011 Census – Key Statistics* (2013), https://www.glasgow.gov.uk/CHttpHandler.ashx?id=17543&p=0 (last accessed 2 December 2016); North Lanarkshire Council Key facts: 2016 Demography (2016), http://www.northlanarkshire.gov.uk/index.aspx?articleid=25145 (last accessed 2 December 2016).

24. D. Sim and K. Laughlin, *The Long-Term Integration of Gateway Protection Programme Refugees in Motherwell* (Paisley: UWS/Oxfam, 2014).

25. Sim, 'Refugee onward migration'.

26. M. Rodgers, 'The Lanarkshire Lithuanians', in B. Kay (ed.), *Odyssey: Voices from Scotland's Recent Past* (Edinburgh: Polygon, 1980), pp. 18–25.

27. R. Miles, *Racism after 'Race Relations'* (London: Routledge, 1993).

28. T. Piacentini, 'Refugee solidarity in the everyday', *Soundings: A Journal of Politics and Culture*, 64 (2016), pp. 57–61.

29. A. Fraser and T. Piacentini, 'We belong to Glasgow: The thirdspaces of youth "gangs" and asylum seeker, refugee and migrant groups', in C. Phillips and C. Webster (eds), *New Directions in Race, Ethnicity and Crime* (Abingdon: Routledge, 2014), pp. 55–79.

30. W. W. Daniel, *Racial Discrimination in England* (Harmondsworth: Penguin, 1968).

31. Scottish Refugee Council, *Refugees and British Citizenship*, Policy Briefing (2011), www.scottishrefugeecouncil.org.uk (last accessed 13 July 2016).

32. Sim, *Refugee Onward Migration*.

33. Bloch, *The Migration and Settlement of Refugees*.

34. G. Valentine, 'Living with difference: Reflections on geographies of encounter', *Progress in Human Geography*, 32:3 (2008), pp. 323–37; Hage, 'At home in the entrails of the west'.

35. Sim and Laughlin, *The Long-Term Integration of Gateway Protection Programme Refugees*.
36. Community Development Alliance Scotland, conference presentation 'Sanctuary, Solidarity and Social Capital', online at https://www.commu nitydevelopmentalliancescotland.org/cdas-news/sanctuary-solidarity-and-social-capital-2 (last accessed 2 December 2016).
37. D. Kay, *Chileans in Exile* (Basingstoke: Macmillan Press, 1987).

9

'Race', Place and Territorial Stigmatisation: The Construction of Roma Migrants in and through Govanhill, Scotland

Ashli Mullen

INTRODUCTION

'Object to mass immigration from the EU? Join the Romaphobe club!'

The statement above is not a placard slogan from a far-right protest, nor even a soundbite from one of the many ill-tempered debates that occurred so frequently during the European Union referendum campaign in 2016 (although it may not have seemed out of place in either of these contexts). It is a headline from a newspaper article authored by Tom Harris who, at the time of the article's writing, was a local Labour MP, bemoaning the 'influx' of Roma to Glasgow and warning of dangers to come. Harris' issues with Roma are many:

> filthy and vastly overcrowded living arrangements, organised aggressive begging, the ghetto-isation of local streets where women no longer feel safe to walk due to the presence of large groups of (workless) men, the rifling through domestic wheelie bins by groups of women pushing oddly child-free prams, and a worrying increase in the reporting of aggressive and violent behavior [*sic*] in local schools[.][1]

As the MP for Glasgow South, some of the Romani people that Harris blamed for these problems were in fact his own constituents. Yet he did not appear to recognise them as such: *'my constituents* become angrier and more resentful, because the lives they have worked so hard to build for *themselves and their families are being impinged upon by people* whose culture, way of life and attitude to authority and those around them are *utterly alien'*.[2] This distinction between these so-called legitimate citizens and Romani residents who have arrived more recently permeates media representations and is central to legitimising constructions of Roma as a people whose settlement has resulted in the perceived 'ghettoisation' of Govanhill.

This chapter analyses media representations of Roma migrants in Govanhill from 2007 to 2017. It will examine the portrayal of Roma migrants in Scotland as a problematic population, as articulated through the construction of Govanhill as a problem place. As places produce distinctly local forms of inclusion and exclusion, particular racisms are realised through place, and become taken for granted through them being embedded in the routine fabric of the everyday.[3] Through a process of 'territorial stigmatisation',[4] a 'blemish of place' has been produced with a strong connection forged between Roma and the perceived social ills of Govanhill. A consequence of this racialisation of space is the exacerbation of inequalities, the obscuring of common experiences that Romani people share with other residents, and the creation and exacerbation of divisions, in which Roma are simultaneously subject to and blamed for harsh local conditions.

To explore the ways in which processes of racialisation[5] and place-based stigma intersect and interact, I will begin by describing Romani migration to Scotland, as well as providing a brief sketch of Govanhill. I will then explore early local evidence of the racialisation of Roma migrants in Scotland and how these representations were consolidated through the construction of the 'Govanhill Ghetto'. This will be followed by an analysis of how these ideas have been mobilised by campaigns such as Let's Save Govanhill and amplified by wider political questions in the shadow of the 2014 Scottish Independence Referendum. Throughout, I argue that through a process of territorial stigmatisation, Roma and Govanhill have become inextricably linked, to the extent that it has become possible to evoke the Roma 'problem' without naming Roma at all.

SITUATING ROMA

Roma are historically one of the most systematically oppressed and marginalised populations in Europe and have been subject to centuries of state violence across the continent. Roma continue to experience this legacy today, with discrimination and destitution exacerbating the everyday struggle to survive.[6] The situation of Roma throughout Europe has resulted in concerted political efforts to address the severity of their plight, most notably via the European Decade of Roma Inclusion. Despite such efforts, little in the way of meaningful structural change has been achieved.[7] As Europe's largest transnational minority, Roma are often constructed as a homogenous group, yet the category Roma is an umbrella term that encompasses a wide range of identifications that cut across national, linguistic, occupational and cultural lines. The Council of Europe, for instance, adopts the following common definition: 'Roma, Sinti, Kale and related groups in Europe, including Travellers and the Eastern groups (Dom and Lom), and covers the wide diversity of the groups concerned, including persons who identify themselves as Gypsies.'[8] In this sense, Roma may be more appropriately considered as 'a mosaic of small diverse groups'.[9]

There is a longer history of Romani people migrating westwards in Europe from the fifteenth century onwards and perhaps even earlier.[10] Romani migration from Eastern Europe also occurred throughout the twentieth century, including a small number of refugees from the former Czechoslovakia to the United Kingdom during the 1990s.[11] However, it is primarily the European Union's enlargements of 2004 and 2007 that enabled Roma to move more freely and which eventually led to the establishment of migrant Romani communities in Scotland.[12] Reliable figures on their size are not available.[13] The Scottish Government did,

Figure 9.1 International Roma Day, Govanhill, April 2017. International Roma Day is celebrated internationally and has been held in Govanhill every year since 2014 (organised by the local Roma community organisation, Friends of Romano Lav). It is reported to be the first public procession of Roma in the UK. © Andy Neil.

however, conduct a 'mapping study' in 2013 to establish the scale of Roma immigration.[14] It estimated the total Roma population in Scotland to be between 3,804 and 4,946, with the majority, around 3,500, living in Glasgow, most of whom reside across a small number of streets in Govanhill. This area is Glasgow's most diverse neighbourhood, with approximately fifty-two languages spoken within 'one square mile', as the local refrain commonly goes.

Govanhill has historically been a neighbourhood of settlement for Scotland's new migrant communities and owes much of its diversity to successions of Irish, Jewish, Italian and Pakistani migration from its establishment in the nineteenth century onwards. Its status as a booming industrial economy that was home to 'Dixon's Blazes' (the Govan Iron Works established by the Dixon family in 1837 and closed in 1959) ensured that many seeking work, either via internal migration or from further afield, would set up homes in the tenements which were specifically built to house the industrial labour force.[15] As Suzanne Audrey argues, Govanhill's history is 'inextricably linked to the rise of Glasgow as the Second City of the Empire', and later to the consequences of deindustrialisation.[16] Comparisons are often made between the nineteenth-century reception of Irish migrants and the contemporary situation of Roma; indeed, it is common for Roma migrants in Govanhill to be described as 'the new Irish'.[17] The term is mobilised both pejoratively by those who bemoan the Roma 'influx' and in solidarity[18] by those who appreciate the connections between the contemporary Roma experience and those of their ancestors. The parallels between the two migrant experiences are striking. Audrey describes the conditions that Irish Catholic immigrants in mid-nineteenth-century Glasgow faced as follows:

> They were often the least skilled, undertook the least desirable jobs and lived in the worst housing. Negative stereotypes were in abundance: they were a filthy inferior 'race', arriving in large numbers, multiplying at an alarming rate and turning whole areas into slums; they were immoral yet obsessed with their religion; they were lazy and living off charity, yet taking the jobs of others[.][19]

As we will see, many of the stereotypes within this statement are familiar and could easily be read as a commentary about the reception of Roma migrants in Govanhill today, with the caveat that while still constructed as 'filthy' and 'inferior', the language of 'race' is rarely evoked. Instead, racialised conceptions of cultural difference are articulated and often cited as 'legitimate concerns' about immigration, which function to the same effect.[20]

EARLY LOCAL ARTICULATIONS OF RACIALISATION

As Jan Grill argues in his ethnographic analysis of the 'crystallisation' of the Roma category in Glasgow, Romani migrants were not identified as Roma in the early years of their migration, but were understood within broader categories such as 'Slovaks' or 'Eastern Europeans', or misrecognised as 'asylum seekers' or 'refugees'.[21] This labelling was also reflected in media accounts, but was to change in March 2007. From relative invisibility, Roma migrants were suddenly and dramatically foregrounded in widely publicised accounts of 'race hate gang wars'.[22] The beginnings of the connection forged between Roma and the problems of Govanhill has its roots in a media story that made reference to both. Govanhill was constructed as 'a playground by day', where 'children play unsupervised on busy street corners', and 'a battleground by night', where 'teenagers hurl bricks and bottles at each other'.[23] These battles were said to be 'between groups of Eastern European teenagers and white Scots or Scottish Asians', with violence the response to 'rising racial tensions'.[24] Inter-community tensions were emphasised by the inclusion of quotations from concerned residents, including 'Scots Asians', who were alleged to be 'outspoken about their discomfort with the "Slovakians"', as well as from 'Scots'.[25] Violent imagery of 'nail-studded planks ... spattered with blood' wielded by Slovakian youths who 'charged a group of white Scots' in response to their 'screaming racist insults' was woven throughout these texts to dramatise the allegations.[26]

'Romany groups' were described as incoming communities whose 'cultural differences' were 'adding strain' to the area,[27] but they were afforded no voice, other than indirectly through the mitigating comments of anti-racist campaigners. The 'significant influx of Eastern Europeans over the past 18 months' and the challenges in 'integrating Slovakian Romany families, in particular' became central to the narrative.[28] Despite many of the articles acknowledging that fighting had been instigated by Scottish youth and 'fuelled by rumour and paranoia', the overarching emphasis was on the migrants' 'cultural differences and lack of integration'.[29] This was legitimised through an entire article devoted to the 'huge response' from readers, which reported that 'a discussion has raged over the past week about whether there should be more restrictions on migrants from new European Union states to the UK'.[30] The article asserted that 'the Glasgow South Side community risks being torn apart',[31] and implied that the mere presence of Roma was the provocative cause.

Allegations of child neglect added to this troubled picture, with unidentified residents reported as claiming that 'toddlers and young-sters, originally from Slovakia or the Czech Republic, are allowed to roam the streets unchecked for hours on end'.[32] This was underscored by the observations of journalists: 'We watched as children – the eldest looked no more than five – ran in and out of shops and in front of cars in Allison Street, forcing drivers to make emergency stops. A passing woman who spoke to the children was from the Czech Republic. When asked if she knew where the children's parents were, she pointed to a tenement 50 yards away.'[33]

The theme of child neglect and abuse became central in the months that followed, culminating in an explosive story regarding the alleged sexual exploitation of Roma children. Much of this story centred around a particularly graphic eyewitness account, which recounted in horrific detail an allegation of a nine-year-old girl being sexually assaulted in a tenement close.[34] Further allegations included the following: 'Another Govanhill resident, who wished to remain anonymous, claimed he saw an incident in which two boys aged between seven and nine – who *appeared to be of Roma origin* – were engaged in a sex act together in the backyard of his tenement building.'[35]

Yet crucially, although the article opened with the definitive statement that 'A child prostitution ring which is sexually exploiting immigrant Roma children as young as nine is operating in Glasgow, the Sunday Herald can reveal', no evidence appeared in the article in support of the headline.[36] The police confirmed that they were undertaking an undercover operation based on 'at least six' reports 'involving the alleged abuse of children' that an unnamed senior police source claimed 'specified particular areas in Govanhill and related to the Roma com-munity'.[37] This story did not feature in any other newspaper and did not appear in the *Sunday Herald* again. The only possible reference to this story was in October 2011 when its sister paper, *The Herald*, reported that 'senior police officers are increasingly unhappy with a series of what they say are urban myths springing up in Govanhill over child prostitution involving Roma girls'.[38] To assume that Roma can be identified by their 'appearance', and to foreground ethnicity[39] so strongly is irresponsible reporting that plays into wider racialised stereotypes of Roma criminality and specific accusations regarding their exploitation of children.[40] In a context where dominant discourses 'simultaneously victimize and vilify Romani children, rendering them incapable of experiencing humane childhoods',[41] such stories can lead to the stigmatisation of an entire community.

Efforts to pre-emptively address this potential panic fuelled by racist assumptions were made by the police superintendent in charge of the investigation, who stressed that 'The Roma community would be up in arms itself if the people were aware of these allegations.'[42] Indeed, in an unusual move that may have been an attempt at providing 'balanced' coverage, the author, Neil Mackay, who is the current (2018) editor of the *Sunday Herald*, also published an accompanying piece to the notorious article in the pages that followed it questioning Roma stereotypes and stigma. It included a comment from the police: 'The mistrust of the indigenous community is simply down to ignorance. One or two incidents lead to rumours and soon you have a crime wave that doesn't exist. Things get out of proportion.'[43] Mackay added that 'police were keen to stress that this crime, *if it is happening*, must not be used to tarnish the entire community'.[44] Yet such caution was omitted in the original article itself and indeed was undermined by the inclusion of an unnamed 'senior' police colleague's assertion that there is 'no smoke without fire'.[45]

CONSOLIDATION: CONSTRUCTING THE GOVANHILL GHETTO

Mutual resentment and fear

The idea of the 'ghetto' is a contested concept. Territorial stigmatisation is a necessary condition of a ghetto but is not in and of itself sufficient to constitute one; while definitions vary in emphasis and precise criteria, most focus on ethnic homogeneity as a necessary characteristic, with the caveat that the 'true' ghetto is an ideal type and has rarely existed.[46] As the most ethnically diverse community in Scotland, Govanhill is not a ghetto and indeed might be regarded as its antithesis. Yet the media persistently construct the area as comprised of separate bounded communities united only in mutual resentment and antagonism:

> Walking the network of streets in the heart of Govanhill is a primer for the confused and warring nature of race relations in 21st century Scotland. Local white people and those of Asian origin throw the most appalling slurs at the latest incomers to the area – the Roma community . . . But that's not all. Whites and Asians are daggers drawn at times as well. The word 'Paki' is never long out of earshot and white people are told to 'get back to your white ghettos'.[47]

This latter point was challenged by residents in the readers' letters that followed in the press,[48] yet it proved to be a theme that would be maintained throughout many of the accounts.

Positioned against 'established' communities, Roma were constructed as the archetypal problem neighbour, which was predicated
on assimilationist notions of integration. Their socialising on the streets
was depicted as intimidating, with Roma men especially perceived as a
threat. This gendered aspect of racialisation was articulated through the
reported concerns of local women who 'on their own or even a couple
of women walking past these groups are feeling a bit uncomfortable'.[49]
Such discourses juxtaposing female safety against threatening males is
an old trope, which has its roots in colonial thinking that simultaneously
racialised foreign bodies and constructed white women as vulnerable
subjects in need of patriarchal protection.[50] This construction extended
to children and intimidation was taken to be self-evident: 'Groups of men
and children socialise in the street, chatting in Romanes and gesticulating
largely. You can see that is intimidating.'[51] In addition to the stereotype
of dangerous Roma men, it encodes everyday interactions with loaded
markers of difference and normalises the entitlement of others in the
community to feel threatened by their presence. Conversely, racialising constructions can also intersect with gender in more novel ways:
'You see the Roma women at night with flick-knives, tearing open bin
bags to rifle the rubbish. You can see why that is intimidating.'[52] This
image inverts traditional gender roles,[53] with the animalistic imagery of
scavenging through garbage serving to dehumanise. These discourses
cast the unfamiliar as foreign and threatening. In this sense, Roma are
constructed as disruptive 'bodies out of place'.[54]

Roma were also consistently accused of being a threat to public
services. In the context of education, a schoolteacher contrasted the
right to freedom of movement with the right to education for all and
'made an impassioned appeal' for restrictions on the number of children
who do not speak English in school classrooms. It was a proposal
reportedly rejected as contravening 'race relations' legislation.[55] This
involved playing different communities against one another. One newspaper article claimed that 'the NHS may be "ignoring the majority of
the population" in Glasgow's deprived Govanhill area, while "a lot
of money" is spent on "a very small proportion of the community"',
with 'Eastern European Roma gypsy families' benefiting from 'access
to better health and well being services' than 'the indigenous population' and 'the Asian population'.[56] This distinction is worth considering.
Much of the so-called 'Asian community' are in fact Scottish, yet are
persistently constructed as Other. This distinction would reappear in
several articles that claimed a local school had no Scottish pupils, in
newspapers including the *Scottish Daily Mail*,[57] the *Daily Record*,[58] *The*

Scotsman[59] and *The Herald* (albeit modified as no 'indigenous Scots').[60] In an otherwise positive article on the school challenging this claim, it was stated that the school's register 'might not include a single child born to conventional white Scottish parents', but that many of the children, 'a number of whom were born on these shores', embrace many Scottish traditions and indeed might consider themselves as Scottish.[61] This seems to place a high bar on claims to authentic Scottishness and indicates that despite proclaiming its 'welcoming' and 'inclusive' nature,[62] Scottishness remains implicitly wedded to whiteness in the constructions of many commentators. This tension calls to mind Les Back's idea of 'neighbourhood nationalism',[63] which Alistair Fraser and Teresa Piacentini argue can result in 'particular racisms being muted whilst others flourish'.[64] In this sense, while Govanhill's Scottish 'Asian population' are included within the community aggrieved by the Roma 'influx', and are often strategically quoted as such to deflect from allegations of racism, this inclusion is always partial and their construction as 'Others' never fully disappears from view.

Overcrowding and infestation

Overcrowding and its effects proved to be a determining factor in the direction that discourses of Roma racialisation would take in the early years when Roma made their homes in Govanhill. This was heightened by the constant rehearsal of claims of their 'soaring population'.[65] While there is no means to accurately establish the size of the Roma population, numbers fluctuated across and indeed within the same news outlets, reaching heights of 'between 6000 and 8000',[66] which would double the population and assume around half of Govanhill's residents to be Roma migrants. As one commentator explains, the reporting and contesting of immigration figures is not a neutral conveying of information, but rather is part of a 'numbers game' in which the higher the number, the greater legitimacy that can be afforded to governmental control and 'increasingly "tough" measures, since high numbers fuel a panic of overcrowding'.[67]

This panic would play out over the decade and continues to do so today. Newspapers reported with horror of 'up to four families of three generations, or around 20 people, living in two-bedroom flats', who would 'operate a "hotbedding" system where beds are shared by two people – one who works a day shift and one who works at night'.[68] The director of the Govanhill Housing Association described Govanhill as blighted by 'scenes of poverty comparable to 1960s slums',[69] 'with conditions in some flats "not fit for a dog"'.[70] While multi-generational family living arrangements are common within Romani communities and families might prefer to live with their relatives, it is important to be wary of assuming this to be exclusively a 'cultural' choice, as 'choices' are of course subject to economic constraints and the pooling of rent is often the only viable option for families to avoid outright destitution.[71] Romani residents are disproportionately subject to the worst of local housing conditions and the most egregious of landlords, who often refuse to provide essential maintenance or formal leases. Yet their presence within these rundown flats allowed for an association to be formed between Roma and neighbourhood decline, with Roma blamed for the conditions that are produced by exploitative landlord practices.

The predominant link through which this association between Roma and the problems of Govanhill was consolidated was one of infestation, which provided much fodder for voyeuristic accounts of the 'slums' from within:

> You don't have to look long in the closes in streets on either side of Allison Street, Govanhill's main thoroughfare, to uncover pretty squalid conditions. One close is open to the skies, with rain falling on to stairs and down walls, and a group of pigeons in residence on the top landing. Much of the stair is caked with bird excrement. Piles of rubbish, discarded toys and leaking soil pipes are not uncommon in back courts. Some closes have smashed windows all the way up, with stair railings broken and "secured" with plywood. Others have signs up warning that council officers have laid rat poison.[72]

Another examines a flat rented by an SNP councillor 'to a family of five Romanian Big Issue sellers':

> Furious locals told them the street has become a dumping ground with rubbish and faeces in the backyards attracting rats and infestations of cockroaches and maggots. Hanif's flat stands at the top of a dilapidated common close, where the ceiling has gaping holes and the plaster is falling off the walls. All owners share responsibility for the communal entrance. It is infested with flies and has a shooting gallery for heroin addicts on the ground floor ... there is a strong stench of urine throughout the building. The walls are filthy and daubed with graffiti and the stairs are caked in grime ... There is rubbish, including a mattress, piling up in back yards and spilling on to the street. The overcrowding has led to reports of human faeces being found in gardens.[73]

Further, in an expose of a particularly exploitative landlord, it was reported that:

Conditions in the close leading to it are even worse than when the Evening Times revealed the disgusting living conditions suffered by some of Mr Aslam's tenants last year. The walls of the close in Allison Street are covered in graffiti, from front door to top floor, and through to the rear exit. About half appears to have been written by Roma children, with the rest messages, poems and abuse from Scots youths . . . cockroaches and other insects swarmed over the walls, inches from a sleeping baby.[74]

Readers online were invited to visually engage with this spectacle through viewing 'a walkthrough video of 221 Allison Street' via an embedded link.[75] These extracts are worth reproducing at length as exemplars of this affective journalistic style, where the dominant themes of filth, despair and decay are persistently narrated in all of their inglorious gratuitous detail. The effect of this is to produce an archetypal set of representations that would serve as the dominant frames through which accounts of the Roma 'problem' would be reified and sustained.

Moreover, the language of ghettoisation transcended the sensationalising accounts of local journalism and everyday street discourses to be given official sanctioning. In a high-profile intervention by the Govanhill Housing Association at the Scottish Parliament, a report was presented to MSPs which claimed 'slum housing' had resulted in 'the area becoming a "breeding ground" for crime, exploitation, poor health and education and cockroaches', with 750 properties 'below tolerable standard' and 131 'in the area bounded by Westmoreland Street, Dixon Avenue, Langside Road and Allison Street – dubbed 'Ground Zero' by residents' where many Roma families live requiring 'comprehensive improvement'.[76] Overcrowding was described as a problem that produces 'anti-social behaviour and race relations conflicts'[77] through immigration 'mainly of Slovakian Roma people'.[78] This framing echoes media representations that suggest a connection between the presence of Roma migrants and the outbreak of tensions, and operates through constructing Roma in opposition to 'the community' and as a burden to long-standing residents. This logic was implicit in the evidence given at Holyrood. It was argued that persistent issues in Govanhill (conceived of here as domestic violence, substance abuse and subsequent overdoses, alcohol dependency and high crime rates) had now been exacerbated by 'the addition of at least another 4000 migrants who had "their own issues in terms of not being employable, not understanding their rights, living in overcrowded conditions and being used by unscrupulous landlords and gangmasters" [causing] problems for the entire community'.[79] The director of the Govanhill Housing Association was reported to have 'shocked the Holyrood Petitions Committee' by concluding, 'We feel the south-east of Govanhill has become a ghetto for the Roma migrants and for the community.'[80] As others have put it, 'it is a short step from understanding problems in an area to presenting them as problems of an area and its population'.[81] In the case of Roma and Govanhill, this association solidified to the extent that the 'problem' of Roma would become synonymous with the problems of Govanhill.

LATERAL DENIGRATION AND AMPLIFICATION

As representations of Roma were depicted by their association with the perceived ills of Govanhill, a process of territorial stigmatisation was rendered complete. This was evident in the formation of a range of task forces and working groups, in the establishment of 'a dedicated Hub ... made up of around 20 agencies' which provided 'a drop-in service for concerned locals',[82] in 'bad-tempered' meetings between residents, local authority representatives and the police,[83] in increased surveillance with the rolling out of twenty-seven 'state of the art CCTV cameras' across a handful of streets,[84] as well as in the designation of Govanhill as Scotland's first (and only) 'Enhanced Enforcement Area'.[85] This proliferation of governmental activity is indicative of the portrayal of Govanhill's status as a uniquely problematic place that can only be tackled via a series of targeted interventions and exceptional measures, with some even calling for 'a czar for Govanhill'.[86] This dominant construction of decline was reflected in the formation of a neighbourhood campaign group, 'Let's Save Govanhill'. This organisation was ostensibly set up to allow all residents to share their concerns about the area and exert pressure on the local authority and elected representatives to make improvements. Even so, its methods and rhetoric remain troubling, with its social media pages often functioning as a vehicle to 'blame high crime rates, sub-standard housing and fly-tipping on the influx of Roma migrants'.[87]

'Saving' Govanhill . . . from what or whom?

This group of angry residents regularly takes to the streets to demonstrate the squalor of the area, with images of discarded mattresses, piles of rubbish, and rats collected on a near-daily basis and posted online. Anonymous social media accounts such as 'Visit Govanhill' also contribute to this circulation and regularly post images of Romani people specifically (and particularly groups of Roma men) without their consent. In line with wider trends within racist discourses, Roma are rarely explicitly referred to in the 'official' statements of such groups and instead are evoked via euphemisms, as made possible via the connections forged between Roma and the ills of the area (although the audiences of such accounts tend to show less restraint in their comments posted in response, which rarely fail to demonstrate that the 'message' has been received). This is symptomatic of *'lateral denigration and mutual distanciation'*, defined as:

> the acute sense of social indignity that enshrouds neighbourhoods of rel-
> egation can be attenuated only by thrusting the stigma onto a faceless,
> demonized other – the downstairs neighbours, the immigrant family dwelling
> in an adjacent building, the youths from across the street who 'do drugs' or
> are engaged in street 'hustling', or the residents over on the next block whom
> one suspects of illegally drawing unemployment or welfare support[.][88]

The discursive trope of the ghetto and its associated metaphors and connotations featured heavily in the framing of Let's Save Govanhill's activities, including marches, rallies, 'back court' hustings and street vigils. Residents fumed about rats 'as big as cats . . . so fat they were hopping rather than running', so large they 'pull the bins down'[89]– a notion that would go on to become iconic in depictions. The first march held in March 2015 conflated a range of different issues, with attendees reportedly protesting 'Govanhill's continuing decline and social issues of crime, rubbish dumping, rat infestations and general upkeep' as well as 'bedbugs, cockroaches' and 'rape'.[90] This is reflective of how the inter-relation of these themes is understood as given, as almost synonymous, in the eyes of a vocal minority of the residents of the area. The protest was reported to have attracted 'hundreds of people' as 'men, women, and children chanted "let's save Govanhill" as they marched through the streets, banging pots and pans'.[91] In justifying their plans for further protests, an organiser argued, 'We are trying to control the tempers of angry residents by organising this march, otherwise there is potential for unrest on the streets.'[92] This claim to speak on behalf of a silent majority of residents articulated through the exaggerated trope of tensions on the verge of explosion is a familiar aspect of the stigmatisation of Roma in and *through* place, and is frequently deployed in communities where Roma reside in the UK[93] and beyond.[94]

Exonerating oneself from place-based stigma may also involve claims to the rightful ownership of space via a reimagining of the past, of what 'used to be', through which affective appeals to people 'like us' are made. As Stuart Hall argued, for racialising discourses to function effec-tively, who is *included* is just as salient as who is excluded.[95] Let's Save

Govanhill's narratives of a 'once proud working class neighbourhood' where closes were 'immaculate',[96] the streets safe and the neighbours lived together in harmonious familiarity exemplify this. The irony of nostalgia being put to this use was not lost on one journalist, who noted that 'a glimpse of the auld jelly-piece Glasgow'[97] is exactly what contemporary Govanhill offers, with children playing in the street, generations of family members living together, and the buzz and variety of the local shops in place of faceless chains. Yet residents' quotes redeployed in headlines such as 'We're sick to the back teeth of living in fear',[98] describing themselves as 'prisoners in our homes'[99] who 'refuse to walk down the streets alone',[100] contradicted this. Let's Save Govanhill petitioned police 'to stop gangs of men standing in corners and intimidating our pensioners and other residents'.[101] When two elderly residents did have their purses stolen within one week, this was unhelpfully framed in the press as a 'number of muggings', through the suspects' alleged 'Eastern European appearance', and with significance afforded to this occurring in a 'racially diverse area of the city'.[102] In response, Let's Save Govanhill held a street corner 'vigil for all the Govanhill pensioners who have been attacked, battered and robbed on the streets of Govanhill'.[103] Through the emotive figures of the vulnerable pensioner and the mugger lurking on once-safe street corners, long identified by Stuart Hall as symbolic of a whole range of racialised social anxieties,[104] Let's Save Govanhill was able to tap into a wider racialised fear of crime through mourning for an imagined community now lost. Through this lateral denigration, those affected by the 'blemish of place' were thus most actively involved in its (re)production, albeit through displacement onto 'others'.

'Sturgeon's slums'

This lateral denigration was given oxygen by increasing coverage in conservative-leaning newspapers. In an article in the *Scottish Daily Express*, which had previously featured on 'The Conservative Women' website, the academic Tom Gallagher asserted after his attendance at a street vigil for pensioners that 'Things started to go wrong almost a decade ago thanks to an abrupt shift in its make-up.'[105] Written in April 2016, it is clear that 'almost a decade ago' refers to Romania's accession to the EU in 2007. Gallagher claimed that while 'Scots, Pakistanis and Irish had got along for over a generation', sharing 'the same rules for living' and 'plenty of cross-ethnic friendships', the social fabric of Govanhill had now unravelled. The implicit premise of these barely coded remarks was then made clear: 'A hardcore element among several thousand gypsies or Roma, now nearly all from Romania, who have occupied poorer housing in the area have, so far, been unwilling to abide by the rules for amicable urban living.'[106] The usual clichés are rehearsed here to support this claim: threatening groups of Roma men, littering, loitering, infestation, dirt, decay and decline. A distinction is also made between 'Roma, who pursue a disorderly lifestyle here' and 'others who wish to improve themselves and put aside medieval ways'.[107] This echoes the familiar ideology of the deserving and undeserving poor and is articulated through representing inequalities as emanating 'from the perceived possession of distinct sets of cultural values',[108] as exemplified by the word 'medieval'.

The article goes on to praise Let's Save Govanhill as the 'one thing' Govanhill 'has got going for it' and claims that the founding member's familiarity with conditions in the USA uniquely equips her to tackle the issues, given that she had witnessed 'what worked and didn't work in terms of multiracial living' across the Atlantic. This narrowly interprets Govanhill's structural issues as being those of 'race relations', although the author notes that the founding member of Let's Save Govanhill 'has never framed the problem in ethnic terms but sees it about the unravelling of a once good social and physical environment. She believes a regeneration project is needed involving the cooperation of the Scottish Government and the city council and is confident many Roma in time can adapt to Western cultural ways.'[109]

Locating problems within 'backwards' Roma culture in the final sentence, contrary to those that immediately preceded it and to the 'official' position of the group itself (although it cannot be seriously disputed that this is not what lurks beneath their rhetoric), is indicative of the 'ventriloquisation' of the working class. In other words, claiming to speak for the beleaguered 'ordinary person' is a discursive strategy deployed to claim 'a principled rejection of immigration and the defence against the charge of racism at the same time'.[110] This strategy is adopted by Let's Save Govanhill representatives themselves in declaring they speak on behalf of the besieged community who, along with its institutions, are afraid to act 'for fear of being seen as racist . . . This label has been used to silence people.'[111] In this sense, perceived institutional neglect is constructed as a symptom of the real problem of Roma and, more specifically, their 'culture'. This ensures that any ambivalence regarding the underlying problematisation of Govanhill and what or whom it should be 'saved' from is eliminated.

Moreover, the framing of this story as indicative of 'the nats' 'neglect' of Govanhill is significant, with 'the number of toots from car owners in appreciation as they drove past' the vigil read as evidencing the likelihood of the Scottish National Party's 'reckoning' to come.[112] Conservative newspapers were notably absent in the early years of coverage of Roma in Govanhill, with stories largely appearing in the *Evening Times* and *The Herald* due to their 'local' nature. Yet as territorial stigmatisation took hold, and with increasing attention on Nicola Sturgeon as First Minister, feature pieces on Govanhill and its Roma residents became more prevalent within newspapers hostile to Scottish independence and to the Scottish National Party (SNP) more broadly. Following the *Scottish Daily Express* article discussed above, which referred to Nicola Sturgeon as 'behaving like a negligent parent' and claimed that 'the SNP uses its clout over part of the media and the third sector to discourage any serious assessment of problems',[113] almost every headline featuring the Let's Save Govanhill campaign since[114] has been framed in this way. Headlines include the *Scottish Daily Express*'s 'Scotland's first "ghetto" is in Nicola's backyard',[115] which featured on the same day as the vigil article and 'GOVANHELL; SQUALOR, RATS, FILTH AND SEX CRIME . . . WHAT IT'S LIKE TO LIVE IN STURGEON'S SLUMS';[116] the *Daily Record*'s 'It smells something rotten in Nic's back yard, say her binmen';[117] the *Scottish Mail on Sunday*'s 'The MSP for Glasgow Ghetto';[118] and the *Scottish Daily Mail*'s 'Squalor of the city ghetto in Sturgeon's back yard', which concluded that 'No wonder those living in the Dickensian nightmare of Govanhill are so angry at the politician supposed to represent them.'[119] Throughout this period, Let's Save Govanhill would also exploit this political opportunity to render their campaign more visible. In a protest outside the 2015 SNP conference, Let's Save Govanhill protestors wielded 'a 7ft-tall model rat'[120] above their heads to symbolise the slum-like conditions in Nicola Sturgeon's constituency. In a further action, a free bus tour of the 'Govanhill Ghetto'[121] was offered at the 2016 SNP conference, with delegates invited to join Let's Save Govanhill in touring the 'squalid slums'.[122] In this sense, the problems of Govanhill (and implicitly, of a segment of its population) are amplified when constructed as symbolic of failures in SNP governance. 'Race' and place not only intersect to produce specific forms of territorial stigma, but are heightened through connections forged to wider political questions, from which they must not be studied in isolation.

CONCLUSION

Throughout the last decade, Roma have been consistently constructed as a problem people. In the earlier period of their migration to Glasgow from 2004, Roma briefly enjoyed relative invisibility in being identified within broader national categories, but the 'crystallisation' identified by Grill on the ground was also reflected in media accounts by 2007. Through sensationalising and stigmatising constructions, Roma became associated with a variety of issues which culminated in their representation as symptomatic of and synonymous with the problems of Govanhill. This place-based racialisation has resulted in the problems of an area being attributed to Roma explicitly (and often exclusively) and presented as distinctly 'Roma problems' or as symptoms of *The* Roma Problem. Issues regarding overcrowding, infestation and dirt dominate representations, to the effect that a discursive association has been forged between Roma and a totalising sense of neighbourhood decline and decay in Govanhill. These themes, while particularly pronounced here, are far from unique to Govanhill. As a study of racism in Peterborough argues, 'The repeated association of migrants with overcrowding, the failure to maintain private-public distinctions, and with excessive rubbish ... builds on racist tropes that have been well established in Britain since the nineteenth century.'[123] At times, Roma themselves are discussed as if they are 'matter out of place'.[124] This is particularly the case for Roma men, whose mere presence on the streets is automatically perceived as threatening. As well as being discursively constituted as the cause of all local problems, Roma are disproportionately affected by such problems materially and blamed for their poverty. Through a process of territorial stigmatisation over time, Roma have thus been racialised through distinctly place-based constructions, while Govanhill has been constructed as a problem place through its association with Roma, such that it has become possible to evoke the 'Roma problem' locally without naming Roma at all.

Being attentive to place in processes of racialisation reveals departures from as well as convergences with national and supranational constructions of Roma. Common stereotypes of Roma migrants in the UK and throughout Europe often fixate on welfare and the threat of the migrant 'benefits tourist'.[125] Yet while Roma were certainly constructed as a threat to local public services, benefits rarely featured in these discussions and indeed the only major benefits story was that condemning systematic discrimination that Roma faced at the local job centre.[126] This is not to suggest that this rhetoric is absent in Scotland but, rather, is less significant within these highly specific place-based accounts where local markers of difference carry much more weight. In this sense, place is not merely a container of 'context' but is deeply *constitutive* in forming particular racisms. Despite its persistent problematisation, it is important to note that Govanhill is not a ghetto and that many of its residents simply do not recognise its dominant depiction. But this has little bearing on its construction: 'whether or not these areas are in fact dilapidated and dangerous, and their population composed essentially of poor people, minorities and foreigners, matters little in the end: the prejudicial belief that they are suffices to set off the socially noxious consequences.'[127]

On the matter of consequences, territorial stigmatisation often appears as a precursor to gentrification and its devastating effects, acting as a 'convenient alibi for large-scale gentrification and working-class displacement',[128] to the extent that it is argued that 'territorial stigmatisation and "regeneration" through gentrification form two sides of the same conceptual and policy coin'.[129] Govanhill has so far escaped relatively unscathed from the most brutal campaigns of gentrification and regeneration experienced elsewhere in the city, yet is certainly not immune to their encroachments.

As I write this chapter, a story which has dominated the local news in September 2017 is Glasgow City Council's planned enforcement of compulsory purchase orders which will force approximately five hundred properties in Govanhill from the hands of 'unscrupulous slum landlords'[130] to the council. This news has been well-received locally, yet what has been elided in the discussions so far are the consequences for the residents who live there. The presumption is that tenants will be invited to reapply for their homes, yet due to the much stricter occupancy criteria that operate in assessing social housing applications, it is unlikely that the larger Roma families who live there currently can be housed there. While such families often prefer to live together, this is also necessitated by poverty, and exacerbated by welfare restrictions. This seemingly benign and indeed progressive policy may produce homelessness or displacement which will disproportionately affect Romani residents.

If this seems like an outlandish claim, it is worth noting that Glasgow City Council's own equality impact assessment of the Glasgow Housing Strategy 2017–21 spells out this possibility. Under 'raise management standards in the private sector' in relation to potential impacts on ethnic minorities, a potential negative consequence is noted:

> if landlords fail to cooperate and improve the quality it may lead to enforcement action to be taken and therefore the numbers of properties available may reduce which could be a negative impact on this group of displacement/ homelessness.[131]

This document was published in January 2017 by the previous administration prior to the decision to enforce compulsory purchases and it was deemed insufficiently concerning at that time to affect the strategy. This material change in the council's strategy demands urgent attention. The recently established Govanhill Regeneration Group has published its ten-year plan for a 'Better Govanhill' which emphasises that:

> Our aspiration is not to deliver the sort of regeneration that leaves existing communities behind but, rather, to work together with all of Govanhill's communities to build on its distinctive strengths and to overcome its weaknesses – not to create a different Govanhill but a Better Govanhill.[132]

While this is a laudable aspiration, progressive policies often have unintended consequences and are not always benign or evenly distributed in their effects. With many Roma families subject to the harshest of housing conditions locally, at the sharp end of poverty, and disproportionately concentrated within the streets marked for enforcement, it is imperative that Govanhill's territorial stigmatisation vis-à-vis its Roma residents does not provide a 'convenient alibi' for their displacement.

NOTES

1. T. Harris, 'Object to mass immigration from the EU? Join the Romaphobe club!', *The Telegraph* (27 November 2013), http://www.telegraph.co.uk/news/uknews/immigration/10477858/Object-to-mass-immigration-from-the-EU-Join-the-Romaphobe-club.html (last accessed 12 October 2017).
2. Ibid; my emphasis. Glasgow South is the neighbouring constituency of Glasgow Central, where Govanhill is located.
3. Sherene Razack, *Race, Space, and the Law: Unmapping a White Settler Society* (Toronto: Between the Lines, 2002); Satnam Virdee, Christopher Kyriakides and Tariq Modood, 'Codes of cultural belonging: Racialised national identities in a multi-ethnic Scottish neighbourhood', *Sociological Research Online*, 11:4 (2006).
4. Loïc Wacquant, 'Territorial stigmatization in the age of advanced marginality', *Thesis Eleven*, 91:1 (2007), pp. 66–77.
5. As a system of signification, racism arbitrarily constructs elements of human variance such as skin colour, mode of dress, religion or 'cultural' attributes as important markers of difference. This differentiation is then consolidated through essentialism: these attributes are imbued with significance and read as indicative of deeper characteristics through stereotypes that are naturalised as inherent to those signified (thus, *essential*). As there is, of course, no such thing as 'races', this relies on a social process of *racialisation*, through which social actors become differentiated, categorised and constructed as 'Others'. See Robert Miles, *Racism After 'Race*

Relations' (London: Routledge, 1993) and Colette Guillaumin, *Racism, Sexism, Power and Ideology* (London: Routledge, 1995).

6. FRA (European Union Agency for Fundamental Rights), EU-MIDIS II – Second European Union Minorities and Discrimination Survey. Roma – Selected Findings, 2016, http://fra.europa.eu/en/publication/2016/eumidis-ii-roma-selected-findings (last accessed 12 October 2017).

7. See Bernard Rorke and Orhan Usein (eds), *A Lost Decade? Reflections on Roma Inclusion 2005–2015* (Budapest: Decade of Roma Inclusion Secretariat Foundation, 2015); special issue of *European Education*, 49:1 (2017) and editors' introduction: Christian Brüggemann and Eben Friedman, 'The decade of Roma inclusion: origins, actors, and legacies', *European Education*, 49:1 (2017), pp. 1–9.

8. Council of Europe, 'Council of Europe descriptive glossary of terms relating to Roma issues' (18 May 2012), http://a.cs.coe.int/team20/cahrom/documents/Glossary%20Roma%20EN%20version%2018%20May%202012.pdf (last accessed 14 October 2017).

9. Jean Pierre Liégeois, *Gypsies: An Illustrated History* (London: Al Saqi Books, 1986), pp. 49–50.

10. Judith Okely, *The Traveller-Gypsies* (Cambridge: Cambridge University Press, 1983). See 'Contaminated grounds: Disputing the Roma's origins', in Huub van Baar, *The European Roma: Minority Representation, Memory, and the Limits of Transnational Governmentality* (Amsterdam: F. & N. Eigen Beheer, 2007), pp. 77–105, for an overview of the 'origins debate' in Romani Studies.

11. See Colin Clark and Elaine Campbell, '"Gypsy invasion": A critical analysis of newspaper reaction to Czech and Slovak Romani asylum-seekers in Britain, 1997', *Romani Studies*, 10:1 (2000), pp. 23–47.

12. Colin Clark, 'Glasgow's Ellis Island? The integration and stigmatisation of Govanhill's Roma population', *People, Place and Policy*, 8:1 (2014), pp. 34–50.

13. See Philip Brown, Philip Martin and Lisa Scullion, 'Migrant Roma in the United Kingdom and the need to estimate population size', *People, Place and Policy Online*, 8:1 (2014), pp. 19–33, for a discussion of the problems in estimating the Roma population.

14. Social Marketing Gateway, 'Mapping the Roma community in Scotland: Final report' (26 September 2013), http://www.migrationscotland.org.uk/uploads/files/documents/mappingtheromacommunityinscotlandreport-2.pdf (last accessed 10 October 2017). This study was methodologically unconventional and, in the absence of reliable statistics, was based on a series of interviews and focus groups with a range of stakeholders who work with Roma communities. Their estimates were then aggregated to produce lower and upper estimates by local authority and an overall population estimate. This approach has been critiqued on methodological grounds as well as in its tendency to essentialise. See Taulant Guma, 'The

ethnicisation of need: questioning the role of ethnicity in the provision of support and services for post-accession migrants in Glasgow', Policy paper, University of Glasgow and Glasgow City Council (September 2015), http://cadair.aber.ac.uk/dspace/bitstream/handle/2160/44587/med ia_427566_en.pdf?sequence=1&isAllowed=y. However, as Clark notes, these numbers are broadly accepted by those working with Roma as 'reliable and credible' (see Clark, 'Glasgow's Ellis Island?', p. 40).

15. Suzanne Audrey, *Multiculturalism in Practice: Irish, Jewish, Italian and Pakistani Migration to Scotland*, Interdisciplinary Research Series in Ethnic, Gender and Class Relations (Aldershot: Ashgate, 2000).

16. Ibid., p. 85.

17. Clark, 'Glasgow's Ellis Island', p. 40.

18. When expressed in solidarity, this is at times ambiguous when offered as an afterthought to contextualise the alleged problems that the Roma communities bring.

19. Audrey, *Multiculturalism in Practice*, p. 21.

20. Etienne Balibar, 'Is there a "neo-racism"?', in Etienne Balibar and Immanuel Wallerstein, *Race, Nation, Class: Ambiguous Identities* (London: Verso, 1991), pp. 17–27.

21. Jan Grill, '"It's building up to something and it won't be nice when it erupts": The making of Roma/Gypsy migrants in post-industrial Scotland', *Focaal*, 62 (2012), p. 42.

22. 'Crackdown on race hate gang wars', *Evening Times*, 17 March 2007, p. 1. Author unspecified.

23. C. Musson, 'A playground by day . . . Battleground by night; Communities split by racial tensions', *Evening Times*, 16 March 2007, p. 4.

24. C. Musson, 'Rising tensions spark a huge response', *Evening Times*, 24 March 2007, p. 4.

25. Musson, 'A playground by day'.

26. C. Musson and J. McCann, 'Caught in the middle of race hate violence: As taunts spark fury, teenager brandishes nail-studded weapon', *Evening Times,* 17 March 2007, p. 8.

27. Musson, 'Rising tensions spark a huge response'.

28. Musson and McCann, 'Caught in the middle of race hate violence'.

29. Musson, 'Rising tensions spark a huge response'.

30. Ibid.

31. Musson and McCann, 'Caught in the middle of race hate violence'.

32. Musson, 'A playground by day'.

33. Ibid.

34. N. Mackay, 'The child sex scandal on the streets of Scotland; Major police probe as immigrant Roma children exploited', *Sunday Herald*, 5 August 2007, p. 8. This is a story that would be resurrected by *The Times* ten years later, just weeks after this chapter was completed. *The Times* published a four-part investigation that claimed, on the basis of allega-

tions from unnamed sources and barstool testimonies from a local pub, that Roma children in Govanhill are being prostituted by their parents. See M. Horne, 'Govanhill child sex trade: "there are so many . . . it's easy pickings for child abusers"', *The Times*, 17 November 2017, https://www.thetimes.co.uk/article/govanhill-child-sex-trade-there-are-so-many-it-s-easy-pickings-for-child-abusers-m2swzc63h (last accessed 1 February 2018). Many pieces have since been published condemning this.

35. Ibid.; my emphasis.

36. Ibid.

37. Ibid.

38. D. Leask, 'Unit offers support for Roma', *The Herald*, 7 October 2011, p. 26.

39. Indeed, as Waqas Tufail argues in 'Rotherham, Rochdale, and the racialised threat of the "Muslim grooming gang"', *International Journal for Crime Justice and Social Democracy*, 4:3 (2015), pp. 30–43, while coverage of child exploitation in Rotherham and Rochdale was consistently framed through Muslim 'culture', it is difficult to imagine similar extrapolations being made to 'the white community'.

40. Judith Okely, 'Recycled (mis)representations: Gypsies, Travellers or Roma treated as objects, rarely subjects', *People, Place and Policy*, 8:1 (2014), pp. 65–85.

41. Mary Christianakis, 'Victimization and vilification of Romani children in media and human rights organizations discourses', *Social Inclusion*, 3:5 (2015), p. 48.

42. Mackay, 'The child sex scandal on the streets of Scotland'.

43. N. Mackay, 'Isolated, abused, and victims of decades of persecution; The Rome community in Scotland', *Sunday Herald*, 5 August 2007, p. 10.

44. Ibid.; my emphasis.

45. Mackay, 'The child sex scandal on the streets of Scotland'.

46. Ryan Powell, 'Loïc Wacquant's "Ghetto" and ethnic minority segregation in the UK: the neglected case of Gypsy-Travellers', *International Journal of Urban and Regional Research*, 37:1 (2013), pp. 115–34.

47. Mackay, 'Isolated, abused, and victims of decades of persecution', p. 10.

48. One resident responded, 'I accept that Asian residents of Govanhill may be better placed to comment, I have never heard "Paki" used on the streets of Govanhill and I can categorically state that I have never been told to get back to my "white ghetto".' See 'Mail in print and online', *Sunday Herald*, 12 August 2007, p. 40.

49. 'Stamp out the slums', *Evening Times*, 29 October 2011, p. 6. Author unspecified.

50. Anne McClintock, *Imperial Leather: Race, Gender and Sexuality in the Colonial Contest* (Oxon: Routledge, 1995). See also Shannon Woodcock, 'Gender as catalyst for violence against Roma in contemporary Italy', *Patterns of Prejudice*, 44:5 (2010), pp. 469–88, for an incisive discus-

sion of how this trope plays out to legitimise violence against Roma in Italy.

51. 'Making the Roma at home in our city', *The Herald*, 23 November, 2013, p. 13. Author unspecified.

52. Ibid.

53. Floya Anthias, 'Rethinking social divisions: Some notes towards a theoretical framework', *The Sociological Review*, 46:3 (1998), pp. 505–35.

54. Nirmal Puwar, *Space Invaders: Race, Gender and Bodies Out of Place* (Oxford: Berg, 2004).

55. J. Bynorth, 'Revealed: the 4000 migrant children in our schools who can't speak English', *Sunday Herald*, 31 August 2008, p. 8.

56. P. Gilbride, 'Migrants are given "better" NHS care; Health experts' warning to MSPs', *Scottish Daily Express*, 31 January 2013, p. 1. See also D. Herbert, 'Anger at health board's £15,000 gypsy project', *Scottish Daily Express*, 3 January 2012, p. 15.

57. G. Grant, 'Cash appeal by primary with no Scots pupils', *Scottish Daily Mail*, 2 May 2016, p. 19.

58. 'School with no Scots kids in funds call', *Daily Record*, 2 May 2016, p. 20. Author unspecified.

59. 'Glasgow school has no "Scottish" students, headteacher reveals', *The Scotsman*, 2 May 2016. Author unspecified; unpaginated (online version).

60. S. Naysmith, 'Youtube bid to help migrant pupils', *The Herald*, 2 May 2016, p. 14.

61. P. English, 'Watch as Govanhill primary pupils hit back at "No Scots" claims by singing Flower of Scotland', *Daily Record*, 12 May 2016, unpaginated (online).

62. See David McCollum, Beata Nowok and Scott Tindal, 'Public attitudes towards migration in Scotland: Exceptionality and possible policy implications', *Scottish Affairs*, 23:1 (2014), pp. 79–102, for an analysis of Scottish exceptionalism.

63. Les Back, *New Ethnicities and Urban Culture: Racisms and Multiculture in Young Lives* (London: UCL, 1996).

64. Alistair Fraser and Teresa Piacentini, 'We belong to Glasgow: The third-spaces of youth "gangs" and asylum seeker, refugee and migrant groups', in Coretta Phillips and Colin Webster (eds), *New Directions in Race, Ethnicity and Crime* (Oxon: Routledge, 2014), p. 64.

65. D. Leask, 'Violence falling in city hot spot', *Evening Times*, 28 October 2011, p. 16.

66. 'Making the Roma at home in our city', *The Herald*, 23 November, 2013, p. 13. Author unspecified.

67. Bastian A. Vollmer, 'Policy discourses on irregular migration in the EU – "number games" and "political games"', *European Journal of Migration and Law*, 13 (2011), p. 327.

68. Mackay, 'Isolated, abused, and victims of decades of persecution'.

69. S. Naysmith, 'The European workers paying GBP650 a month to live in a Glasgow slum', *The Herald*, 1 April 2008, p. 16.

70. B. Currie, '"Govanhill flats are not fit for a dog": City scheme is being turned into ghetto MSPS told', *Evening Times*, 8 October 2008, p. 7.

71. Philip Brown, Peter Dwyer and Lisa Scullion, 'The limits of inclusion? Exploring the views of Roma and non Roma in six European member states' (Roma Source: University of Salford, March 2013), http://usir. salford.ac.uk/35826/1/Roma_full%20report.pdf (last accessed 12 October 2017).

72. Naysmith, 'The European workers paying GBP650 a month to live in a Glasgow slum'.

73. A. Brown, 'Exposed: Housing campaigner who is slum landlord; Exclusive Nat's £500-a-month flat in "Ground Zero" street', *Daily Record*, 11 July 2008, p. 12.

74. J. McCann, 'Slum landlord to fight council ban: Legal appeal means he can again charge tenants in his flats; Exclusive', *Evening Times*, 23 January 2009, p. 19.

75. Ibid.

76. B. Currie, 'Govanhill's a breeding ground for exploitation, crime, poor health . . . and cockroaches', *Evening Times*, 7 October, 2008, p. 19.

77. Ibid.

78. Currie, 'Govanhill flats are not fit for a dog', p. 7.

79. Ibid.

80. Ibid.

81. Neil Gray and Gerry Mooney, 'Glasgow's new urban frontier: "Civilising" the population of "Glasgow East"', *City*, 15:1 (2011), pp. 4–24.

82. C. Stewart, 'Residents in talks to solve area's issues', *Evening Times*, 15 November 2013, p. 23.

83. P. Swindon and C. Stewart, '"We're sick to the back teeth of living in fear"', *Evening Times*, 30 May 2014, p. 4.

84. P. Swindon, 'Council's CCTV privacy pledge', *Evening Times*, 27 July 2015, p. 7.

85. D. Herbert, 'Squalor of the city ghetto in Sturgeon's back yard', *Scottish Daily Mail*, 3 June 2017, pp. 22–3.

86. P. Swindon, 'Residents demand action to clean up "filthy" district', *Evening Times*, 6 June 2015, p. 11.

87. Stewart, 'Residents in talks to solve area's issues'.

88. Wacquant, 'Territorial stigmatization in the age of advanced marginality', p. 68; original emphasis.

89. C. Woollard, 'Residents up in arms over rubbish left in city streets', *Evening Times*, 18 March 2015, p. 18.

90. C. Woollard, 'Hundreds turn out in Govanhill protest', *Evening Times*, 23 March 2015, p. 11.

91. Ibid.

92. P. Swindon, 'Residents back safer streets call', *Evening Times*, 30 July 2015, p. 5.
93. See Grill, '"It's building up to something and it won't be nice when it erupts"', and Jo Richardson, 'Roma in the news: an examination of media and political discourse and what needs to change', *People, Place and Policy*, 8:1 (2014), pp. 51–64.
94. Giovanni Picker, '"That neighbourhood is an ethnic bomb!" The emergence of an urban governance apparatus in Western Europe', *European Urban and Regional Studies*, 23:2 (2016), pp. 136–48.
95. Stuart Hall (ed.), *Representation. Cultural Representations and Signifying Practices*, (London: Sage/Open University, 1997), p. 56.
96. Herbert, 'Squalor of the city ghetto in Sturgeon's back yard'.
97. P. Ross, 'Govanhill: Glasgow's Ellis Island', *Scotland on Sunday*, 10 February 2013, unpaginated.
98. P. Swindon and C. Stewart, 'We're sick to the back teeth of living in fear'.
99. C. Woollard, 'Hundreds turn out in Govanhill protest'.
100. D. Campbell, 'Let's Save Govanhill trio challenge First Minister', *Evening Times*, 27 May 2015, p. 12.
101. Swindon, 'Residents back safer streets call'.
102. D. O'Leary, 'Police increase patrols after Govanhill gang muggings', *The Scotsman*, 7 April 2016, unpaginated.
103. P. Swindon, 'Appeal after pensioner's purse taken', *Evening Times*, 28 March 2016, p. 7.
104. Stuart Hall, Chas Critcher, Tony Jefferson, John Clarke and Brian Roberts, *Policing the Crisis: Mugging, the State and Law and Order* (London: Palgrave Macmillan, 2013, first pub. 1978).
105. T. Gallagher, 'Nats will pay for neglect', *Scottish Daily Express*, 3 April 2016, unpaginated. The author, Professor Tom Gallagher, is not a regular *Express* journalist but is Emeritus Professor of Politics at the University of Bradford.
106. Ibid. Although precise numbers are not available, this assertion that Roma in Govanhill are 'nearly all from Romania' is almost certainly inaccurate. At the last estimate in 2013, the local Slovakian Roma population was approximated to be double that of Romanian Roma (2,000 to 1,000). While Romanian Romani migration has increased since then, there remains an established Slovak Romani community.
107. Ibid.
108. James Rhodes, 'Stigmatization, space, and boundaries in de-industrial Burnley', *Ethnic and Racial Studies*, 35:4 (2012), p. 701.
109. Gallagher, 'Nats will pay for neglect'.
110. Anita Biressi and Heather Nunn, '"Are you thinking what we're thinking?": Class, immigration and belonging', in Anita Biressi and Heather Nunn, *Class and Contemporary British Culture* (London: Palgrave Macmillan, 2013), p. 148.

111. B. Borland, 'Scotland's first "ghetto" is in Nicola's backyard', *Scottish Daily Express*, 3 April 2016, p. 7.

112. Gallagher, 'Nats will pay for neglect'.

113. Ibid.

114. There have been ten articles featuring Let's Save Govanhill since the *Scottish Daily Express* article between April 2016 and September 2017. Of these, nine frame their stories with reference to the SNP or Nicola Sturgeon. The exception is an article on Let's Save Govanhill's critique of the recent Govanhill Against Racism concert and Govanhill International Carnival, which were described as 'psychological abuse' while the streets remained dilapidated.

115. Borland, 'Scotland's first "ghetto" is in Nicola's backyard'.

116. B. Borland, Govanhell; Squalor, rats, filth and sex crime … What it's like to live in Sturgeon's slums', *Scottish Daily Express*, 9 October 2016, pp. 1, 6, 7.

117. S. Hind and C. Clement, 'It smells something rotten in Nic's back yard, say her binmen', *Daily Record*, 13 October 2016, p. 9.

118. H. Macdonell, 'The MSP for Glasgow Ghetto', *Scottish Mail on Sunday*, 16 October 2016, p. 41.

119. Herbert, 'Squalor of the city ghetto in Sturgeon's back yard'.

120. M. Aitken, 'The long game: An SNP revolt? No danger of SNP revolt as newbies hold the line on indy vote', *Daily Record*, 18 October 2015, pp. 16–17.

121. Macdonell, 'The MSP for Glasgow Ghetto'.

122. Borland, 'Govanhell; Squalor, rats, filth and sex crime'.

123. Umut Erel, 'Complex belongings: Racialization and migration in a small English city', *Ethnic and Racial Studies*, 34:12 (2011), p. 2059.

124. Mary Douglas, *Purity and Danger. An Analysis of Concepts of Pollution and Taboo* (London: Routledge & Kegan Paul, 1966).

125. Nira Yuval-Davis, Viktor Varjú, Miika Tervonen, Jamie Hakim and Mastoureh Fathi, 'Press discourses on Roma in the UK, Finland and Hungary', *Ethnic and Racial Studies*, 40:7 (2017), pp. 1151–69.

126. B. Briggs, 'Revealed: Abuse of Roma at Glasgow job centre routine', *Scotland on Sunday*, 19 May 2012, unpaginated.

127. Wacquant, 'Territorial stigmatization in the age of advanced marginality', p. 68.

128. Gray and Mooney, 'Glasgow's new urban frontier', p. 11; see also Kirsteen Paton, Vikki McCall and Gerry Mooney, 'Place revisited: Class, stigma and urban restructuring in the case of Glasgow's Commonwealth Games', *The Sociological Review*, published online first: 1 February 2017, https://doi.org/10.1111/1467-954X.12423.

129. Hamish Kallin and Tom Slater, 'Activating territorial stigma: Gentrifying marginality on Edinburgh's periphery', *Environment and Planning A*, 46 (2014), p. 1351.

130. S. Dick, 'Hundreds of Govanhill homes to be seized under £50m slum landlord crackdown in deprived Glasgow community', *The Herald*, 18 September 2017, http://www.heraldscotland.com/news/15540746. Hundreds_of_homes_to_be_seized_under___50m_slum_landlord_crack down/ (last accessed 10 October 2017).
131. Equality Impact Screening Assessment, Glasgow City Council 'Glasgow Housing Strategy – 2017–2021', 9 January 2017, https://www.glasgow. gov.uk/CHttpHandler.ashx?id=37514&p=0 (last accessed 13 October 2017).
132. Govanhill Regeneration Group, A Better Govanhill: A 10-year Vision and Community Plan for Govanhill, http://www.glasgow.gov.uk/council lorsandcommittees/viewSelectedDocument.asp?c=P62AFQDNDNNT0 GZLZ3 (last accessed 13 October 2017).

10

Migration, Engagement and Constitutional Preferences: Evidence from the 2014 Scottish Independence Referendum

Ailsa Henderson, Chris Carman, Rob Johns and James Mitchell

There was a debate within the pages of Scotland's newspapers in early 2017 about the inclusiveness of Scottish nationalism. For some, it can be equated with racism, especially against the English, rooted in ethnicity and, to a certain extent, religion. For others, it is a model of a civic and inclusive movement, open to all those who live within Scotland's borders.[1] The extent to which Scottish nationalism is civic or ethnic appears in the academic literature, and from time to time features in the popular press.[2] However, the issue was noteworthy for its relative absence in the year before and after the 2014 independence referendum. Before the referendum there was limited analysis that the result might be determined by residents not born in Scotland. After the referendum there was never any hint that it was lost to the Yes side by 'money and the ethnic vote', as was claimed following the 1995 referendum on sovereignty partnership in Quebec.[3] These points offer, of course, two related issues to consider. The first is the perceived inclusiveness or exclusiveness of Scottish nationalism and whether its markers of national identity excludes, explicitly or implicitly, certain types of residents. If it is exclusive, what is the basis for exclusion? Is it 'race'? Residence? Values? Religion? The second issue to consider is how diversity relates to engagement and constitutional preferences.

This chapter focuses on place of birth and its impact on engagement with the 2014 referendum as well as its influence on support for independence. Before proceeding, it is useful to examine the numerical importance of migrants in the Scottish electorate (see Table 10.1). Among the 'usual suspect' substate nations with vibrant independence movements, such as Catalonia or Quebec, Scotland has experienced a relatively low rate of migration from outside the UK.

The results in Table 10.1 list the countries of origin for the total

Table 10.1 Scotland by place of birth

Place of birth	Number	% of population
All	5,295,403	100
Scotland	4,411,884	83.4
England	459,486	9.0
Northern Ireland	36,655	0.7
Wales	17,381	0.3
Poland	55,231	1.0
India	23,489	0.4
Ireland	22,952	0.4
Germany	22,274	0.4
Pakistan	20,039	0.4
United States	15,919	0.3
China	15,338	0.3
South Africa	10,607	0.2
Nigeria	9,458	0.2
Canada	9,435	0.2
Australia	8,279	0.2
Hong Kong	7,586	0.1
France	7,147	0.1
Italy	6,048	0.1

Bold = EU member state

Scottish population (incorporating only those locations where 5,000 or more residents now live in Scotland). In the last Scottish census of 2011, 93 per of Scotland's population was born in the UK, with 83 per cent natives of Scotland itself. Only 7 per cent were born outside the UK. Of the 883,000 residents not born in Scotland, 58 per cent were from elsewhere in the UK, with over half from England alone. Of those born outside the UK, half had arrived no more than a decade before the 2014 referendum.[4] In Catalonia, by contrast, 83 per cent of residents were born in Spain, with 65 per cent of them born in Catalonia and 17 per cent born outside Spain.

For Quebec we have annual intra-provincial figures rather than totals by province of birth, so a comparison is harder to identify. Nonetheless, 13.6 per cent of Quebecers were born outside Canada and in any given year twice as many migrants to Quebec were from outside Canada as from elsewhere in Canada. This suggests that interprovincial migrants form around 7 per cent of the population.[5] In other words, Scotland's migration pattern is distinct compared to these two examples, first because such a large proportion of the population is born in Scotland and, second, because the majority of migrants to Scotland are from elsewhere in the UK. In Catalonia, for example, those from outside Spain are roughly 50 per cent of total migrants. In any given year, Quebec attracts roughly twice as many migrants from outside Canada as it does from within Canada. This might well be a function of the way that language can act as a barrier to intrastate migration, as might be perceived to be the case in Catalonia and Quebec. In any event, migrants to Scotland are predominantly from elsewhere within the UK rather than from outside it.

If we are interested in diversity and the constitutional question in Scotland, there are a number of issues we can evaluate. First, we might, for example, look to see how inclusive the nationalist project actually is, whether it is perceived to be tied to ethnic or civic markers or if it excludes migrants or not. Nationalist movements, in general, vary in the extent to which they adopt civic, inclusive definitions of nationalist membership. There is something of a schism between the resolutely civic and inclusive messages of the Scottish National Party (including in its internal structures) and the more ethnic markers of belonging that Scottish residents (of all political stripes) believe should enable access to Scottish citizenship and passports.[6] For all that, though, the official messages of the pro-independence movement (both the political parties and associated groups such as Women for Independence) have emphasised civic and inclusive markers of belonging. The White Paper on independence, *Scotland's Future*, refers to 'We, the people who live here', clearly a deliberately inclusive framing of national membership. It suggests that Scottish citizenship would be extended to all British citizens 'habitually resident' in Scotland as well as to Scottish-born British citizens living outside Scotland. Second, we might focus on engagement with the referendum process. To what extent did different voters engage with referendum issues or with the different campaigns? Did we see greater involvement on the part of those born in Scotland? Third, we might focus on constitutional attitudes. What follows will focus predominantly on the latter two rather than the first.

LITERATURE REVIEW

A considerable body of research tracks the process by which immigrants integrate into new political environments. Part of this is learning new orientations or modes of participation that are appropriate to the new political context. For adult migrants, this can involve shedding the political views acquired in their previous state of residence, as well as the acquisition of values reflecting dominant modes of thought or action in the host state.[7] For this reason researchers have been interested to observe the integration processes of individuals moving across different political systems, from, for example, authoritarian regimes to democracies,[8] as well as following the integration processes of less dramatic transitions, for example from countries without compulsory voting to those with compulsory voting.[9]

Within multi-level (non-unitary), multi-national states there is an additional layer of complexity. To what extent do immigrants integrate themselves into a state-level political culture or into the 'small world' of a substate/regional/national political culture?[10] For a comparison with Scotland and the UK in relation to that question, Canadian research proves particularly useful. One study from the 1980s found that Canadian immigrants gradually acquired a sense of trust and efficacy that reflected dominant preferences in their host province.[11] In other words, immigrants became integrated within the wider substate political culture within which they lived. To the extent that different parts of the same state held different values, that diversity would also be broadly reflected in the attitudes of migrants. Related to this is the issue of frames of reference. Another study sought to determine whether immigrants adopt a substate frame of reference to their political worlds.[12] In other words, they looked to see whether immigrants adopt the dominant provincial interpretation of federal-provincial relations, including a sense of regional grievance should one be present. The authors found that the attitudes of migrants and Canadian-born respondents differ across provinces and by issue. Outside Quebec, the two groups tend to share similar views. Within Quebec, migrants are less likely to mirror Canadian-born respondents. They are also less likely to hold negative views of the federal government and its treatment of provinces. In general, they conclude that 'regional outlooks are reproduced among immigrants, notwithstanding the differences between immigrants and Canadian-born populations within provinces'.[13] Their analysis focuses on the distinction between those born in Canada and those outside. It does not explore possible influences of inter-provincial migration on attitudes to federal-provincial relations. In Scotland, however, it is typical to compare the attitudes not just of those born in Scotland and those born outside the UK, but of those who have migrated from elsewhere in the UK.

In a UK context there has been comparatively little focus on the political behaviour of migrants. There is a rich vein of research on 'race' and dominant ethnicity, but not typically on its relationship to voter choice, notwithstanding research on BAME support for the Labour

Party which can overlap with migration status.[14] There has been rather more work on the relationship between attitudes to immigration and other political output variables, such as policy preferences, than on the attitudes of migrants themselves.[15] Much of the work in Scotland has focused on the perceived benefits of migration,[16] the attitudes of parties to migration[17] rather than on the voting behaviour of migrants, and on the way that migrants align themselves with markers of Scottish national identity.[18] For the most part, studies of Scottish voting behaviour have not included place of birth as a key independent variable.[19]

Despite these gaps, we have reason to believe that immigrants on the whole might be less likely to support substate independence. There are four possible reasons for this. First, immigrants might hold greater attachment to the state that facilitated their immigration. Second, they might be less likely to adopt dominant perceptions of regional grievance within a state. These first two assumptions are consistent with the literature on migrant attitudes to politics.[20] Third, migrants might well have left countries undergoing violent political debate, and therefore they might have an aversion to political discord over constitutional change as well as a greater degree of support for the governing party. Last, if they are economic migrants they might well have an aversion to economic risk that might be associated with constitutional change.

On the other hand, there could also be reasons why migrants might be more supportive of substate independence if they hail from a country that sought to shake off the imperial attentions of other states (including the British state) or if they are attracted to the policy preferences – including about immigration – advocated by those who favour independence. Then they might well find themselves more supportive of change than those born within the region. Migrants are not an undifferentiated group. They vary by age, wealth, education, political views and country of origin – and indeed whether they are from within or outside the state. In order to understand what role place of birth plays in structuring constitutional attitudes we must evaluate it in terms of other known aspects of attitudes to independence, including those related to risk, partisan identification and national identity.

Given what we know from the comparative literature noted above, what might we expect of migrants to Scotland and their engagement with the referendum? We should first distinguish between migrants from elsewhere in the UK and those from beyond the UK. We would expect migrants from elsewhere in the UK to be as engaged with the referendum process as Scottish-born residents, due to a familiarity with the axes of political debate and the key runners and riders, and would expect migrants from outside the UK to be less engaged. On the issue of independence itself, however, we would anticipate greater variation between Scottish-born residents and those from elsewhere in the UK. If we believe that migrants are less likely to adopt a substate lens through which to evaluate political life, this might be expected to be particularly true for those born elsewhere in the state.

METHODOLOGY

The data for this chapter were collected as part of the ESRC-funded Scottish Referendum Study (SRS) involving researchers at universities in Edinburgh, Glasgow and Essex. Data for the SRS were collected by YouGov as part of their online panel. Wave one was conducted as a rolling cross-section design from 22 August until 17 September 2014. Wave two was conducted immediately after the referendum (22–26 September 2014), while the third wave was conducted one year after the referendum (28 September–15 October 2015). The relative sample sizes are 4,849, 3,719 and 2,610.

The YouGov questionnaire included items intended to probe variables such as place of birth but also included educational qualifications, income, religious observance and social class, as well as attitudes and behaviours related to the independence referendum. This included contact with and assessments of the campaigns, knowledge of key issues and preferences for the distribution of legislative competence. We also included a range of political control variables that have been shown to influence vote choice in elections, including partisan identification, political interest and attitudes to leaders. The result is a comprehensive dataset (sourced from the YouGov panel) that allows us to evaluate the impact of place of birth on constitutional attitudes.

RESULTS

We are interested in two facets of migration and constitutional attitudes. First, we are interested in levels of engagement with and satisfaction with the referendum campaign process and, second, in constitutional preferences themselves. On the first issue we would expect the key distinction to be between those from the UK and those outside, and on the second between those from elsewhere in the UK and those from Scotland or outside the UK.

Table 10.2 Campaign engagement by place of birth (% very often)

	Born in Scotland	Born in rest of UK	Born outside UK
Discussed the referendum with family and friends	51.3	49.3	39.3
Read about the referendum in newspapers or magazines	41.8	37.1	28.8
Discussed the referendum via social media or online forums	22.2	17.2	21.4
Attended public meetings about the referendum	7.4	6.5	4.6
Got involved in grassroots referendum campaigning	7.0	3.3	4.1

Engagement

Our measures of engagement explore whether respondents discussed the referendum with other people, the methods by which they did so, and whether they adopted particular behaviours during the referendum campaign (see Table 10.2).

In terms of levels of campaign engagement, those born outside the UK were consistently less likely to be involved than those of Scottish birth. But whether they were markedly less involved or whether they were more involved than those born in the rest of the UK varies by type of engagement. With respect to discussing the referendum with family and friends, fewer than four in ten immigrants from non-UK destinations to Scotland said they did so, compared to over half of the Scottish-born respondents and almost half of those born in the rest of the UK. The same pattern holds for reading about the referendum in newspapers or magazines, although the levels of engagement are lower here. Just over one-quarter of non-UK-born migrants read about the referendum, while over 40 per cent of Scottish-born respondents did so. There is a similar pattern for attending public meetings, although here all three groups by place of birth record levels of participation that suggest less than one in ten took part. Those born outside the UK were more likely to become involved in grassroots campaigning than those born in the rest of the UK. The striking findings, however, are for social media engagement. Here we see that those born outside the UK were as likely to engage online as were Scottish-born in the electorate. These results might well reflect the various barriers to participation felt by different groups, but with easier access to online activities.

In light of these findings it is perhaps unsurprising that we see

Table 10.3 Satisfaction with referendum process by place of birth

	Born in Scotland	Born in rest of UK	Born outside UK
The independence referendum was more important than any other vote in Scotland in the last fifty years	89.4	84.5	86.7
The independence debate has given ordinary people a say in Scotland's future	81.5	79.4	75.9
It was a good idea to allow 16- and 17-year-olds to vote in the referendum	60.6	49.3	40.7
Both sides of the referendum debate have had a fair chance to present their point of view	66.2	69.3	47.1
Although I was on one side of the debate I must admit that the other side had some strong points	41.1	43.1	31.5

differences across the three groups in terms of their subjective evaluations of knowledge about the referendum. Here we see that more than 58 per cent of Scottish-born respondents felt 'I know enough' about the referendum issues to make an informed choice. This figure dropped to just over 54 per cent for those born in the rest of the UK and to just over 50 per cent for those born outside the UK.

Given differing levels of engagement with the referendum, we might expect to see varying levels of satisfaction with the referendum process. Yet the extent to which this is true varies (see Table 10.3). All groups were equally likely to say that the referendum was the most important vote in the last fifty years in Scotland and all believed that the debate about independence was giving ordinary people a say in the future of the nation. The groups differ in their assessments of the quality of debate, perceived opportunities for deliberation and changes to the electoral franchise. Those born outside the UK were significantly less likely (40 per cent) to say that they thought it was a good idea to lower the franchise to 16 and 17 year-olds, compared to 60 per cent of those born in Scotland. Those born outside the UK were also less likely to believe that both sides had a fair chance to present their point of view in the referendum debate (less than 50 per cent compared to almost 70 per cent for other groups) and were less likely to say that the other side had strong points (30 per cent compared to 40 per cent for other groups).

If we look at levels of engagement, then, we can distinguish, for many of the indicators, between those born within the UK, regardless of whether they were born in Scotland or not, and those born outside the UK, with lower levels of engagement from migrants outside the UK and lower levels of satisfaction. It is worth noting, however, that there are exceptions to this general pattern.

Referendums vary in the extent to which they pose new or well-known issues to voters. They are often criticised for the fact that they provide limited opportunities for deliberation, and offer to voters the opportunity merely to cast a ballot on government performance rather than the referendum issue itself. In that way, independence referendums may be considered unique. They offer opportunities where the stakes are high – in other words, on issues that are meaningful to voters – and on questions where voters typically have a view before the referendum date approaches. In light of this, we might expect those born in Scotland to have decided earlier how they would vote than those from elsewhere in the UK or outside the UK. What we find, however, is that those born in the rest of the UK were significantly more likely to have known all along how they would vote, and significantly less likely to have made up their minds in the last few weeks (see Table 10.4). To the extent that the campaign sought to change hearts and minds, this was least likely to have an effect on those born in the rest of the UK. Those born outside the UK appeared to be the opposite of those born in England, Wales or Northern Ireland, for they were the least likely to have known all along how they would vote. It is worth noting, however, that even though the differences across the groups are large – approximately ten percentage points when we compare those born in the rest of the UK and those born outside the UK – a majority of all groups knew 'all along' how they would vote. Thereafter, the most prevalent response is 'reaching a decision in the last few weeks of the campaign'.

We know that the flourishing extent of democratic participation during the referendum campaign was perceived to have transformed Scotland. Elsewhere we have noted that there are significant differences between Yes and No voters, with No voters significantly less likely to say that they will stay more engaged or that Scotland as a whole has

Table 10.4 Timing of vote choice by place of birth

	Born in Scotland	Born in rest of UK	Born outside UK
I've known all along how I would vote	59.7	64.2	52.1
Once referendum was announced	5.2	5.8	9.0
Year before referendum	7.3	6.6	7.7
Few months before referendum	10.0	9.1	9.5
Last few weeks	17.7	14.4	21.6

Table 10.5 Post-referendum engagement by place of birth (% will state more involved)

	Born in Scotland	Born in rest of UK	Born outside UK
Scotland as a country will stay involved	46.6	40.3	41.1
Self as an individual will stay involved	48.8	41.3	41.6

changed. Over 60 per cent of Yes voters indicated that they were likely to stay more involved, while this was true of just under one-third of No voters. The gap in perceptions of whether Scotland was transformed by the referendum is similarly large (just over 15 per cent for No voters and over 50 per cent for Yes voters believing that Scotland will remain more engaged). We also see in Table 10.5 significant variations by place of birth. Scottish-born respondents were significantly more likely to say that they will stay more involved and that Scotland as a whole is more likely to stay more involved. On this issue, those born outside the UK and those born in the UK outside of Scotland were very similar, with roughly four in ten saying that they will stay more involved (compared to almost half of all those born in Scotland). Thus, while we see gaps by place of birth, the range of responses is nothing like the difference we see between Yes and No voters in Scotland.

Support for independence

If we wish to understand the relationship between migration and constitutional attitudes we can of course evaluate support for independence by place of birth. Those born in Scotland were more likely to back independence (52.7 per cent Yes vs 47.3 per cent No), while those born outside the UK were more likely to back the status quo, and by a bigger margin (42.9 per cent Yes vs 57.1 per cent No). The biggest gap between Yes and No supporters can be seen among those born outside Scotland but born elsewhere in the UK. Here we see 27.9 per cent support for Yes and 72.1 per cent support for No. We cannot therefore distinguish between assorted migrants, but can distinguish between those born in Scotland, those born in the rest of the UK and those born outside the UK. It is clear that migrants to Scotland hold different attitudes to constitutional matters. It is also worth noting that the gaps we see by place of birth are similar to the variations across other demographic groups. Support for Yes and No among those born outside the UK is most similar to levels of support by women in Scotland (with No favoured over Yes), with Scottish-born respondents most similar to the

Table 10.6 National identity by place of birth

	Born in Scotland	Born in rest of UK	Born outside UK
Scottish not British	30.9	4.5	11.9
More Scottish than British	30.1	8.8	14.9
Equally Scottish and British	31.9	17.7	15.7
More British than Scottish	4.3	15.4	5.7
British not Scottish	1.3	34.6	13.7
Other	1.1	15.4	24.5

balance of support for Yes and No among men (with Yes favoured over No). The outliers, as such, in other words those least similar to the domestic-born population, are those born in the rest of the UK, who have a balance of attitudes to Yes and No that are more polarised than those found in any other demographic group with the exception of religious denomination.[21]

When we wish to explain the correlates of support for independence we look at attitudes such as national identity, perceptions of regional grievance and attitudes to risk. These help us to understand the frames of reference that different groups might use when engaging with the referendum issue. Before determining whether these have an independent impact on referendum vote choice it is worth verifying whether different respondents, by their place of birth, hold different national identities or different political attitudes (see Table 10.6).

Surveys typically evaluate attitudes to national identity in a number of different ways. We sometimes ask individuals on a scale of 0 to 10 and so on which among a list of possible national identities they would use to describe themselves, or which single identity best describes how they feel, or how attached they are to particular places. One common measure of national identity requires individuals to state whether they hold state and substate identities and, if both, whether one is more important than the other. Developed from a scale used by Juan Linz in Spain, the Moreno question has been employed consistently in Scottish attitudes research. It is particularly useful as it enables us to understand the affinity that different groups of migrants might feel towards the state or to the substate region/nation. The results in Table 10.6 reveal that those born outside the UK are almost three times as likely to describe themselves as Scottish rather than British as those born in the rest of the UK. Those born in the rest of the UK are the only group to prioritise their sense of Britishness over other identities (50 per cent compared to 5.6 per cent for those born in Scotland). Admittedly the question forces

Table 10.7 Holyrood voting intention by place of birth

	Born in Scotland	Born in rest of UK	Born outside UK
SNP	43.7	21.0	38.4
Labour	32.0	28.8	32.1
Conservative	13.2	19.8	11.9
LibDem	3.1	7.8	5.3

respondents to choose between Scottish and British poles, and therefore we might have had significantly fewer British responses to a question that asked respondents to compare their English or Welsh identity and a British identity. If we recall the Bilodeau et al. research about frames of reference, we can see that those born in Scotland are more likely to prioritise their Scottish identity than other voters.[22]

We can also evaluate voting intention by place of birth (see Table 10.7). We know that support for the SNP correlates strongly with support for independence. We might therefore expect to see higher rates of support for the SNP among Scottish-born respondents. In our sample, those born in Scotland were indeed more likely to vote for the SNP (almost 45 per cent in our sample). The figure is lower but not substantially so among those born outside the UK, and both groups were as likely to say that they were going to vote Labour. Those born in Scotland were only slightly more likely to say that they were going to vote for the Conservative Party than were those born outside the UK. It is those born in the rest of the UK who stand out, both in terms of being significantly less likely to vote for the SNP (something which can be considered a demographic obstacle for SNP support) and significantly more likely to vote for the Conservatives than other residents.

We know from research in Canada that one reason migrants have been slow to support independence in Quebec is because they have been slow to adopt a lens of regional grievance through which to evaluate state-level politics.[23] We can explore the same issues in Scotland. One typical question explores whether respondents believe that Scotland obtains less than its fair share or more than its fair share of UK funding (see Table 10.8). Here we see that those born in Scotland and those born outside the UK are more likely to say that Scotland gets much less than its fair share, and less likely to say that it gets more than its fair share. Those born in the rest of the UK are significantly more likely to say that Scotland gets more than its fair share. Less clear is whether this is because, having lived elsewhere in the UK, they retain a UK-wide lens for evaluating resource distribution, or whether they retain a territorial

Table 10.8 Regional grievance by place of birth

	Born in Scotland	Born in rest of UK	Born outside UK
Scotland gets much less than its fair share	21.7	11.8	17.3
A little less than its fair share	29.7	21.2	30.5
More or less its fair share	30.0	31.2	28.5
A little more than its fair share	15.6	26.7	20.2
Scotland gets much more than its fair share	3.1	9.1	3.5

Table 10.9 Attitudes to specific risks by place of birth

	Born in Scotland	Born in rest of UK	Born outside UK
The general election situation in Scotland would be worse (% likely)	40.5	59.7	43.3
Scotland could keep using pound (% unlikely)	24.9	39.6	32.5
Scotland would be able to retain EU membership (% unlikely)	36.8	54.4	37.0

lens through which to view things but the territory in question is not Scotland. In any event, newcomers to Scotland are less likely to believe the country gets a poor deal if they have lived elsewhere in the UK.

We know from research on the referendum that risk perceptions matter (see Table 10.9). Those more tolerant of generalised risk are more likely to vote for change in a range of referendum settings.[24] We can see that those born in Scotland and migrants from outside the UK were less likely to foresee risks in the event of independence. They were less likely to believe that the general economic situation would deteriorate, less likely to believe it unlikely that Scotland would be able to continue to use the pound sterling as currency, and less likely to believe it unlikely that Scotland would retain membership in the EU. Of course, whether these are considered to be risks or opportunities depends on one's perspective. One might see EU membership as a risk (to parliamentary sovereignty, to specific economic sectors, in terms of uncontrolled migration) or might see its loss as a risk. Risk is also relevant because one argument for the status quo bias in referendums is that migrants are more likely to be risk averse as a result of their economic situation, although here variation among migrants in terms of income and employment status is obviously relevant.[25]

The results in Table 10.10 allow us to compare attitudes to specific

Table 10.10 Reaction to Yes and No arguments by place of birth (% extremely convincing)

	Born in Scotland	Born in rest of UK	Born outside UK
Yes arguments			
Scottish problems are bound to be better understood in Edinburgh than in London	40.5	22.7	27.9
Without independence, Scotland will keep on getting governments it hasn't voted for	41.8	21.6	33.0
Scotland should be free to shape its own role in the world	36.7	19.5	27.0
Independence is the natural state of nations like Scotland	28.1	12.8	18.0
Scottish political values are different from those in the rest of the UK	26.1	14.7	15.0
No arguments			
There are too many unanswered questions about what an independent Scotland would look like	33.4	48.5	30.7
Nations are stronger when they work together rather than going it alone	26.5	36.6	23.2
For as long as Scotland uses the pound and the Bank of England sets its interest rates, it won't really be independent	22.1	30.3	17.5
An independent Scotland would be too reliant on oil	19.9	27.8	16.0
Further devolution will give Scotland more autonomy without the risks of separation	15.7	22.9	13.2

Yes arguments by place of birth. Here we see that Scottish-born voters found all Yes arguments more convincing than migrants. Indeed, over 40 per cent found it 'extremely convincing' that Scotland's problems are better understood in Edinburgh, and that Scotland would continue to get the governments it has not voted for without independence. In each instance, respondents from the rest of the UK found the arguments least convincing. They were also least likely to believe that Scottish political values are different from those in the rest of the UK. This is an issue on which migrants fwrom within and beyond the UK agree.

The same patterns hold for No arguments, with those born in the rest of the UK most likely to find it extremely convincing that Scotland would not benefit from more autonomy but that an independent Scotland would be too reliant on oil, faces too many unanswered questions, and should work together with the rest of the UK. It is not particularly surprising that Scottish-born respondents, who we know were more likely to vote Yes, find Yes arguments more convincing than other respondents. For this reason we would not wish to include such questions in any models seeking to account for referendum preferences. Attitudes to the arguments might explain support for Yes, or support for Yes might lead to positive evaluation of messages about independence. What is worth highlighting, however, is the nature of the gap, the issues that divide the Scottish-born and migrants, as well as the issues on which different types of migrants agree or differ. In almost all cases, those born outside the UK typically possess attitudes that place them between those born in Scotland and those born in the rest of the UK in terms of reactions to Yes arguments, attitudes to specific risks and Holyrood voting intention. We can distinguish, therefore, not between Scottish-born and migrants, but between a polarised vision of politics held by those born in different parts of the UK and the middle ground views of those from outside the UK.

Of course, if we want to understand voting preferences we should explore issues not just in a bivariate sense (the relationship between place of birth and one other issue at a time). In order to explain the different influences on constitutional preferences we can build a model of vote choice while holding a range of different issues constant. If we construct a demographic model of vote choice we see that those born outside Scotland were less likely to vote Yes, but for only those born in the rest of the UK is the coefficient significant (in other words, we can be reasonably confident we are not making errors when we say that the variable influences vote choice). The only variable influencing greater impact on support for No is that of religious denomination as a member of the Church of England. To a certain extent, these results are consistent with the academic literature. Migrants from beyond the UK had lower levels of engagement and were less likely to perceive a sense of regional or national grievance. There were no signs that migrants were unduly influenced by risks of independence. In most cases the group with lower levels of engagement, or disaffection, were those born in the rest of the UK.

If we add in other variables, including a sense of national identity, regional grievance (measured in this case by a perception that Scotland gets less than its fair share) and attitudes to specific risks related to a Yes vote, we see that place of birth does not matter. In other words, once we control for the fact that people who are born in different places hold different views, then place of birth ceases to exert an independent influence on vote choice.

Table 10.11 Predictors of support for independence

	Demographic variables	All variables
Age		
Gender	Women less likely to vote	Women less likely to vote
Degree	Yes	Yes
Place of birth		
Born in rest of UK		
Born outside the UK	Less likely to vote Yes	
Housing status		
Owner occupier		
Social renter	Less likely to vote Yes	
Religious denomination		
Presbyterian/C of Scotland		
Catholic	Less likely to vote Yes	Less likely to vote Yes
Anglican/C of England		
Other Religion	Less likely to vote Yes	Less likely to vote Yes
Income		
Lowest income quartile		
Highest income quartile	More likely to vote Yes	
Scottish more than/not British		More likely to vote Yes
Regional grievance		More likely to vote Yes
Specific risks		More likely to vote Yes

There are of course limitations to any study and the same is true of our survey. Despite what might be considered a large sample size for a referendum study, levels of migration to Scotland ensure that we have very small numbers for some categories of migrant. This makes it difficult for us to extend our analysis within particular migrant groups. Our sample size is too small, for example, to explore the impact of parental country of birth, or the influence of migrating from different democratic regions. We also have no way to identify migrants by the length of time they have spent in Scotland or by form of migration: whether they arrived in Scotland as economic migrants, as part of family reunification or to seek asylum. We know that the economic context of migration could well produce situations in which attitudes to risk might vary significantly. Future studies would do well to include such variables and to oversample among migrants, as well as to examine how migration status and place of birth interacts with race and religious denomination.

These limitations notwithstanding, what might we make of these findings? Our expectations were that those born in the UK would have similar attitudes to and similar levels of engagement, with those born outside the UK less engaged. To a certain extent our results suggest that this is the case. We also expected those born elsewhere in the UK to hold less supportive attitudes to constitutional change, in part because of the frames of reference they employ for national identity and for a sense of regional grievance. Such findings are consistent with the wider literature on migration and attitudes to constitutional politics. This indeed appears to be the case and it likewise appears to be variations in territorial frames of reference that influence constitutional attitudes rather than place of birth itself.

Might we then conclude that migration played a role in the 2014 independence referendum? If we are interested purely in the result, then yes. A franchise that was restricted not to residents of Scotland but to those born in Scotland would, on the basis of our research findings, have resulted in a Yes vote. But no such franchise was pursued, nor can such a franchise be considered defensible in light of the deliberately civic construction of Scottish national identity as outlined by both the SNP and the Scottish Government's White Paper on independence. Did a particular group of migrants swing the result for the No side? No. Even if all those residents born in the rest of the UK had similar preferences to those born outside the UK the result would not have been different. What the results suggest, however, is that different groups of voters engage with the political process differently. Not only do they come to different conclusions about the ideal constitutional arrangements for the polity but they participate with differing levels of engagement and deliberation.

NOTES

1. F. Bechhofer and D. McCrone, 'Choosing national identity', *Sociological Research Online*, 15:3 (2010), http://www.socresonline.org.uk/15/3/3.html.
2. J. McKee, 'Scottish nationalism isn't racist – but Sadiq Khan has a point', *New Statesman*, 1 March 2017; Claire Heuchan, 'The parallels between Scottish nationalism and racism are clear', *The Guardian*, 27 February 2017; David Torrance, 'Curious case of SNP's shift from ethnic nationalism', *The Herald*, 14 April 2014.
3. Allan Woods, '"Money and ethnic votes": The words that shape Jacques Parizeau's legacy', *Toronto Star*, 2 June 2014.
4. National Records of Scotland, *Country of Birth (detailed), Scotland's Census* (Edinburgh: NRS, 2013), www.scotlandscensus.gov.uk/.../census-results/.../rel2a_COB_detailed_Scotland.pdf.
5. There are ten times as many people born in Italy living in Quebec (58,750) as living in Scotland (6,048). Ministère de l'Immigration, de la Diversité et

de l'Inclusion, *Immigration et Démographie au Québec* (Quebec, 2015), www.midi.gouv.qc.ca/.../fr/.../

6. Ailsa Henderson, *Hierarchies of Belonging: National Identity and Political Culture in* Scotland and Quebec (Montreal: McGill-Queen's University Press, 2007). Pub_Immigration_et_demo_2015.pdf.

7. J. W. Berry, 'Immigration, acculturation, and adaptation', *Applied Psychology: An International Review*, 46:1 (1997), pp. 5–69; J. W. Berry, 'A psychology of immigration', *Journal of Social Issues*, 57:3 (2001), pp. 615–31; A. Bilodeau, *Just Ordinary Citizens? Towards a Comparative Portrait of the Political Immigrant* (Toronto: University of Toronto Press, 2015); J. H. Black, 'The practice of politics in two settings: Political transferability among recent immigrants to Canada', *Canadian Journal of Politics*, 20:4 (1987), pp. 731–54; J. H. Black, R. G. Niemi and G. B. Powell Jr, 'Age, resistance, and political learning in a new environment: The case of Canadian immigrants', *Comparative Politics*, 20:1 (1987), pp. 73–84; M. Fennema and J. Tillie, 'Political participation and political trust in Amsterdam: Civic communities and ethnic networks', *Journal of Ethnic and Migration Studies*, 25:4 (1999), pp. 703–26; R. Huckfelt, and J. Sprague, 'Networks in context: The social flow of political information', *American Political Science Review*, 81:4 (1987), pp. 1197–1216; M. MacKuen and C. Brown, 'Political context and attitude change', *American Political Science Review*, 81:2 (1987), pp. 471–90; I. McAllister and T. Makkai, 'Resource and social learning theories of political participation: Ethnic patterns in Australia', *Canadian Journal of Political Science*, 25:2 (1992), pp. 269–93; S. McClung, 'Social networks and political participation: The role of social interaction in explaining political participation', *Political Research Quarterly*, 56:4 (2003), pp. 449–64; J. G. Reitz, R. Banerjee, M. Phan and J. Thompson, 'Race, religion, and the social integration of new immigrant minorities in Canada', *International Migration Review*, 43:4 (2009), pp. 695–726; S. White, A. Bilodeau and N. Nevitte, 'Earning their support: Feelings towards Canada among recent immigrants', *Ethnic and Racial Studies*, 38:2 (2015), pp. 292–308.

8. A. Bilodeau and N. Nevitte, 'Political trust for a new regime: The case of immigrants from non-democratic countries in Canada', unpublished paper presented at the annual meeting of the American Political Association, 2003; A. Bilodeau, 'Immigrants' voice through protest politics in Canada and Australia: Assessing the impact of pre-migration political repression', *Journal of Ethnic and Migration Studies*, 34:6 (2008), pp. 975–1002.

9. A. Finifter and B. Finifter, 'Party identification and political adaptation of American migrants in Australia', *Journal of Politics*, 51:3 (1989), pp. 599–630.

10. D. J. Elkins and R. Simeon (eds), *Small Worlds: Provinces and Parties in Canadian Political Life* (Toronto: Methuen, 1980).

11. D. J. Elkins, 'The horizontal mosaic: Immigrants and migrants in the

provincial political cultures', in D. J. Elkins and R. Simeon (eds), *Small Worlds: Provinces and Parties in Canadian Political* Life (Toronto: Methuen, 1980), pp. 106–30.

12. A. Bilodeau, S. White and N. Nevitte, 'The development of dual loyalties: Immigrants' integration to Canadian regional dynamics', *Canadian Journal of Political Science*, 43:3 (2010), pp. 515–44.

13. Ibid., p. 528.

14. Electoral Commission, *Black and Minority Ethnic Survey* (London: Electoral Commission, 2005).

15. See, for example, A. F. Heath and J. R. Tilley, 'British national identity and attitudes towards immigration', *International Journal on Multicultural Societies*, 7:2 (2005), pp. 119–32; D. Cutts, R. Ford and M. J. Goodwin, 'Anti-immigrant, politically disaffected or still racist after all? Examining the attitudinal drivers of extreme right support in Britain in the 2009 European elections', *European Journal of Political Research*, 50:3 (2011), pp. 418–40; R. Ford, M. J. Goodwin and D. Cutts, 'Strategic Eurosceptics and polite xenophobes: Support for the United Kingdom Independence Party (UKIP) in the 2009 European Parliament elections', *European Journal of Political Research*, 51:2 (2012), pp. 204–34.

16. D. McCollum, B. Nowak and S. Tindal, 'Perceptions of migration: How "different" is Scotland from the rest of the UK?', *Research brief for AQMeN and ScotCen* (2014), http://aqmen.ac.uk/sites/default/files/SSA_Briefs_3_McCollum_Nowok_Tindal.pdf.

17. E. Hepburn and M. Rosie, 'Immigration, nationalism and political parties in Scotland', in E. Hepburn and Ricard Zapata-Barrero (eds), *The Politics of Immigration in Multi-level States: Governance and Political Parties* (Basingstoke: Palgrave Macmillan 2014).

18. A. Saeed, N. Blain and D. Forbes, 'New ethnic and national questions in Scotland: Post-British identities among Glasgow Pakistani teenagers', *Ethnic and Racial Studies*, 22:5 (1999), pp. 821–44; R. Bond, 'Belonging and becoming: National identity and exclusion', *Sociology*, 40:4 (2006); A. Henderson, *Hierarchies of Belonging* (Montreal: McGill-Queen's University Press, 2007).

19. See, for example, C. Carman, R. Johns and J. Mitchell, *More Scottish than British: The 2011 Scottish Parliament Election* (Basingstoke: Palgrave, 2014); J. Curtice, D. McCrone, N. McEwen, M. Marsh and R. Ormston, *Revolution or Evolution: The 2007 Scottish Elections* (Edinburgh: Edinburgh University Press, 2009).

20. Bilodeau et al., 'The development of dual loyalties', pp. 515–44.

21. Among those describing their religious denomination as Catholic or Roman Catholic, the balance of support for No and Yes was 44 per cent to 56 per cent respectively. This becomes 82 per cent No and 18 per cent Yes among those describing their religious denomination as Anglican or Church of England.

THE 2014 SCOTTISH INDEPENDENCE REFERENDUM

22. Bilodeau et al., 'The development of dual loyalties', pp. 515–44.
23. Ibid.
24. Richard Nadeau, Pierre Martin and André Blais, 'Attitude towards risk-taking and individual choice in the Quebec referendum on sovereignty', *British Journal of Political Science*, 29 (1999), pp. 523–39.
25. Ibid., pp. 523–39.

11

Immigration to Scotland since 1945: The Global Context

Enda Delaney

INTRODUCTION

The decades after 1945 were an era of mass migration across the globe.[1] The end of the Second World War initiated huge population movements across Europe, as did events in Asia, including the partition of India in 1947 and the establishment of the People's Republic of China in 1949. Demobilisation, and fears for the future under the new dispensations held by ethnic and religious minorities such as Jews in Poland and other parts of Eastern Europe, created a major international refugee crisis. Combined with labour shortages in the immediate post-war period in the major industrial powers such as West Germany, the UK and France, migration emerged as a defining feature of the post-war years.[2] These events in faraway places were part of the wider global context in which the history of immigration to Scotland since 1945 occurred. The ethnic composition of Scotland, along with the other parts of the UK, was shaped with the arrival of significant numbers of migrants and refugees from Europe, Asia and Africa. This, by necessity, involved a reconfiguration of what it meant to be Scottish. What had seemed like certainties in terms of national identities at the start of the twentieth century were challenged by immigration and the consequent need to revisit what it meant to be Scottish, English, Welsh or indeed Irish.

Scotland's immigration history after 1945 can be best understood in three overlapping spheres. Migrants from within the United Kingdom have always been an important component of Scotland's immigrant population, and that has remained the case up to the present day, as people born in England, Wales and Northern Ireland make up about a tenth of the total population.[3] Second, migrants from Scotland's European neighbours have a long history, including the Irish, Italians,

Poles and many other groups. Scotland, as a part of the UK, was a member of the European Union (or European Economic Community) from 1973. In 2016 just over 7 per cent of the Scottish population was born outside the UK. The enlargement of the European Union in 2004 meant that migrants from accession states settled in Scotland in significant numbers. In 2016, of the estimated 181,000 EU migrants living in Scotland, two-thirds were from accession countries, around a half of which were Polish.[4] Finally, Scotland, like England and Wales, had a long and complex imperial past. In the late 1940s relatively small numbers of Caribbean migrants arriving in Britain attracted much public attention. From the 1960s, immigrants from South Asia and former African colonies also came to Scotland, albeit in smaller numbers, settling primarily in the urban conurbations of lowland Scotland. The Chinese who settled in Scotland in the 1950s came primarily from Hong Kong, where the Scottish influence was very strong prior to independence in 1997.[5]

In the 2011 census, one in six of the people resident in Scotland were born outside the country.[6] Contrary to the widespread assumption since the mid-nineteenth century, when migrants from other parts of the UK are included Scotland has always had a slightly higher proportion of immigrants than England and Wales.[7] The significant share of migrants from within the UK compares with relatively low levels of immigration from the New Commonwealth from the 1950s onwards. As Michael Anderson argues, it was about the choices made in terms of locations by Commonwealth immigrants:

> The key reason why England had net immigration flows from the 1950s onwards was not that its natives did not emigrate in large numbers: they did, though not on as large scale as from Scotland. England also attracted growing numbers of immigrants from outside the UK: by contrast, until well into the twenty-first century, disproportionately far fewer of these migrants came to Scotland.[8]

Within a global context a noteworthy feature of Scotland's demographic experience after 1945 is the coexistence of emigration and immigration over much of the post-war era. In a European context, a number of southern European countries such as Italy, Spain and Portugal exported large numbers of people to the advanced economies of Western Europe but were also destinations of choice for non-European migrants, particularly in the later stages of the twentieth century.[9] Equally, after the financial crash that occurred in Ireland in 2008, for the following nine years the emigration of Irish-born people occurred at the same time as migration from Europe, Africa and elsewhere.[10] It may well seem contradictory that some people leave a country at the same time that others choose to settle, but these patterns tell us more about the fragmentation of labour markets and the differential opportunities available to individuals depending on skills and education. Low-paid, unskilled jobs are often the forms of employment that are most readily accessible to immigrants.

THE PAST AND THE PRESENT

Scotland's long history of accommodating, if not entirely welcoming, immigrants establishes the broader context for the responses to the arrival of 'new' immigrants after 1945.[11] Five groups in particular should be mentioned here: the English, discussed by T. M. Devine, whose deep and entangled connections with Scotland ensured they were the most numerous and arguably powerful migrant group; the Irish, who since time immemorial had settled in Scotland, but who arrived in large numbers from the mid-1840s onwards; Jews from Eastern Europe who arrived from the 1880s onwards; the Poles who came to Scotland across the twentieth century but especially during and immediately after the Second World War; and finally the Italians, who had made Scotland their home in the interwar years. Each of these groups had experienced acute hostility at times: for the Italians the Second World War proved an especially hostile time as many were interned as enemy aliens; Jews experienced occasional outbreaks of anti-Semitism; and the Poles along with the Irish and Italians experienced anti-Catholicism as well as other forms of religious intolerance. These European migrants were the most obvious manifestation of immigration until the 1950s and 1960s. Sectarianism reached its most brutal form in the anti-Irishness that was such an endemic feature of modern Scotland and which continues to linger on in certain forms to the present day.

Immigration was therefore nothing new to Scotland after 1945, even if the place of origin was different or indeed the 'new' migrants looked unlike previous waves of settlers. Those arriving in Scotland come to a society that while hardly embracing past immigrations certainly understood the necessity of welcoming newcomers, not least due to demographic considerations. Scotland's population growth in the twenty-first century is largely a consequence of immigration. While the numbers born in other parts of the UK living in Scotland have remained relatively stable between 2001 and 2011, the total of people born outside the UK has nearly doubled.[12] This marks a new phase in the history of Scottish immigration.

SHARED SPACES

One of the issues which does not emerge in the preceding chapters is how immigrants to Scotland after 1945 inhabited shared urban and rural spaces. There was, as is often the case with the arrival of new immigrants, residential clustering, as is clear from the chapters by Eona Bell, Stefano Bonino and Emilia Piętka-Nykaza. To say that the English migrants occupied very different worlds to the Poles and Chinese is almost a cliché. What is different about Scotland after 1945, and much the same can be said for England and Wales, is the ethnic diversity of the population. Before the Second World War the Irish and Jews were the largest migrant populations, and while each group had a distinctive sense of their own identity and attracted considerable antipathy and occasionally racial violence, the post-war experience was very different. In the UK more generally, relatively small numbers of migrants from the New Commonwealth coming in the 1940s and 1950s attracted disproportionate attention in everyday interactions and in the press and political sphere, leading ultimately to the introduction of restrictionist immigration controls in the Commonwealth Immigrants Act, passed in 1962.

Presumably the English did not see themselves as migrants to Scotland but rather as people 'relocating' within the UK for work or family reasons. The stereotype of the 'immigrant' was a racialised one, often based on skin colour and a sense of innate difference. The chapters on African refugees and asylum seekers by Teresa Piacentini shows how images and stereotypes, many of which were racist, conditioned not just the response of the society at large but also the migrants themselves. An intriguing theme which emerges tangentially in this chapter and in other work on Africans in Scotland is the complex colonial relationship between Scotland and Africa forged through imperialism and mission-ary evangelical activity.[13] One of the reasons why Scotland was known to prospective newcomers was the links that had been established over the previous centuries through colonial governance, education and evan-gelicalism. This was not perhaps the 'mother country' that Caribbean immigrants imagined England to be. Yet Scotland's role in the empire did ensure that there was knowledge about the society in many distant places. In the twentieth century Britain's colonial past in Africa and South East Asia began to shape domestic society, not least as immigrants from the colonies came to settle in Britain, including Scotland, as they were legally entitled to do under the British Nationality Act of 1948.[14] This point comes out in Bonino's chapter on Pakistanis and Indians, when he underlines how the imperial past influenced the connections of people and place after 1945.

What is arguably the next logical stage in the development of studies of migration to Scotland after 1945 is an assessment of the cultural effects of this movement beyond the traditional conventional wisdom relating to the growth of ethnic food and stereotypical types of businesses associated with Chinese, Indians, Pakistanis and Italians. A more sophisticated exploration of the encounter between 'old' and 'new' Scots would examine topics such as multi-generational cultural production, how Scottish culture and society was reformulated as a consequence of immigration, and how immigration challenged notions of what it meant to be Scottish in the contemporary world. Bell's research on the Chinese in Scotland summarised in her chapter demonstrates the potential of such finely grained ethnographic work undertaken by a social anthropologist.

Looking more broadly to scholarship on the English, Scots and Irish overseas, a conspicuous absence is any detailed investigation of the relationships between these groups in the new environments in which they settled, let alone sustained historical analysis of how they related to other migrant groups. There are tantalising glimpses, for instance, of the often fractious relations between the Irish and the Chinese in San Francisco in the later nineteenth century or between the Irish and African-Americans in mid-nineteenth-century New York City.[15] Competing often for housing and work in the same spheres must have created tensions between immigrant groups in Scotland after 1945, as it did in the nineteenth century, yet we know relatively little about these dimensions.

Naturally historians must circumscribe the coverage to a particular group at a particular point in time. Another approach would be to explore the history of a place to identify how migrants interacted with each other. A recent study of New York City as an immigrant destination gives an indication of the numerous benefits of such an approach.[16] Both Glasgow and Edinburgh have well-established historiographies yet immigrants rarely feature in most studies of social and cultural life in either city. The social scientific research which is represented in this book in the chapters by Bell and Piacentini indicates the potential of seeing migrants from the inside out, or more precisely how the world-view of those who settled in Scotland after 1945 was shaped by encounters with other immigrants, either 'new' groups or more established ethnic communities such as the Irish or Italians.

And even more intriguing is to investigate inter-generational relations between groups who settled at different points in time, and how they saw both those who arrived before and after them. There is some fascinating if fragmentary evidence, for instance, that the Irish who arrived in the United States in the 1950s did not forge common cause with established Irish-Americans, not least because, as one Irish consular official put it, 'a great deal of the sentimentalism and romanticism of so many Irish-Americans grates on the younger people coming to this country'.[17] The basic point here is that the Ireland they had come from was very different, as indeed was the society they had now settled in. How, for instance, did the established Polish community who settled in Scotland in the 1940s and 1950s respond to the 'new' Poles who came to Scotland after EU accession in 2004? Did this generation have different attitudes towards the Catholic Church, a key community institution for the older generation? Similarly, Bonino's chapter reminds us of the importance of institutions and associational culture within the lives of migrants, largely based around religious denominations, and this also emerges in other chapters.

We have very few multi-generational histories of migrants in Scotland, or Britain more generally. Inevitably we focus on the first and most obvious generations, leaving out those who while being born in Scotland do not see themselves primarily as 'white Scottish' or 'white: other British', to use the classifications employed by recent census enumerations. How these questions might be teased out in the context of Scotland's immigration history after 1945 would involve developing an analytical and conceptual framework that is both horizontal in capturing a cross-section of immigrants and ethnic groups, and vertical in charting changes across time for specific groups. Some work has been done using oral history, and the benefits of this approach are obvious for tracing multi-generational histories and how ethnic identities were shaped over time.[18] Nicholas J. Evans and Angela McCarthy in their chapter on 'New' Jews use oral testimony very effectively to give a sense of Scottish Jewish identity and how this changed over time. Jewish identity is a particularly intriguing case study given its multi-generational nature and there is potential to make comparisons across Jewish communities in England, the United States and many other places.

One final point that might be added is the tendency of historians and social scientists to see immigrant groups as monolithic entities. Differences of class, geographical origin, religion and sense of integration within the receiving society often created divisions within what seemed to outsiders to be cohesive groups. To an external observer all members of a group can appear to display similar characteristics and this lumping together of sometimes very diverse people into ethnic categories can unintentionally flatten out these subtle yet very important differences.

THE POLITICS OF IMMIGRATION

Scotland's immigration policy was determined by the wider British move towards restrictionism from the early 1960s onwards, culminating in the Immigration Act of 1971, effectively cutting off unrestricted access to migrants from the New Commonwealth. Nativism never featured in Scottish political or public discourse after 1945, but some of the debates surrounding Irish immigration in the 1920s had distinct racial and sectarian dimensions. Nativism inspired by racism reached its nadir in the 1919 'race' riots in Glasgow.[19] These riots were fuelled by racial hatred as well as by concerns about employment. Arguably the sectarianism associated with the Old Firm rivalry provided a focus for the playing out of ritualistic ethnic tensions between the descendants of Irish Protestants and Irish Catholics in a set-piece format. While these chapters undoubtedly do not suggest that there was a universal Scottish response to different waves of immigrants, nativist responses were rare and exceptional.

Across the Western world from the 1950s and 1960s, governments introduced legislation to restrict the entry of immigrants. The McCarran-Walter Act of 1952 established the terms of US immigration policy up until the present day, though subsequent measures introduced in 1965 and 1990 modified its provisions. Nevertheless the emphasis was on selective entry and restriction. Similarly in the UK, the Commonwealth Immigrants Acts introduced a set of provisions in 1962 and 1968 which established immigration controls, though this was largely directed at Black and Asian arrivals. Likewise, Australia and New Zealand introduced immigration policies in the 1960s and 1970s, privileging white British and Irish migrants over other groups from Europe, Asia and Africa.

A counter-prevailing tendency was the freedom of the movement of labour enshrined as a foundational principle in the formation of the European Economic Community. When the UK joined the EEC in 1973, Scotland, as with other parts of the UK, was bound to observe this principle and, in large part, benefited from workers from EU countries in the context of a decreasing population. Devolution in 1999 gave the Scottish Executive very limited powers over aspects of immigration control, which is a 'reserved' subject under the control of the UK

Government. Nevertheless, the Fresh Talent initiative in operation from 2005 to 2008 was designed to address immigration with specifically Scottish concerns.[20] It aimed to retain high-skilled migrants who had studied in Scotland and was therefore a very selective and targeted initiative. It raises, however, a more general point which applies equally to Scotland as with most European countries, namely the imperative to attract and retain highly skilled migrants, an issue covered in Ima Jackson's chapter on nurse migration. Across Europe and the Western world from the 1970s onwards, high-skilled migrants were highly sought after, the entry of which to any society rarely attracted any public attention.[21] The assumption was that this 'talent', to use the inelegant vocabulary of human resources, was beneficial to the economy of the receiving country and that these individuals were unlikely to become reliant on state welfare.

Politics also could take other forms as migrants maintained political links with the homeland. Diasporic nationalism was associated with a number of groups in the nineteenth century, including Irish, Jewish and Polish immigrants settled in the United States.[22] But the politics of the homeland was also a feature of post-1945 migrant flows. Less is known than might be expected about Irish Catholics and Irish Protestants living in Scotland who were involved in the political conflict that erupted in Northern Ireland in the late 1960s.[23] Bonino shows how political division within the Indian and Pakistani communities was in large part fuelled by ethnic and religious tensions in South Asia. Poles in Scotland had also deep connections with politics at home, especially during periods of acute crisis such as during the Solidarity movement of the 1980s. But as Ailsa Henderson and her colleagues show, using the unique event of the Scottish referendum of 2014, political engagement with the new society can be equally important, as they demonstrate using data on place of birth.

Public opinion within Scotland about immigration also differs from the situation in England and Wales.[24] Social scientists who have investigated this subject are unclear about the precise reasons for this:

> Firstly, for reasons that are difficult to pinpoint with any great certainty, the general public in Scotland is less opposed to immigration than most other parts of Britain. Policymakers north of the border can therefore legitimately promote Scotland as a relatively welcoming place for migrants.[25]

But despite this overall favourable picture, this study using data from social attitudes surveys also found that disadvantaged groups within Scotland express hostility towards migrants as they see themselves as 'losing out'.[26] That said, immigration was never a major political issue in Scotland and all the political parties are broadly supportive of encouraging people to come to Scotland.

CONCLUSION

Scotland, as part of one of the world's advanced economies, was not exceptional in any sense in that it experienced significant immigration from the end of the Second World War until the present day, and continues to be a destination for EU and other migrants. The consensus is that immigration has benefited Scotland in economic, social and cultural terms, bringing to the country rich cultures, ethnic diversity and a sense of Scottish identity that is rooted in a civic rather than an ethnic or racial identity.[27] Unlike England, however, there has been relatively little in terms of nativist reaction to the 'new' Scots who have made the country their home. Why that is the case is arguably to do with a combination of factors: a tradition of liberal tolerance and equalitarianism stretching back to the early nineteenth century, a national church that has promoted tolerance (certainly in the last half-century), the dominance of a centrist political establishment, and the absence of the stoking of political tensions around the issues of access to housing and welfare services that has divided other societies. To say that Scotland has accommodated migrants and ethnic minorities with relative ease probably overstates the degree of acceptance. But there is no doubt that immigration has not become a political issue as in other countries and that immigrants themselves say that they have experienced relatively little hostility or racial prejudice.

What is surprising is how little of this features in the Scottish national story. For instance, a recent volume on everyday life in twentieth-century Scotland includes only a handful of references to immigrants, when arguably one of the greatest changes in the quotidian experience were encounters with people from different ethnic backgrounds.[28] An inclusive history of post-war Scotland will need to incorporate the multi-layered histories of groups who have made Scotland their home in the second half of the twentieth century. The chapters in this collection add much to our understanding of these diverse experiences. But the migration of people is intrinsically never circumscribed by the boundaries of one nation-state and the challenge will be to disentangle the extent to which the working out of these processes of movement and settlement was shaped by transnational flows of capital, information and people.

NOTES

1. For an overview, see Stephen Castles, Hein de Hass and Mark J. Miller, *The Age of Migration: International Population Movements in the Modern World* (Basingstoke: Palgrave, 5th edn, 2014).
2. An early geographical perspective can be found in John Salt and Hugh Clout (eds), *Migration in Post-war Europe: Geographical Essays* (London: Oxford University Press, 1976).
3. Ibid.
4. *Financial Scrutiny Unit Briefing, EU Nationals Living in Scotland* (Edinburgh: Scottish Parliament, 2016) (http://www.parliament.scot/ResearchBriefingsAndFactsheets/S5/SB_16-86_EU_nationals_living_in_Scotland.pdf).
5. See Iain Watson, 'Changed lives, flexible identities and adaptable responses: A comparative history of post-1950 Scottish migrants in New Zealand and Hong Kong', PhD, University of Edinburgh, 2017.
6. Michael Anderson, 'Migrants in Scotland's population histories since 1850', in *Scotland's Population: The Registrar General's Annual Review of Demographic Trends, 2015* (Edinburgh: National Records of Scotland, 2016), p. 80.
7. Ibid., p. 81.
8. Ibid., p.104.
9. See Russell King (ed.), *Mass Migrations in Europe: The Legacy and the Future* (Chichester: Wiley, 1995).
10. *Population and Migration Estimates, April 2017* (Dublin: Central Statistics Office, 2017) http://www.cso.ie/en/releasesandpublications/er/pme/populationandmigrationestimatesapril2017/ (accessed 1 October 2017).
11. For the broader context of Scottish immigration, see Ben Braber, 'Immigrants', in T. M. Devine and Jenny Wormald (eds), *The Oxford Handbook of Modern Scottish History* (Oxford: Oxford University Press, 2012), pp. 491–509.
12. *The Impacts [sic] of Migrants and Migration into Scotland* (Edinburgh: Scottish Government, 2016), p. 12.
13. Afeosemime U. Adogame and Andrew G. Lawrence (eds), *Africa in Scotland, Scotland in Africa: Historical Legacies and Contemporary Hybridities* (Leiden: Brill, 2014).
14. See Randall Hansen, *Citizenship and Immigration in Post-war Britain* (Oxford: Oxford University Press, 2000), pp. 35–61.
15. Graham Hodges, '"Desirable companions and lovers": Irish and African Americans in the sixth ward, 1830–1870', in Ronald H. Bayor and Timothy J. Meagher (eds), *The New York Irish* (Baltimore: The Johns Hopkins University Press, 1996), pp. 107–22; R. A. Burchell, *The San Francisco Irish, 1848–1880* (Manchester: Manchester University Press, 1979), pp. 180–1.

16. Tyler Anbinder, *City of Dreams: The Four-Hundred Year Epic History of Immigrant New York* (Boston: Houghton Mifflin Harcourt, 2016).

17. Quoted in Mary E. Daly, 'Nationalism, sentiment, and economics: Relations between Ireland and Irish-America in the postwar years', in Kevin Kenny (ed.), *New Directions in Irish-American History* (Madison: University of Wisconsin Press, 2003), p. 263.

18. Mark Boyle, *Metropolitan Anxieties: On the Meaning of the Irish Catholic Adventure in Scotland* (Farnham: Ashgate, 2011); Murray Watson, *Being English in Scotland* (Edinburgh: Edinburgh University Press, 2003).

19. Jacqueline Jenkinson, 'The Glasgow race disturbances of 1919', in Kenneth Lunn (ed.), *Race and Labour in Twentieth-Century Britain* (London: Routledge, 1986), pp. 43–67.

20. Fiona Barker, *Nationalism, Identity and the Governance of Diversity: Old Politics, New Arrivals* (Basingstoke: Palgrave Macmillan, 2015), pp. 127–56; P. Skilling, 'New Scots: The Fresh Talent Initiative and post-devolution immigration policy', *Scottish Affairs*, 61 (Autumn 2007), pp. 101–20; Edwige Camp-Pietrain, 'Scotland's devolved institutions and immigration', in Romain Garbaye and Pauline Schnapper (ed.), *The Politics of Ethnic Diversity in the British Isles* (Basingstoke: Palgrave, 2014), pp. 116–35.

21. Tito Boeri et al. (eds), *Brain Drain and Brain Gain: The Global Competition to Attract High-Skilled Migrants* (Oxford: Oxford University Press, 2012).

22. Matthew Jacobson, *Special Sorrows: The Diasporic Imagination of Irish, Polish, and Jewish Immigrants in the United States* (Cambridge, MA: Harvard University Press, 1995).

23. Graham Walker, *Intimate Strangers: Political and Cultural Interaction between Scotland and Ulster in Modern Times* (Edinburgh: John Donald, 1995), p. 149f.

24. Some fascinating insights into attitudes within Scotland can be found in Asifa Hussain and W. L. Miller, *Multicultural Nationalism: Islamophobia, Anglophobia, and Devolution* (Oxford: Oxford University Press, 2016).

25. David McCollum, Beata Nowak and Scott Tindal, 'Public attitudes towards migration in Scotland: Exceptionality and possible policy implications', *Scottish Affairs*, 23:1 (2014), p. 99.

26. Ibid.

27. See *The Impacts [sic] of Migrants and Migration into Scotland*, p. 74.

28. Lynn Abrams and Callum G. Brown (eds), *A History of Everyday Life in Twentieth-Century Scotland* (Edinburgh: Edinburgh University Press, 2010).

Index